ASIA IN EUROPE AND THE MAKING OF THE WEST

*A series in four volumes examining the spread of cultures
from the East into Europe*

Volume 1

D1585858

OUT OF ARABIA
*Phoenicians, Arabs
and the Discovery of Europe*

Warwick Ball

To fellow travellers, east and west

OUT OF ARABIA
Phoenicians, Arabs
and the Discovery of Europe

Warwick Ball

EAST & WEST
PUBLISHING
LONDON

OUT OF ARABIA
Phoenicians, Arabs and the Discovery of Europe
First published 2009 by
EAST & WEST PUBLISHING LTD
London
ISBN 978 1 907318 00 9

eastandwestpublishing.com

Cover design: Eleanor Ball
Editor: Leonard Harrow
Produced by Fox Communications and Publications
Printed and bound in England at the Cromwell Press Group

CONTENTS

SERIES INTRODUCTION

Every culture looks at history in relation to itself, and so it is not surprising that since the nineteenth century our view of world history has been Eurocentric. Perhaps this bias has been overplayed because so many of the world's more powerful nations are rooted in European culture and so the concept of the 'West' and being 'Western' has become almost stereotypical and a crude packaging of a whole complex set of cultures.

Whether or not such a view is correct, this questions whether the 'West' is truly 'Western'. Or, to put it another way, being 'Western' also incorporates a huge amount that is 'Eastern'. Hence, regardless of whether the Eurocentric view is correct or not (and in its own terms it can be correct), the traditional view of the European worldwide spread must be balanced by two considerations. First, by the spread of peoples from the East into Europe. And second, that so much of the civilisation we consider to be 'European' is equally Asiatic. In describing the ensuing contact and assessing the affect, much of what it means to be 'European' is challenged. Ultimately, 'eastern' and 'western' civilisations are neither exclusive nor confrontational. In short, it poses the question, what is 'Europe'?

To deny that Arabs and Turks—or Phoenicians, Scythians, Persians, Jews, Huns, and Mongols—are a part of European as well as Asiatic civilisation is not only to fly in the face of evidence, it is to deny some of the greatest achievements of our civilisation: they are integral parts to be acknowledged as much as our Greek, Roman, Norman or Slavic parts. Phoenicians, Persians, Arabs, Turks, Mongols, all form a part of European history, a part that is both European and Asiatic, a part that defines and makes Europe what it is. Arab and Turkish invasions were no more 'attacks on Europe' than Roman or Norman invasions were.

In this series I do not wish to match East against West nor to demonstrate that 'everything came out of the East.' I wish simply to explore the affect of those cultures from beyond the conventional boundaries of Europe that, to a greater or lesser extent, expanded westwards—the counterpart of the 'European expansion'. Since the earliest times, the history of Europe has been inextricably bound up with peoples and cultures from the East. It is an extraordinarily rich and complex relationship. Not only was Europe born and defined out of this relationship, but at every stage in its history it was intimately affected by the lands to the east. This is the story of that relationship: it is the story of Europe itself.

ACKNOWLEDGEMENTS

It is a pleasure to thank Wendy Ball, Peter D'Ews Thompson, Monika Raudnitz and David Whitehouse for comments on earlier drafts or answers to specific questions on aspects of this book (with apologies for suggestions I ignored or errors that crept in afterwards), as well as Oliver Ball for producing the maps. I would also like to thank Sahar Huneidi, Alan Ball and Leonard Harrow of East and West Publications, the former whose vision made this book possible, and latter who put it into practice.

Above all I would like to thank numerous fellow travellers over the years who have had to endure my talking of many of the ideas expressed in this book. Their inexhaustible curiosity led me to first to pose many of the questions raised in this book, and their invaluable feedback prevented my worst pitfalls. It is to them that this series is rightly dedicated.

Warwick Ball
Stow
October 2009

LIST OF MAPS

LIST OF PLATES

1. The excavations at the Phoenician port of Tyre in Lebanon. Mainly Roman remains are on the surface.

2. The huge hippodrome dating from the time of Septimius Severus' rebuilding of Tyre, built on the mole constructed by Alexander of Macedon to connect the island to the mainland.

3. The harbour at Sidon. Although partially obscured by the medieval castle on the mole and the modern Lebanese port facilities, the harbour still preserves its original Phoenician form.

4. The Phoenician temple of Eshmoun inland from Sidon. The square sanctuary is in the foreground, the terrace wall in the background is from the Persian period. Note the cubic form of the sanctuary.

5. The overgrown excavations of the Phoenician city of Ugarit in Syria.

6. The excavated Phoenician port of Byblos in Lebanon. The city ramparts are on the right; a later Roman colonnade is in the background.

7. The Phoenician temple at Amrit in Syria. Note the cubic form of the central sanctuary.

8. Phoenician tombs at Amrit.

9. The remains of Carthage outside Tunis. The large pillars are the supports for the forum which the Romans built over the ancient Carthaginian remains deliberately to obscure them. In the background is the 19th century French Cathedral of St Louis.

10. Excavated Punic slipways at the naval harbour at Carthage.

11. Stele representing child sacrifice at the Carthage *tophet*.

12. The site of Hannibal's burial place in Bithynia in Turkey.

13. The excavated Punic site of Kerkouane in Tunisia.

14. Punic Kerkouane. Note the bathroom in the foreground and the ordered layout

in the background.

15. Newly excavated remains of ancient Roman Beirut, possibly the site of its famous law school.

16. The Arab delegation on the Persepolis reliefs—the clothing, not to mention the camel, still characterise the Arabs today.

17. The line of monoliths forming the propyleum of the Temple of Awwam at Marib in Yemen.

18. Monoliths of the Temple of 'Almaqah at Ma'reb. Note the 'cubic' form of the capitals.

19. The great dam at Marib. The overflow is in the foreground and in the background is one of the sluice gates.

20. The ancient Minnaean city of Yathil, modern Barraqish in Yemen.

21. A stylised ibex frieze at Sirwah near Marib.

22. The great temple complex at Baalbek in Lebanon. The huge colonnade in the background is part of the Temple of Jupiter Heliopolitanus, and the temple to the right is the so-called Temple of Bacchus.

23. The dedicatory inscription to the Emesene 'Great King Samsigeramus' at Baalbek.

24. The elaborately decorated courtyard of the Temple of Jupiter at Baalbek.

25. The courtyard of the Temple of Jupiter at Baalbek. The single standing column is one of originally a pair of dedicatory columns, possibly relating to ancient Phoenician practice. The inscription in the foreground reads *IOMH*: 'Iupiter Optimus Magnus Heliopolitanus'.

26. The city of Petra in Jordan, with the great royal facades in the distance.

27. The older style of tomb facades at Petra.

28. The *baetyl* in the Siq at Petra representing Dushares and his consorts al-Uzza and Allat.

29. The so-called 'god blocks' at the entrance to Petra.

30. The new Nabatean capital at Bosra in Syria. Although ostensibly a Roman style of monumental arch, the capitals are Nabatean.

31. The twin pillars standing on the citadel overlooking the modern city of Urfa in Turkey, ancient Edessa.

32. The 'Fish-pools of Abraham' with their sacred carp at Urfa, probably originally part of the cult of Atargatis.

33. The great Temple of Bel at Palmyra in the Syrian desert.

34. The start of the great colonnade at Palmyra, with the tomb towers and the desert beyond.

35. The courtyard of the Temple of Bel at Palmyra.

INTRODUCTION
An Unsound Compass

In the battle between truth and prejudice, waged in the field of
history books, it must be confessed that the latter usually wins.
Stephen Runciman 1929[1]

Picture two archetypal figures from seemingly opposite ends of the
conventional east-west spectrum: an Arab Caliph and a Roman Emperor.
Both easily slip into popular, almost cliché images, familiar from Roman
portrait busts and coins to illustrations of the *Arabian Nights*. But the rulers
I have in mind belie the images: a Caliph who was blond-haired and blue-
eyed, and a Roman Emperor who was the son of a sheikh from a provincial
Syrian village bordering the desert. The former was Caliph 'Abd al-Rahman
III, one of the greatest princes of Arab history ruling over al-Andalus at
its height in the tenth century, one of the most magnificent courts of the
Islamic world.* The latter was the Emperor Philip the Arab, presiding over
the greatest triumph in Roman imperial history when he celebrated Rome's
Millennium in the third century (Pl. 45). At once both European and Arab,
both figures illustrate the complexities of a shared history covering thousands
of years of how closely intertwined Europe has been with Arabia and the
Near East.

Arab history is often viewed as beginning with Islam. But the Arabs
have a history going back thousands of years before that world changing
event—one, furthermore, intimately bound up with European history and
identity. They also have a history of world penetration parallel to that of
the European. Islam, therefore, was a culmination as much as a beginning.
Nor did Islam cause the Arabs to turn away from Europe: on the contrary,
Islam's first outward movement was towards the West as much as (or more

---

* There are no portraits of 'Abd al-Rahman III, but contemporary descriptions record his blond
  and blue-eyed appearance. See Kennedy 1996: 82.

1

than) the East, and Islam's first Caliphate was revived in Spain after a second Caliphate was created in Baghdad. The Arabs' occidental orientation did not end with the decline of the Caliphate or the expulsion of the Moors from Spain. On the contrary, Islamic learning and ideas changed the course of European development, whilst Arab powers—and their ideas—continued to rival European overseas expansion until the modern era.

In examining a world that appears increasingly dominated by European values ever since the 'Age of Expansion,' complexities become apparent. For example, questions as to who actually 'discovered' America—Vikings, Italians, Spanish, Welsh, Egyptians or Chinese—become irrelevant when we ask: who discovered Europe? In an age when European powers were penetrating throughout the world, peoples from Arabia and the Near East had penetrated first, remained longer, and had conquered and colonised parts of Europe long before. Arabs, for example, had advanced as far as France and Switzerland by the tenth century, whilst the last Arab colonial possession in the Indian Subcontinent remained after the last European.*

In one important survey of the interaction of East and West, the historian J M Roberts makes the point that 'when the ports of China and India were full of European and North American shipping, no junk or dhow had ever been seen in Seville, Bristol or Boston.'2 Perhaps not Bristol or Boston (although the Ottomans occupied a part of the Bristol Channel at the height of the European Age of Expansion), and perhaps not in dhows. But Phoenician vessels probably sailed up the Dart (and doubtless the Bristol Channel)—and certainly colonised parts of Spain and Africa—in the first millennium BC. And Arabs were not only 'seen' in Seville but throughout the rest of Spain and much of the Mediterranean as well. Indeed, another Asiatic power was later to make the Mediterranean a Turkish lake. As for the 'ports of China and India', they were certainly full of 'dhows' a thousand years before European caravels were seen there, while 'junks' were seen on the coasts of East Africa and the Middle East long before any of our Portuguese, Spanish, Dutch or North American ships reached Canton. Europe, in other words, has been engaged with a complex relationship with the Arabs and their immediate forbears throughout its history.

Much of the Near East became a part of the European world for almost a millennium with its conquest in the last centuries BC at first by the Macedonians and then by the Romans. But there was always a two-way

---

* The last European possession in the Indian Subcontinent was Goa, becoming a part of India in 1961; the Omani possession of Gwadar came under Pakistani rule in 1974.

process. Hellenistic civilisation, born of the Macedonian conquests, was by definition a hybrid one, and the great Hellenistic centres of Alexandria, Antioch and Pergamon displayed as many Egyptian, Syrian and Anatolian elements as they did Greek. When it all became a part of the Roman world, this complex interaction between the peoples of Europe and the Near East was accelerated. Out of it, European civilisation itself became a hybrid one with the adoption of a Near Eastern religion as its main identity, but even before that the relationship was changing Europe. Philip the Arab forms a part of that story—and he was not the first Arab to rule in Rome.

Nor was Philip the last Arab to rule a European country. For the emergence of Islam in the seventh century did not represent the opening of a division between Europe and the Near East. On the contrary, the Arabs under Islam continued a tradition already millennia old of maintaining this complex relationship, and established Emirates in Sicily and Italy and a Caliphate in Spain. The Caliphate, perhaps Islam's most venerable institution, was to return to Europe for a further four centuries when the Ottomans transferred it from Cairo to Constantinople in the sixteenth century. Today, there are Muslim countries, communities and regions within Europe: Albania, Bosnia, Kosovo, Thrace, Tatarstan, Daghestan, Chechnya—communities which many were unaware of (often to our cost) until recently.* Such regions, of course, are only indirectly an Arab legacy and belong more to the histories of the Turks and Mongols (to be examined in Volumes 3 and 4 of this series). But they do underline the fact that Arabs and Islam form an integral part of European identity.

There has long been many works on the Arabs in Spain and the brilliant civilisation it produced. The achievements of Moorish Andalusia are now widely recognised, so hardly require retelling here. More recently, works have been appearing that now recognise the broader implications that arose as a consequence, mainly the impact of Islam upon Europe.† But the more one examines these issues, the more it becomes apparent that even a huge subject like Islam was only a part of a much broader picture, and that the arrival of the Arabs in Spain in 711 can only be understood as a part of a process that had already been under way for several thousands of years. Hence, Islam is not introduced until halfway through this book. The first

---

* Muslims in some countries such as Bosnia might form a minority—but so too did Muslims in some of the greatest Muslim societies of the past.

† The titles of a selection of such books illustrate the point: Jack Goody's *The East in the West* (1996) and *Islam in Europe* (2004), Franco Cardini's *Europe and Islam* (1999), Nabil Matar's *In the Lands of the Christians* (2003), Ian Almond's *Two Faiths One Banner* (2009).

movements of the Phoenicians out of their Near Eastern homeland towards the west form an essential background to the later movements of their Arab descendants in the same direction. Even after the rise of Rome brought an end to Phoenician expansion, the unification of the Mediterranean under the Romans meant that the movement—of ideas as well as people—continued, maintaining a complex two-way relationship. The Arab conquest of Spain in the eighth century was as much the culmination of an old relationship as the beginning of a new one; only the religion had changed. This book is an account of that relationship.

Of course, whilst Islam only forms a part of the broader picture of the Arab interrelationship with the West, the Arabs equally form only a part of the broader picture of Islam in Europe. This account is limited, therefore, just to the part played by the Arabs in this. The part played by Turks and Mongols in bringing Islam into Europe is left to later volumes,* although there are naturally overlaps. Hence, some of the later history of the Arabs in the west—the revolt of the Moriscos in Spain in the sixteenth century, for example, or the Barbary corsairs of the sixteenth and seventeenth centuries—are better understood in the context of Ottoman hegemony in the Mediterranean at that time.

THE CONFINES OF DEFINITIONS

The approach of this book is in a sense archaeological: to analyse the layers of civilisation to reveal how they are connected and add up to the whole picture. In doing so, terms—civilisation, East, West, Europe, Asia, Arab—are bandied around with a casualness that belies their imprecision, so it might be worth here examining some definitions if only to recognise their limitations.

How do the Phoenicians relate to the Arabs: are they two separate people or the same? To begin with, it is necessary to clarify terminology. 'Phoenicia' is a Greek term, not native. It is supposedly named after an eponymous legendary king of Tyre, the main Phoenician city-state, called King Phoenix. The name itself is obscure, possibly deriving from an Indo-European root word for 'red', referring to the famous purple dye: the 'tyrian purple' with which that coast was associated in antiquity.† The Phoenicians'

---

* Volume 3, *Sultans of Rome* and Volume 4, *The Gates of Europe*.
† The mythical phoenix, a fabled bird said to live 600 years in the Arabian desert before immolating itself then rising from the ashes, is possibly a cognate word relating to the red of the fire. The Arabian connections, as well as the themes of immolation and resurrection, were to be constant

own native term for themselves was 'Canaanites'—the Bible also refers to them under this name. Even as late as the fifth century AD, St Augustine mentions that the Punic people of North Africa still called themselves 'Canaanites'. Both Homer and some native Phoenician sources also refer to them as 'Sidonians', despite Tyre being the more important city. Later, when the Phoenicians colonised much of North Africa, the Romans referred to them as either 'Punic' (derived from Phoenician) or 'Carthaginian' after the main city they founded there. It is important to remember, therefore, that the differences between 'Canaanite', 'Phoenician', 'Punic' and 'Carthaginian' are artificial and often simply confuse a continuous history of just the one people.

The Phoenician language is a Semitic one, belonging to the North-western Semitic group. Other languages in this group include Hebrew, Amorite, Nabatean, Aramaic and Syriac, and it is from this group that Arabic derives. A language, of course, is not necessarily the same as a people, but by the first few centuries AD all of these language-speakers (with the exception of the Hebrews) were beginning to be lumped together as 'Arabs' or 'Saracens'. Whilst it might not be correct to refer to Phoenicians as 'Arabs,' they were at least immediate ancestors, with their differences increasingly blurred until they merge imperceptibly into the present-day Arabs of the Levantine coast.

Arabs are mentioned as a distinctive people in Assyrian texts of the early first millennium BC, and are depicted on Assyrian reliefs of the seventh and Persepolis reliefs of the sixth centuries BC (Pl. 16). These earliest references to the Arabs do not necessarily correspond to the rather ill-defined region we now know as 'Arabia,' but seem to refer to the tribes who inhabited the desert area of Syria, Jordan and southern Iraq—roughly northern Arabia. This is the same general homeland of other major ancient Semitic peoples such as the Assyrians—described in their own annals of the early second millennium as 'peoples who dwell in tents' west of the Euphrates—as well as Amorites and Aramaeans. Whilst it would be inaccurate to call the ancient Semitic peoples of the Near East—Amorites, Canaanites, Phoenicians or Aramaeans—'Arab', the Arabs can at least be described as their descendants: by the first century AD contemporary writers were beginning to refer to most of the indigenous inhabitants of the Levant as 'Arabs' or 'Saracens'.

---

themes of the Phoenicians in the west, as we will see in Chapters 1 and 2. The name survives in the small port of Finike, ancient Phoinikos, on the south-western coast of Turkey. Phoinikos was the port of the ancient Lycian city of Limyra just inland, although very little ancient remains survive in Finike today.

The term 'Arab,' therefore, has become a fairly general ethnic designation, now referring to all speakers of the Arabic language broadly from Morocco to Oman. 'Arabic' came to be used even more broadly as a religious, cultural and international language of Muslims in general, especially by Persians, Turks, Berbers—and Andalusians, whether of Latin, Visigothic or Iberian descent. Hence, 'Arab' has acquired an even broader cultural term meaning Arab-derived, particularly under Islam. In discussions, for example, of Moorish Spain, 'Arab Spain' and 'Muslim Spain' become virtually interchangeable. 'Arabia' is a more specific geographical designation, nowadays generally confined to Saudi Arabia, but it is used here in its nineteenth-century sense when 'Arabia' was a more general term referring to the Arabic-speaking lands of the Ottoman Empire, roughly all the land between the Mediterranean and the Persian Gulf. In this sense, 'Arabian' is used here in a broader, but more ill-defined and non-ethnic sense, than 'Arab'.

How can we define a civilisation? The art historian Kenneth Clark famously found it difficult to *define* civilisation but had no hesitation in defining its opposite: barbarism. But he could *recognise* civilisation, as well as appreciate both its complexity and fragility. Its fragility was also recognised by J Bronowski, who further defined its requirements: confidence, vigour, energy, vitality.[3] Many recognise civilisation as referring to a particular stage of human development. However, on once being asked in Australia as to why, as an archaeologist, I never excavated there, my innocent answer that it had no 'ancient civilisations' was received with outrage as denigrating Aboriginal achievement. Hence, the historian Felipe Fernández-Armesto in his magisterial *Civilizations* has gone to the opposite extreme: all human societies from remote stone-age tribes or Arctic hunter-gathers to the most developed and complex states are now 'civilisations,' which is perhaps like the mad-hatters tea party in *Alice in Wonderland* where everybody gets first prize. On the other hand, 'civilisation' has become a politically incorrect term in many archaeological circles as being judgemental, as implying that other cultures were not 'civilised,' and terms such as 'developed societies' or 'cultural complexes' are used instead.*

The more one looks at civilisation, therefore, the more ephemeral it becomes. Fernand Braudel described it as a 'miscellany of trivia and daily happenings which rises like a cloud of dust' and further points out, 'No

---

* A good example is the recently identified ancient Oxus Civilisation of Central Asia—recently identified in comparison with the conventionally recognised ancient civilisations of Greece, Rome, Egypt, Mesopotamia, etc.—where the term 'Bactro-Margiana Cultural Complex' or 'BMAC' is preferred in academic contexts.

sooner does the historian think he has isolated the particular quality of a civilization than it gives proof of the exact opposite. Civilizations may be fraternal and liberal, yet at the same time exclusive and unwelcoming; they receive visits and return them; they can be pacific yet militant; in many ways astonishingly stable, they are nevertheless constantly shifting and straying, their surface disturbed by a thousand eddies and whirlpools, the tiny particles of their daily life subject to random "Brownian movements"...'[4] Civilisation is the minutiae as well as the broader picture, the woods as well as the trees, belonging to everyone and no-one.

How can one define the 'West?' Of course we all *know* what it is: it is a term that we use or read about daily, one of the most important—probably *the* most important—of our cultural self-definitions. But what exactly is this 'West'? Herodian, writing in the third century, put the dividing line between East and West at the Taurus Mountains in Anatolia.[5] The T'ang Chinese regarded all Persians, Arabs and Indians as 'Westerners'.[6] To the Arabs of the Middle Ages, the 'West' was just north-west Africa, *al-Maghreb*, corresponding to Tunisia, Algeria and Morocco. Is the 'West,' therefore, simply a matter of perspective?[7]

The position of Malta provides a brief, if perhaps superficial, illustration of the inherent contradictions of such definitions. Lying off the coast of Africa to the south of Algiers and Tunis, the Maltese speak a Semitic language related to ancient Phoenician, surviving here long after the Phoenician language in its homeland had been swamped successively by Aramaic and Arabic. They practise an eastern religion (Christianity) and pray to Allah. Is Malta, therefore, European, African or Asian? Of course few would question that Malta may not be 'Western:' it is significant, for example, that in Malta's application to join the European Union there was none of the agonising that characterises Turkey's (except, significantly, by the Maltese themselves). Far beyond the opposite end of the Mediterranean, two countries lying to the east of Turkey whose capitals are on roughly the same longitude as Baghdad are routinely considered 'Western': Georgia and Armenia; Turkey and Azerbaijan on either side are rarely so considered.

The imprecision is illustrated by what is probably the most thorough export of European culture: the discovery, conquest and colonisation of the Americas.* So successful has this process been that it is now invariably

---

* One is relieved that in 1507 the German geographer Martin Waldseemüller named America after the Italian Amerigo Vespucci, rather than his more deserving fellow countryman Christopher Columbus, who has prior claim to its discovery. An entire continent—two actually—named 'Chris' would not have worked.

considered to be a part of the 'West': a sort of honorary Europe.* But even this definition is highly subjective: the 'West' is generally only confined to United States and Canada. Central and South America, whilst equally European in culture, are simply not rich enough to belong to the 'Western Club': New Orleans is honorary Europe, Bogota is not. Even in this most successful implant of European culture, however, the process was never one way. Western Europe may have conquered the Aztecs and Incas and extinguished their civilisations, but all the world now enjoys the potato, the tomato and other plants that those civilisations domesticated, not to mention the more dubious blessings of coca and tobacco. Where would the Renaissance have been without the New World silver and gold brought in by the Spanish, which underpinned it? The process is more complex now than ever. That most European of arts, for example, formal 'classical' music rooted in the traditions of Hildegard of Bingen, Bach and Beethoven, was radically altered in the twentieth century by African music that came by way of New World jazz and Latin rhythms ('Latin' now, ironically, applying more to Rio de Janeiro than to Rome), and the music of Shostakovich, Milhaud and Bartok owes as much to this as to the cultures of Russia, France and Hungary respectively. That most 'Western' of film genres, the Western, was revamped and given a complete change of direction in the 1960s by an Italian remake of a Japanese samurai movie.†

The 'West,' therefore, becomes as ill-defined as civilisation. What of 'Europe,' 'Asia' and the 'East?' Europe's shifting boundaries are discussed more in Volume 4 and the origin of the name 'Europe' from a Phoenician princess raped by Zeus is discussed in the context of Phoenician colonisation in Chapter 2. The definition of Europe in terms of (Latin) Christendom is discussed in Chapter 6. The historian Eric Hobsbaum emphasises that Europe 'exists *exclusively* as an intellectual construct.'[8] It is simply a self-perception and without the rest of the world—mainly Asia—as a mirror to hold up to itself, Europe would not even exist as an intellectual construct. This is emphasised by Braudel when he writes: 'Perhaps the merit of the West, confined as it was on its narrow "cape of Asia", was that it "needed" the rest of the world, needed to venture outside its own front door. ... The West soon became a kind of luxury of the world. ... Specifying that something is superior means referring either to something inferior, ...

---

* Even so discerning an historian as Eric Hobsbawm, 1983, in a paper entitled 'Europe', discusses the USA without feeling the need to explain or to justify. 'Mass-Producing Traditions: Europe 1870-1914'.

† Sergio Leone's 1964 classic *For a Fistful of Dollars* was a remake of Akira Kurosawa's 1961 *Yojimbo*.

moving on sooner or later to an uncomfortable and deceptive comparison with the rest of the world. ... Europe has never stopped explaining itself "in relation to other continents".[9] It is not until almost at the end of his *History of Europe* that J M Roberts defines Europe as 'a historically changing series of meanings filled out differently as different needs and challenges presented themselves to the European peoples.'[10]

The idea of 'Asia' is even more elusive. The origin of its name illustrates exactly how contradictory—and ultimately meaningless—Asia is as a construct. Some three and a half thousand years ago the Hittite imperial archives in the highlands of Anatolia recorded the names of the various peoples and places in and beyond their empire. Amongst these, the Hittites referred to a minor region in the western-most part of Anatolia: the region of *Assuwa*. The origin of the name is uncertain, but it was probably based upon an Indo-European root word that simply meant 'the west.' The Greeks, who came to occupy this region long after the collapse of the Hittite Empire, Hellenised this name to *Asia*.

Today, this name of this obscure western region has expanded to refer to a super-continent, the entire land mass *east* of the Hittite homeland stretching all the way to the Pacific: the east rather than the west. More specifically, we now tend to think of 'Asians' as belonging to the *Far* East: Chinese, Japanese, Filipinos are 'Asians' but Iranians, Arabs and—least of all—Turks, the present inhabitants of 'Assuwa', would not consider themselves 'Asians'. Ironically, the original 'Asia' is no longer considered 'Asian'. A further irony is that amongst the first 'Asians' that we learn about—the inhabitants of Assuwa—were Greeks.

Eric Hobsbaum expresses the contradictions of 'Asia' when he writes: 'Since 1980, if I am not mistaken, the census of the USA has granted its inhabitants the option of describing themselves as "Asian-Americans", a classification presumably by analogy with "African-Americans", the term by which black Americans currently prefer to be described. Presumably an Asian-American is an American born in Asia or descended from Asians. But what is the sense in classifying immigrants from Turkey under the same heading as those from Cambodia, Korea, the Philippines or Pakistan, not to mention the unquestionably Asian territory of Israel, though its inhabitants do not like to be reminded of this geographical fact? In practice these groups have nothing in common.'[11]

To lump 'Asia' or 'the East' under a single label therefore has no geographical, cultural, ethnic or historical foundation. The Middle East and Far East are more different in every way than, say, the Middle East and Europe, and the East's other components—Central Asia, Indian Subcontinent, Southeast Asia—are similarly distinct. It is as if the Chinese were to divide the world up into 'The East' and 'The West:' the 'East' being themselves, along with Korea, Japan and perhaps Vietnam, and the 'West' being all the rest: Central Asia, Indian Subcontinent, the Middle East and Europe (as indeed, the T'ang Chinese did as we have seen).[12] The use of labels—Europe, Asia, America—by all means have momentary usefulness if one always remembers their limitations.

LITERARY CONFLICT AND COLLUSION

There is nothing more factual than the past: that which has happened is unalterable, it becomes incontrovertible. Yet nothing is more subject to differing interpretations. Even recent, verifiable factual history with many eyewitnesses can often be subject to huge uncertainty: the history of court cases is witness to the difficulties of establishing exactly what has happened. The more distant the past, the more the uncertainty, the wider the interpretations. In the end, the past becomes subject to almost as much change as the present: there is no such thing as history that is fixed. Ultimately, it becomes a creation of the present.

Works presenting the Eastern viewpoint have been criticised as apologist or revisionist: as 'a false humility, a hypocritical egalitarianism'[13] or more recently as 'moral posturing against the West'.[14] Such works (including my own) are often dismissed as 'yet another which claims that everything comes from the east.' This is to miss the point. The achievements of Western civilisation are not called into question and the superiority or primacy of East over West—or the other way around—is not an issue. The real issue is that there is no exclusively 'Eastern' or 'Western' civilisation; civilisation is not a weapon of confrontation, to be glibly defined and then 'claimed' as some sort of intellectual property by one cultural group or another. Even authors who are at pains to present the eastern viewpoint frequently fall into the trap of contrasting, hence ultimately missing, the issue and widening the gap.

The works of Edward Said—mainly *Orientalism* and its sequel, *Culture and Imperialism*—have become 'international bestsellers' (to cite their rear cover publicity). It is certainly true that they have become fashionable reading throughout the West: it is right to feel guilty. Not only is this a part of the self-flagellation that so many like to indulge in, Said's works have ironically become a part of the ammunition of cultural superiority: one is smugly superior enough to recognise criticism and to take it on the jaw. Criticising Said is to risk being branded a cultural imperialist. Accordingly, many books even remotely concerning the Middle East now contain the obligatory token reference to Said in the introduction, and *Orientalism* is duly there to be seen in the bibliography to advertise the author's political correctness.

Orientalism is rightly one of the most influential books of its era. Since its publication in 1978 nobody has been able to look at the subject in quite the same way: it has forced us to examine the opposite viewpoint more than ever; it has helped to redefine terms such as 'oriental', 'eastern' and 'Asian',* and it has given the entire field a much-needed shake-up—the field has lost both its innocence and its complacency, and Said deserves to be read. However, Said goes both too far and not far enough. He goes too far in tarring all European 'Orientalists' with the same imperialist brush. It might—and only might—be valid for British, French or American scholars, but there have been prominent Czech, Hungarian, Polish, Finnish and other Orientalists as well, often from countries that have experienced more foreign exploitation and suffering than Arab countries have. And Said goes not far enough in limiting his study almost solely to the Arab Middle East, a fraction of the whole field of Oriental Studies. Furthermore, the West held no monopoly of cultural arrogance: attitudes of the Ottoman Turks, for example, towards their Arab colonies were as bad as or worse than their other European imperial counterparts. Edward Said can be as guilty of ethnocentricism as the people he accuses.

In fact Western prejudice and consequent 'cultural imperialism' towards the Middle East—Said's orientalism—was no different to its views of other non-European cultures, be they African, Inuit or Polynesian (and in some cases merely non-English cultures: Welsh and Irish might feel 'oriental' in Said's terms). In other words, non-European cultures are merely the 'other,' and in this way Europeans are no different to any other culture: Arabs too have their 'other'. Another author, Jared Diamond, who more recently became a 'best seller' in writing from the non-European perspective, writes: 'The history of interactions amongst disparate peoples is what shaped the modern world through conquests, epidemics and genocide. Those collisions created reverberations that have still not died down.'[15] History and contact between peoples is defined right from the start in terms of *confrontation*, when in fact

---

* Interestingly, the School of Oriental and African Studies (SOAS) at the University of London now has to officially redefine itself in terms of 'Africa, Asia and the Middle East'; Asia has shifted, and Edward Said has turned 'oriental' into a dirty word. If SOAS were founded now instead of 1916, its acronym would need to be SAAMES.

the opposite was true. Although Diamond's very worthwhile *Guns, Germs and Steel* is generally regarded to be in the opposite camp of, say, Huntingdon's *Clash of Civilizations*, the basic premise is the same: East and West is viewed in terms of confrontation, collision, clash. Ultimately, in exaggerating the confrontation,[16] such critiques unwittingly contribute to it: simply reinstating a 'them and us' division, as much as the writers whom they condemn.

Edward Said includes writers such as Jane Austin and Charles Dickens as a part of the baggage of cultural superiority and Jack Goody further includes such historians as Gordon Childe, Moses Finley, Fernand Braudel and Jospeh Needham. They may be right and such critiques of course offer necessary correctives. But all writers are products of their time and place, Goody and Said as much as Huntingdon, Austin or Childe, and it is a mistake to criticise Napoleon for not using nuclear submarines at the Battle of Waterloo (to paraphrase Mortimer Wheeler). In writing of one's own culture there is nothing wrong in recognising its merits, distinctiveness or even superiority; indeed, cultural self-confidence and assertion is one of the essential ingredients of civilisation that Bronowski recognised. All cultures are 'dignified by difference' as Britain's chief rabbi, Jonathan Sachs, so fairly put it.[17]

Orientalism in its worst aspects is without doubt cultural arrogance, but it can also be a manifestation of curiosity. The nineteenth century fascination for Chinoiserie, Turquerie and romantic Orientalism generally, for example, formed some of the sources for the Art Nouveau movement. But good or bad, Orientalism in all its forms is a part of European culture. Orientalist paintings by Delacroix and others, operas from Mozart's *Die Entführung aus dem Serail* to Puccini's *Turandot* set in some perceived fantasy 'orient', or the huge range of eighteenth- and nineteenth-century European romantic Orientalism of all manners and genres, continued with the romantic thirst for all things superficially 'eastern' in the hippy movement of the sixties and seventies or the fashions for Japanese *manga* today. This may be superficial and transient. At the same time it must not be underestimated. Even the ancient Greeks had their 'orientalist' phase, their 'Medizers' and their 'Perserie', and the Roman fascination for oriental cults transformed its empire. And 'Orientalism' is not confined to the occident: the Arabs of the 'Abbasid Caliphate were fascinated by Chinese porcelain and romanticised the barbaric Turk, the Ethiopians of the sixteenth century copied Portuguese fashion, many Iranians of the sixties and seventies were *gharbzadeh*, or 'West-struck'. 'Orientalism' and its counterparts are a part of all cultures.

THE OTHER

A perceived East-West conflict ever since the Trojan Wars is viewed as part of Europe's identity. In our own times this is just as true as in the past: a Communist threat—a perceived 'Red Terror'—had to be invented, and when that collapsed it had to be replaced by another 'Other': perceived Islamic fundamentalists, terrorists and a state of perpetual 'war on terror' or 'clash of civilisations' regarded as so self-evident that it requires no justification.

A perceived 'Other', of course, is common to most societies: Greeks versus 'barbarians', for example, or the Muslim *dar as-salam* versus the *dar al-harb* or the 'house of serenity' versus 'house of chaos', or the division between Chinese and non-Chinese—usually those beyond the Great Wall. The need to define oneself in terms of perceived differences with and consequent struggles against the outsider is a universal trait. The idea of Europe is similarly constructed in terms of an opposite 'Other', in this case the artificial construct of polyglot Asia. But defining Europe in terms of an East-West divide can be dangerous.

History is a weapon that can be as destructive as artillery: the invention and distortion of history to legitimise political ends is as old as the first empty boasts of kings and pharaohs. Defining Europe is now an acute political issue and the current idea of Europe in the political sense is one of the more admirable experiments of recent history. But such grand ideas can go badly wrong, and it is essential to guard against the idea deteriorating into some exclusive 'fortress Europe'. European civilisation has bequeathed a great legacy to the world, a legacy that needs no reassertion here. But probably Europe's most destructive legacy has been the perversion of patriotism into extreme nationalism. An exclusive 'fortress Europe' therefore could risk becoming the ultimate grotesque descendant of Europe's worst nightmare, a huge monolithic—and monstrous—extreme nationalism.

Few would seriously doubt that two of the great ages in Europe— on a par with fifth-century Athens or Renaissance Italy—were Islamic: Cordoba in the age of the Umayyad Caliphate and Constantinople in the age of Süleyman the Magnificent. That they were European is a simple statement of fact: they took place on European soil. That they were Islamic is another obvious statement. By not recognising that Islamic civilisation is a part of Europe is to deny some of the greatest achievements of European civilisation. Phoenicians, Persians, Arabs, Turks, Mongols, all form a part of European history, a part that is both European and Asiatic, a part that defines and makes Europe what it is—cultures that can no more be excluded from Europe than the Viking, Roman or Greek.

The great Muslim-Christian confrontations—Hattin in 1187, Constantinople in 1453, Lepanto in 1571, Smyrna in 1923, Kosovo in 1389 and again in 1999—are all too often remembered. But the far greater periods of co-existence that more truly characterised the history between the two faiths—Cordoba of 'Abd al-Rahman III, Palermo of Roger II, Constantinople of Suleiman the Magnificent, and even Tatarstan or Dubai of the twenty-first century—are all too often overlooked. Even many of the 'confrontations' themselves were not always so one-sided: Sultan Bayazit 'Thunderbolt' only won the Battle of Kosovo through the assistance of his Christian allies, and even during the siege of Constantinople, there were Muslim Turks within Constantinople fighting against Mehmet the Conqueror alongside the Christian defenders. It would be a huge mistake, therefore, to think of the contact solely in terms of conflict. Throughout, bigotry was tempered by pragmatism and intolerance by open mindedness, on both sides.

Edward Said is still a voice that demands to be heard. Partly because it is the voice of the 'other', but more important, his is ultimately a plea for sanity, for pluralism, for cultural diversity. Said rightly concludes *Culture and Imperialism* with the words:

> 'Only through this attitude can a historian, for example, begin to grasp human experience and its written records in all its diversity and particularity; otherwise one would remain committed more to the exclusions and reactions of prejudice than to the negative freedom of real knowledge. ... No one today is purely *one* thing. Labels like Indian, or woman, or Muslim, or American are no more than starting-points, which if followed into actual experience for only a moment are quickly left behind.'[18]

In 1938 Danish author Karen Blixen wrote a novel, *Out of Africa*, that has since become a minor classic. The title has also come to be a convenient shorthand term for the theory of human origins and dispersal 'out of Africa'. *Out of Arabia* is more modest on both counts—but equally makes reference to both. For this work is the story of a complex, intimate relationship, as well as a dispersal.

Chapter 1

THE DISCOVERY OF EUROPE
The First Travellers Out of Arabia

Ships plying to Tarshish ... bringing gold and silver, ivory, apes, and monkeys.

2 Chronicles 9: 21

In the last decade of the last millennium, the greatest Western power of the twentieth century celebrated one of the high points in its history, the American half millennium: five hundred years since the discovery of America by Christopher Columbus in 1492. The celebrations also opened up anew that old can of worms as to exactly *who* (if anybody) discovered America before Christopher Columbus. Speculation ranged from the Vikings, the Irish and the Welsh through to ancient Egyptians, Phoenicians, Atlanteans and men from outer space, the debate often extending to the ridiculous.

But the speculation, even its silliest aspects, did raise a more serious question of viewpoint: the last centuries of world-wide European exploration and expansion have led us to look upon everything in terms of 'us' and 'our' discoveries. The real question which needs to be asked, is not who of 'us' discovered America, but who discovered Europe: who discovered 'us'?[*]

Describing Western European expansion as the 'Age of Discovery' may or may not be one-sided. 'We' were by no means the first to discover the world. The people of south-east Asia discovered and colonised Australia over 40,000 years ago, Polynesians discovered and colonised around the Pacific as far as New Zealand and Easter Island, and the Javanese colonised

---

[*] An interesting corrective in perspective is given, in a different context, by an Arab historian Nabil Matar (1999: 59) when he writes 'The Muslim ruler [in the 16th century] kidnapped Britons in order to learn about them in the same manner Drake kidnapped Indians to learn about them; Drake "discovered" the American Indians in the same way the Muslims of North Africa "discovered" the English.'

Madagascar in the Middle Ages, to give just a few examples from the opposite end of the world from Henry the Navigator.

The origins of civilisation in the Near East are well enough known and long acknowledged, so need hardly detain us here. Of more interest is not the primacy of any civilisation over the other, but which of these older civilisations of the East made the first landfalls in Europe, comparable to those of Christopher Columbus (or the Vikings)—and later the Spanish and the Portuguese—in the New World?

Classical sources are littered with references to Asiatic origins and discoveries of Europe. Europa herself, after whom Europe is named, was the daughter of King Agenor of Tyre. The Greek geographer Strabo, for example, writes of African 'discoveries': of Sesostris the Egyptian and Tearco the Ethiopian advancing as far as Thrace in Europe (a salutary lesson, if nothing else, to those who think of Africa solely in terms of 'our' discoveries). But most ancient speculation centred upon Asiatic exploration and 'discoveries'. Strabo also writes that Nebuchadnezzar led an army as far as the Pillars of Hercules; Ammianus Marcellinus and other Roman historians refer to traditions relating to parts of the western Mediterranean being founded by peoples of Asiatic origin, while the legends of Rome itself being founded by Aeneas and his fellow colonisers from Troy are well enough known from Virgil's great epic (and Berlioz' great opera) not to need reiterating here.

According to Greek myth Europe itself is viewed in terms of Asiatic origin: very briefly, Europa was a beautiful Phoenician princess, the sister of King Cadmus of Phoenicia. Zeus fell in love with Europa, inveigled her away disguised as a bull to Crete, and raped her. King Cadmus of Phoenicia with his followers then sailed to Greece in search of his sister and founded the city of Thebes. Henceforth, the continent was named in honour of a Phoenician princess.

A myth is nothing more than just that: a myth. It cannot of course be taken as history or as evidence of Phoenician origins, discoveries, foundations, or even of 'Europe' necessarily being a Phoenician name. However, although one should not perhaps read too much into the foundation of Europe being based on the rape of an Asiatic girl, Phoenician colonisation of the West was real enough and the Phoenician origins of the Greek alphabet beyond doubt. For myths do serve history in one very important way: they are evidence of peoples' self-perception. Hence, it is Greek and Roman *perceptions* of oriental origins, whether myth or not, that are as revealing as fact. What is important here is that the first people in Europe with a voice saw themselves in terms of Asiatic origins; Europe was seen to be defined right from the very beginning in Asiatic terms.

We do know that Phoenicians colonised parts of the Aegean: Prainetos (modern Karamürsel) on the Gulf of Nicomedia, for example, was founded by Phoenicians in the eighth century BC, and others are known. As usual, archaeological evidence fills out the picture considerably. The Uluburun wreck in the Aegean near Bodrum is graphic evidence of Phoenician trading activities as early as the Bronze Age, so it would be indeed surprising if the Phoenicians *did not* colonise parts of Greece. The Phoenicians created the first great colonial empire in history and colonised much of the shores of the Mediterranean—and even some of the Atlantic—at a time when European civilisation was at much the same level as the American which Columbus and his contemporaries found. For we tend to forget that once 'we' were the 'Indians': the savages, the other.[*]

ORIGINS OF THE PHOENICIANS

The original homeland of the Phoenicians is the Levantine littoral (corresponding to the coast of Lebanon today, with parts of Syria and Israel) comprising the ancient city-states of (from north to south) Ugarit, Arvad, Byblos, Tyre, Sidon, Beirut and Gaza, to name just the main ones (Pls 1-8).[†] Being a seaboard people their natural outward expansion was by sea—hence to the West. This was reinforced by the greatest Phoenician city-state, Tyre, being an off-shore island (Pl. 1-2). It gave the Phoenicians an edge in maritime technology, a supremacy they held for over a thousand years. Their ships were the most superior afloat in the Mediterranean, and the Phoenician fleet was the first real navy in history. Much of the science of navigation, astronomy and cartography was invented by the Phoenicians. Ptolemy, on his own admission, based his geography on Phoenician navigational charts, and the science of navigation remained essentially Phoenician until the Middle Ages. Their maritime geography also gave the Phoenicians a lead in

---

[*] Of course by this I mean no disparagement of the great achievements of the North and South American 'Indian' civilisations. Even more I do not intend to diminish the pre-historic European achievement: the Megalithic cultures of Early Europe, to quote just one example, were impressive by any standard, even ancient Egyptian. I am merely trying to put a different perspective.

[†] Although Herodotus and other ancient sources record an unsubstantiated tradition of their origins in Bahrain and adjacent shores of the Gulf.

trading acumen, and the commercial talents of the coastal peoples of the Levant are a characteristic to this day.

An early Semitic people called the Canaanites appear in history along this coastal strip soon after 2000 BC, probably closely related to the earlier indigenous inhabitants. The best documented of the ancient Canaanite city-states is Ugarit, modern Ras Shamra in northern Syria (Pl. 5). Ancient references to Ugarit have been found as widely apart as Mari on the Euphrates, Böğazköy in central Anatolia and Tell el-Amarna in Egypt, dating back to the second millennium BC. Trade rapidly became Ugarit's economic mainstay over the subsequent millennia. Thus, goods from all over the ancient world have been discovered in the excavations: from Egypt, Cyprus, Crete and Greece in the west to Mesopotamia and Persia in the east. Its height was in the latter half of the second millennium, having particular control over the trade of metalwork, timber, grain, wine, and the 'Tyrian' purple dye, which they manufactured locally. The evidence for this trade has come mainly from pottery and cuneiform documents. Its eventual end came at the hands of the 'Sea People'.

The invasions of the Sea Peoples in about 1200 BC is one of the great watersheds of the history of the eastern Mediterranean and Near East. It was probably sparked off by an initial invasion by nomads from the north—possibly the Dorians, one of the ancestors of the Greeks. The exact identity or nature of the invaders is not clearly understood, but this does not matter so much as its ramifications, which had a knock-on effect of displacement, movements and invasions that lasted a considerable time. The 'Sea Peoples', therefore, refers to a fairly general series of events rather than anything or anybody specific. With it, the old powers of Ugarit, Troy, Crete, Mycenae and even great powers like the Hittites disappeared. Egypt itself was destabilised, and in its wake we see the arrival, movement and eventual emergence of new peoples: Dorians, Aramaeans, Hebrews, Philistines, Greeks, a revival of the Assyrians to the east and the emergence of the Etruscans to the west.

After the invasion of the Sea Peoples there followed a Phoenician 'dark age' when commercial activity almost ceased, only to resume after about 1050 in the hands of the port cities of Arvad, Amrit, Byblos, Sidon and Tyre further down the coast (Pls 1-4 and 6-8). This seems to mark the beginning of the western colonial expansion.

TYRE AND THE EXPANSION THROUGHOUT THE MEDITERRANEAN (MAP 1)

This westward colonisation was led, above all, by Tyre, with Sidon following close behind (Pls 1-4). The oldest archaeological evidence of Tyre dates to the Early Bronze Age of about 2900 BC. Following a period of abandonment, very fragmentary traces were found in the Late Bronze Age, although sources (particularly Egyptian) frequently mention Tyre throughout the second millennium. After about 1200 deteriorating climatic conditions led to a decline in agriculture—probably exacerbated by the Sea Peoples—on the Levant coast. This in turn led to over-population in the coastal cities, creating a need for colonial expansion. It was possibly prompted in the eleventh century by Tyre's loss of its Asian markets brought about by the rise of the Middle Assyrian Empire, when commercial contacts with Cyprus were first made (or more likely re-established, as Cyprus had been a close trading partner with Ugarit earlier in the millennium). The Phoenicians also expanded to Rhodes, Crete (which had two ports on the south-west coast known as 'Phoinix') and Sicily during the eleventh and tenth centuries BC.

Further west, literary tradition puts the foundation of Gadir, modern Cadiz in Spain, during the Bronze Age in about 1110 or 1104 BC and Lixus on the Atlantic coast of Morocco a little earlier, with Utica in Tunisia founded in about 1100 as a midway stop to the colonies of the Far West. Biblical references in the time of Solomon mention Tyrian expeditions to Tarshish, which is identified with Tartessus in Spain, the source of tin and other metals (although this the exact meaning of 'tarshish' is interpreted variously; it might also refer to a type of vessel). For many years, archaeological evidence has found nothing earlier than the eighth-seventh century at any of these sites. But the dates have been steadily pushed back as more archaeological evidence emerges: new radiocarbon evidence has now given an end-tenth century date for the Phoenicians in Spain, and the excavation of the Uluburun wreck off the Aegean coast of Turkey provides ample evidence of far-reaching Phoenician maritime activity much earlier in the Bronze Age. Sources are then silent until a second 'wave' of Tyrian colonisation beginning with the foundation of Auza in the ninth century, described below. The foundation of Carthage, where the earliest archaeological finds are eighth century, was a part of this 'second wave'.

Following a decline in Middle Assyrian power, Tyre was able to increase its commercial growth on the Asiatic mainland once more in the mid-tenth century BC under King Ahiram (Hiram) I, who formed close commercial relations with both King David and King Solomon of ancient Israel. It was probably through Solomon that Tyre gained access to lucrative Asian markets and sent a maritime expedition down the Red Sea to 'the Land of Ophir', whilst Solomon's great building project, the Temple in Jerusalem, was built with the aid of materials, craftsmen and architects from Sidon and Tyre. Indeed, the Temple was probably modelled fairly closely on the great Temple of Melqart at Tyre (the rival nature of Phoenician religion to Jehoveh notwithstanding). Relations between Ahiram and Solomon were certainly close and on a personal footing: for long they seemed to have exchanged riddles with each other, with wagers for the right answers. Under Ahiram's successor, Ithobaal I (887-56), territorial expansion in the Near East and Cyprus continued, and Tyre annexed its great rival, Sidon. Tyre's position in the Near East was strengthened with the marriage of Ithobaal's daughter, Jezebel, to Ahab of Israel. With its position in the Near East assured and with centuries of mercantile experience behind it, Tyre was able to turn its attention to more distant horizons: the west.

Tyrian trading activity established a foothold in Cyprus in the eleventh century BC. This culminated in the foundation of Kition as a Phoenician colony in the 820s. Kition was called *Qart-hadasht*, the Phoenician for 'new city' (from which 'Kition' may derive). The ensuing centuries of Phoenician expansion would see more 'Qart-hadashts' established in the west, the name 'Carthage' itself deriving from it. Between about 820 and 600 BC southeastern Cyprus effectively formed a part of the Kingdom of Tyre. Archaeological excavations at Kition have revealed many traces of its Phoenician origin, including a Temple of Astarte in the form of a columned hall.

Ithobaal's reign also saw the Phoenicians' first foothold in North Africa, with the establishment of the colony of Auza in Libya during the long reign of King Pumayyaton of Tyre—better known as Pygmalion—from 820 to 774 BC. The African connection culminated with the foundation of Phoenicia's greatest colony, Carthage, in 814-3 BC. Here for the first time we have a name for one of these early maritime adventurers—a Phoenician Christopher Columbus—but unlike later European explorers, Phoenicia's first great coloniser was a woman. For Carthage was founded, according to legend, by Pumayyaton's sister Elissa, better known to history (and to opera) as Dido.

There ensued large numbers of new foundations all along the Costa del Sol of Spain around Malaga, confirmed by archaeological investigations

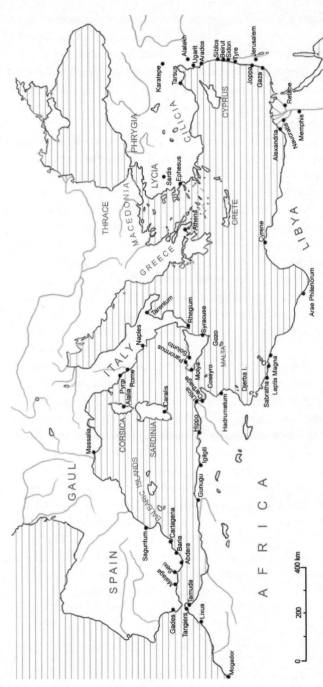

1. *Phoenician expansion in the Mediterranean (after Moscati 1965).*

to be early eighth century, making the south coast of Spain the largest concentration of Phoenician sites outside Lebanon. Ibiza and the Balearics were also colonised, possibly by Phoenicians from Spain rather than directly arriving from the Levant, and extensive traces of ancient metal exploitation have been found there. The Phoenicians then expanded all around the coast of Sicily, typically occupying promontories and off-shore islands. Some retraction was prompted by the arrival of Greek settlers on the island at the end of the eighth century, leading the Phoenicians to concentrate their activities on the north-western part of the island focussed on Motya, which became the main Phoenician colony on Sicily in subsequent centuries. This was followed soon by Malta, where the newcomers intermarried with the indigenous inhabitants, and the Phoenician language remains the main element in the Maltese language today. Another concentration of Phoenician colonies stretched along the coasts of Libya and Tunisia comprising the cities of Leptis Magna, Hippo, Hadrumentum and others (although these might have been Sidonian rather than Tyrian). In Sardinia there is considerable archaeological evidence (including an important Phoenician inscription) for a number of Phoenician colonies of the ninth-eighth centuries BC, probably founded by the arrival of colonists from Carthage under Sardo (who gave his name to the island), as well as others from both Phoenician Spain and Phoenicia itself. More indirect archaeological evidence, however, suggests initial Phoenician trading contacts with Sardinia as early as the eleventh century BC, particularly from Phoenician Cyprus. There is further evidence of Phoenician presence up and down the west coast of Italy, with Phoenician influence even discernable in some elements of Etruscan art, although the presence was never as strong as in other parts of the western Mediterranean.

This Mediterranean wide expansion was made possible by an understanding of the sea currents and prevailing winds that put the Phoenicians far ahead of any rival. The outward journey from Tyre was by way of Cyprus, the Ionian Sea and Sicily to southern Spain. The North African route was not possible for this outward voyage because of the prevailing winds, but was better for the return journey. Hence, many of the North African colonies were later than the Far Western ones.

EXPANSION INTO AFRICA AND THE ATLANTIC

Having encompassed the Mediterranean, the Phoenicians next passed through the Straits of Gibraltar to the Atlantic. Along the Moroccan coast, Lixus was founded in the seventh century BC as a main centre for Phoenician activity in western Africa (mostly trade in gold, ivory and fish). Excavations at modern Larache confirm a seventh century date for Lixus (although the Classical traditions mentioned above record an 1100 BC date), and Tangier (ancient Tingis) was founded as a Carthaginian colony in the sixth century. Further south, a major Phoenician trade entrepôt was established on the island of Mogador (modern Essaouira) from the seventh century, and commercial activity possibly extended as far as the Canaries and Azores (although there is no archaeological proof as yet). The Phoenicians even achieved one of the world's great navigational 'firsts' in 596 when a Phoenician expedition financed by the Pharaoh Necho successfully completed a circumnavigation of Africa from east to west. The account of this is given by Herodotus, who disbelieves it. But the very reasons given by Herodotus for not believing the voyage actually confirms it: that as they sailed around Africa the sun was to the north instead of the south. Indirect evidence for another possible Phoenician circumnavigation in the second century BC was recounted by Strabo, when he reported the discovery of the wreck of a Phoenician ship on the coast of east Africa that could only have come from Cadiz.

Tyre's colonial 'empire' in Africa culminated in about 455 BC with the establishment of a colony at Cerne by the navigator Hanno, probably in Senegal or Cameroon, for importing ivory, gold and skins. Hanno's expedition comprised six vessels and some 3,000 men and women, amply supplied with provisions and equipment. This, therefore, was more than just a voyage of discovery or a commercial adventure: it was an attempt at the colonisation of Africa. Many of the place-names down the west coast of Morocco have been identified from the descriptions given in the account of Hanno's voyage. The island of Cerne was used as a base for further exploration along the coast of West Africa, but the colony was eventually abandoned and many of the settlers returned to Carthage.

Further north along the Atlantic seaboard of Europe, the Phoenician traders' insatiable demands for raw metals resulted in a maritime expedition in the seventh century along the coasts of Portugal, Brittany and possibly Cornwall. This pioneering expedition paved the way for the voyage of

Himilco in about 450 BC, who sailed to Brittany and probably as far as Cornwall, the Scilly Isles, Ireland and the Azores. The tidal island of St Michael's Mount just off the coast of Cornwall has been identified with the ancient island of Ictis where the Phoenicians came to trade for tin, but this has not yet been verified by archaeology.

The first half of the first millennium BC, therefore, sees the Near East establishing permanent footholds across the sea in the 'Far West'. Hence, the later Arab advances into western Europe under Islam were not so much the beginnings of a movement so much as a culmination, and can only be fully understood in the context of the Phoenicians. Just as the Atlantic was to become a West European 'lake' and the Americas a European New world, the precedent for such outward western movements was set thousands of years earlier with the establishment of the Mediterranean as a Phoenician 'lake' and north-west Africa and south-west Europe as the Phoenician 'New World.' It is to this Phoenician New World and its legacy that we turn next.

Chapter 2

THE NEAR EAST'S FAR WEST
The Phoenician New World and its Legacy

Imagine him here—the very end of the world, a sea the colour of
lead, a sky the colour of smoke, a kind of ship about as rigid as a
concertina—and going up this river with stores, or orders, or what
you like. Sand-banks, marshes, forests, savages,—precious little
to eat fit for a civilized man ... cold, fog, tempests, disease, exile,
and death—death skulking in the air, in the water, in the bush.

Joseph Conrad, *Heart of Darkness*[1]

The savage, uncivilised land that Marlow, Joseph Conrad's narrator in
Heart of Darkness, is describing above is not remote, darkest Africa—but
the Thames in England. At the beginning of the book, the old seaman
Marlow is sitting on the deck of a river boat at the mouth of the Thames
and puts himself in the position of a Roman commander on reaching our
shores for the very first time 'nineteen hundred years ago'. The picture
he conjures up is of his younger self, sailing up river into the heart of
Africa in the story he is about to narrate. In trying to put ourselves in
the places of these early Phoenician navigators to form a picture of what
they must have found on the rustic shores of distant Europe, a similar
impact thousands of years later is overwhelmingly brought to mind. For
the Phoenicians encountered much the same conditions—and responded
with much the same reactions—as our own European navigators did when
they first started exploring the coasts of Africa, America and the Pacific
after the Middle Ages. Marlow's Thames—or the Dart or the Guadalquivir,
which the Phoenicians penetrated—was ultimately not much different
from the Amazon.

THE PHOENICIAN NEW WORLD

By the seventh century BC a colonial and commercial 'Phoenician triangle' was established in the western Mediterranean comprising Sicily, Carthage, Sardinia and Andalusia that was virtually impregnable to competitors. It gave the Phoenicians a monopoly in the west, and formed the basis of future Carthaginian power. The jewel in the crown of the Phoenicians' overseas empire was southern Spain. Jewellery certainly forms an appropriate metaphor, for it was the search for tin and silver above all that brought them here (not to mention iron, copper, lead and gold as well). One is reminded—most appropriately—of the later passion that similarly drove the Spanish colonists to America in search of gold. More than any other colony, Cadiz was Tyre's gateway to Phoenicia's own New World Eldorado. It remained very much an 'oriental' city until long after the Phoenicians had left, right down to the first century AD according to Latin accounts. Indeed, these accounts give an impression of a rough, tough opulent boom-town made rich from the silver trade, reminding one overwhelmingly of descriptions of Spain's own New World 'gold-rush' cities. It had a famous temple dedicated to the Phoenician god Melqart. This temple preserved its Semitic characteristics right through to the end, long after it had been absorbed into the Roman cult of Hercules: the absence of figural representation (an Arabian concept that survives in Islam) puzzled the Classical authors, and the central feature of the Melqart cult, both in Cadiz and elsewhere in Phoenician Spain, was the cycle of annual resurrection. This religious impact is explored more in Chapter 6.

Phoenician exploitation of the natives of Spain for their silver bears all the similarities of late Spanish exploitation of New World people for their gold. Diodorus of Sicily, for example, writes how the gullible natives were totally unaware of the value of silver so that the Phoenicians were able to buy it for negligible amounts, usually trinkets—beads for the natives indeed! Such were the quantities of silver bought for next to nothing that, according to one account, Phoenician sea captains even cast their anchors in solid silver when their holds could carry no more—tales of Eldorado again.

The south Mediterranean coast of Spain around Granada, Malaga and Almeria became the richest concentration of Phoenician sites outside Lebanon, with many settlements as close as a kilometre apart. Most of these, however, were just small fishing and agricultural communities, rather than the larger settlements found elsewhere, as there were little or no mineral resources, and most of them were abandoned after 550 BC. The archaeological evidence—of which there is an abundance—reveals a picture of fairly large, substantial houses with the funerary remains reinforcing the picture of wealthy family groups. There was some commercial activity with the hinterland, but nothing on the scale of Cadiz. The coastal strip had good agricultural and fishing potential, so all indications suggest self-supporting settlements purely for the purposes of colonisation rather than commercial activity, dominated by groups of large wealthy families—once again, the comparison with Spanish New World ranching communities is striking.

After about 550 there seems to have been a crisis in the Spanish colonies and a subsequent decline, possibly prompted by a decline in the value of silver (or perhaps the natives had simply learnt to demand its true value at last). There may also have been more competition from the Phocaeans and other Greek colonial powers.

The literary and mythological evidence that puts the foundation of Cadiz and other far western colonies as early as the twelfth century are now usually dismissed by most scholars, as archaeological evidence favours eighth, or at earliest ninth, century foundations. Myth they might be, but that is to miss the point: it is the ancient perception of their origin that is of importance here. One must also remember that archaeology can only really reveal concrete evidence of colonies and settlements, rather than discovery and exploration, which are far more intangible—the first landfall of a pioneering discoverer by its very nature can rarely survive in archaeology, but only in literature and myth.* The archaeological evidence for these colonies, therefore, must date some time—even many centuries—after the initial discoveries that made their eventual settlement possible, so the literary evidence may be nearer the truth after all. The gap between the traditional dates and the archaeological evidence is in any case narrowing with more archaeological discoveries. '… it is quite natural to expect archaeology to indicate the consolidation rather than the first foundation of the colonies, and there might be decades, if not centuries, between the two phases.'[2] The passing of the alphabet, for example, to the Greeks from the Phoenicians in the eighth century must be seen as the *culmination* of a process of diffusion, rather than the beginning.

---

* The archaeological evidence for Captain Cook's landfall on the coast of Queensland being an exception to this.

CARTHAGE AND THE BEGINNINGS OF EUROPE'S FIRST GREAT POWER

By the beginning of the seventh century Tyre had lost virtually all of its mainland Asiatic possession to the resurgent Neo-Assyrian Empire, and by about 640 BC all of mainland Tyre was made an Assyrian province. After the end of the sixth century Tyre declined even further and its arch rival Sidon took over much of the Phoenician trade. But Tyre had left behind a daughter city that was to soon eclipse even the founder. This was Carthage (Pls 9-11).

The foundation of Carthage was one of the most celebrated myths of the ancient world—a myth that still has enormous dramatic appeal today. According to this, the king of Tyre, Pumayatton or Pygmalion, kills his brother-in-law, forcing his sister, Elishat or Elissa or Dido, to flee. In founding Carthage as a consequence, there is the justly famous encounter with Aeneas, approximately linking two famous episodes: the destruction of Troy and the foundation of Rome. Indeed, the *Aeneid* contains a vivid 'eyewitness' description of the construction of Carthage:

'The Trojans hurried along their way, guided by the path. They were now climbing a massive hill which overhung the city and commanded a view of the citadel. Aeneas looked wonderingly at the solid structures springing up where there had been only African huts, and at the gates, the turmoil, and the paved streets. The Tyrians were hurrying about busily, some tracing a line for the walls and manhandling stones up the slopes as they strained to build their citadel, and others siting some building and marking its outline by ploughing a furrow. And they were making choice of laws, of officers of state, and of councillors to command their respect. At one spot they were excavating the harbour, and at another a party was laying out an area for the deep foundations of a theatre; they were also hewing from quarries mighty pillars to stand tall and handsome beside the stage which was still to be built. It was like the work which keeps the bees hard at their tasks about the flowering countryside as the sun shines in the calm of early summer, when they escort the new generation, now fully grown, into the open air, or squeeze clear honey into bulging cells, packing them with sweet nectar; or else take over loads brought by their foragers; or sometimes form up to drive a flock of lazy drones from their farmstead. All is a ferment of activity; and the scent of honey rises with the perfume of thyme.

Aeneas looked up at the buildings. "Ah, fortunate people," he exclaimed, "for your city-walls are already rising!" "[3]

Although mythological, the encounter has important ramifications. For regardless of its historical accuracy, what is important is that the Romans themselves, Europe's first great power, saw themselves as being founded—'discovered'—from the East: founded by Trojans from Asia Minor, with Phoenician elements added. The Phoenicians' outward expansion that resulted in the discovery of Europe and the foundation of Carthage anticipates the foundation of Rome and European civilisation. Thus, Carthage becomes a catalyst where Phoenician, Anatolian, Greek and Roman mythologies draw together.

In addition to the well known encounter with Aeneas, Elissa/Dido is pursued by Hiarbas, the king of the Libyans, on whose lands the enclave of Carthage is founded. Hiarbas wished to marry her, but rather than be unfaithful to her first husband, whose murder by Pygmalion led to the founding of Carthage, Elissa commits suicide by self-immolation on a funeral pyre just outside the city. This episode was to have important echoes in the later history of Carthage. Sacrifice by fire—usually the sacrifice of babies and young children—was to feature largely in later Carthaginian history and was to have important ramifications for the spread of Christianity as we shall see (Chapter 6). The location of Elissa's funerary pyre outside the city probably corresponds to the *tophet*, the place for ritual child-sacrifice, that has been located by archaeology (Pl. 11). Following the final capture of Carthage by Scipio Aemelianus in 146 BC, at the conclusion of the Third Punic War with Rome, the widow of the defeated Carthaginian general Hasdrubal, casts herself and her children into a funerary pyre. Thus, 'myth and history came together full circle, with a similar emblematic female figure in both cases.'[4]

According to Greek tradition, Carthage was founded about fifty years before the fall of Troy, which would put its foundation at about 1215 BC. Tyre's own records (preserved in Greek history) mark the traditional foundation at 814 BC, which corresponds more closely to the archaeological evidence, where the earliest burials are eighth century BC and the earliest *tophet* finds might be as late as the ninth century BC. The rise of Carthage after the eighth century was, unlike the other Tyrian colonies, as a military and naval power rather than a purely commercial one. This was to offset the rise of the Greeks as challengers to Phoenician colonial power, whom Carthage defeated in Sicily in 550 BC (although it is significant that the Sicilian Greeks later united with Carthage against the Romans in both the

First and Second Punic Wars). In general, the character of Carthage and the central Mediterranean colonies seem quite different to those of the Far West, which appear culturally much closer to the Phoenician homeland. Carthage appears more independent than the western colonies such as Cadiz. Carthage, in alliance with the Etruscans, defeated the Greeks once more in 535 BC, and the following century was marked by many wars between Carthage and the Greek states to decide who would rule the waves. With the decline of Tyrian power in Spain, it was the daughter colony of Carthage that stepped into the vacuum. Over the fifth and fourth centuries BC all of southern Spain and much of North Africa became a neo-Phoenician empire under Carthage, with bases extending into southern France.

Carthage's maritime supremacy inevitably brought it into conflict with the rising new power on the European mainland, Rome. This culminated in Rome's Punic Wars in the third and second centuries which finally brought about the end of Carthage—and the age of Phoenician expansion as a whole. Before that, in about 480 BC, Carthage had made a treaty with the Persian Empire under Xerxes to carve up the entire Mediterranean between them. With Xerxes' subsequent defeat in Greece this never came about and Rome was able to expand within Italy fairly unhindered during the fifth and fourth centuries. The first treaty between Carthage and Rome was in 509 BC, restricting Rome's maritime trade and confirming Carthage's control of Sardinia. Sardinia and Africa were further confirmed as belonging within Carthage's sphere of influence in another treaty with Rome in 438 BC. The two powers first clashed openly over rival interests in Sicily, culminating in the First Punic War of 264-41 BC (although significantly, the Greek King Hiero II of Syracuse at first allied himself with Carthage against the Romans—and his grandson King Hieronymus also allied Syracuse with Carthage in the Second Punic War). Initially, Rome suffered massive naval losses at the hands of the Phoenicians, but it was able to strike back with a landing on Africa by Regulus. Regulus, however, was defeated and Rome's ambitions to establish a foothold on Africa were thwarted, but the Carthaginians for their part were forced out of all but a tip of Sicily. Ostensibly, therefore, the First Punic War was stalemate. But the results were important for both sides. For the Romans, it forced them for the first time to become a naval power, beginning a mastery of the seas that would eventually see the entire Mediterranean littoral under Rome. For Carthage, it resulted in the establishment of Carthaginian territory in Phoenician Spain and the foundation of New Carthage—Cartagena—by Hasdrubal, a firm bridgehead on the European mainland. Thus, with Rome becoming a Mediterranean sea-power and Carthage becoming a European land power, the stage was set for the Second Punic War.

The Second Punic War created one of the history's greatest generals and probably Phoenicia's most famous son, the legendary Hannibal. The story does not need to be retold here, as it is well enough known and forms more a part of Rome's history. But it must be emphasised that in confronting and overcoming Carthage, Rome, hitherto a local power, was thrust centre stage: the beginning of Roman expansion had arrived as a direct response to the end of the Phoenician. When Hannibal was finally defeated by the Romans and had to flee for his life, he sailed back to the Phoenician homeland to Tyre where he was greeted as a hero. 'Almost symbolically Carthage's greatest man found his first refuge in the Phoenician mother country from which Dido had departed over six centuries before.'[5]

Despite some of the most dazzling military victories the world had seen, Hannibal was in the end totally defeated. With his defeat ended forever the possibility of the Phoenicians' establishing an empire in Europe. Thus, this final stage of the Phoenicians' outward expansion ended up a complete disaster, with even the total destruction of their city, Carthage, at the end of the Third Punic War in 146 BC.

Or was it such a disaster? It was the end of Phoenician expansion, it is true. But the end of over half a millennium of unrivalled success in expansion from tiny Levantine bases to all corners of the Mediterranean and beyond to southern Europe, the North Atlantic and around Africa can hardly be counted a disaster. The effect of this expansion had already changed Europe ineradicably—and was to continue to change it in the future. The legacy of this we will examine more below. But most of all, it thrust a little known European power on to the world scene. Up until now the centre of civilisation lay in the lands of the East. It was the Phoenicians more than anybody else who had brought it west. With that, we see the birth of civilisation in Western Europe.

THE CONQUERORS CONQUERED:
ROME AND THE AFTERMATH OF THE PUNIC WARS

Phoenician power was at an end, but the Phoenicians as a people did not simply disappear—indeed, they survive as the Lebanese (not to mention Lebanese business acumen) of today, along with the other people of the Levant coast (and the language survives in modern Maltese). The subsequent history of the Phoenicians in their homeland we will have cause to return to. But the Phoenicians of North Africa—the Carthaginians—and their legacy affected subsequent history in several curious but important ways. For the wars between Carthage and Rome had some surprising footnotes centuries after the final conflict.

Hannibal's dazzling campaigns in Spain and Italy may have been the last episodes in the long history of the discovery and colonisation of Europe from the Near East. After Rome had crushed his armies and occupied his capital, Hannibal was forced to flee eastwards to the lands of his Phoenician roots, first to Tyre and then seeking sanctuary at the court of the only other power in the Mediterranean that might resist Rome, the Seleucid kingdom of Antiochus III—Antiochus the Great, whose campaigns reached as far as India—at Antioch. Warning Antiochus of the new threat from the West, Hannibal urged him to turn his might against Italy. The combination of Antiochus and Hannibal brought Rome to the East for the first time, and in 190 BC a mighty Roman army commanded by the great Scipio brothers crossed into Asia. In the ensuing Battle of Magnesia the following year, Rome won its first battle on Asiatic soil. Antiochus' army of 75,000 suffered complete defeat at the hands of Rome's army of only 30,000, with Hannibal's naval squadron suffering similar defeat. Hounded by the Romans demanding blood, Hannibal fled yet again to the court of the Armenian king and eventually to the sanctuary of the King of Bithynia in western Anatolia. Here the last great Carthaginian committed suicide in 183, a military genius of the finest order and one of the ancient world's greatest heroes but ultimately, having unwittingly brought his enemy Rome into Asia where it was to stay for nearly 1,700 years, a tragic figure.

Hannibal may have been the last great Carthaginian, but another great Phoenician from North Africa was to succeed where Hannibal had failed. In the late second century AD a new dynasty assumed the purple in Rome: the Severans. But unlike the Julio-Claudians, the Severan dynasty hailed from distant corners of the empire, not from Rome itself nor even Italy. Its founder was Septimius Severus, a member of the Phoenician aristocracy of Leptis Magna in North Africa, originally a Phoenician colony (Pl. 38). We will discuss this remarkable family further in Chapter 5, but for the moment we need only emphasise that there can be little doubt of Septimius' Phoenician sentiments. In 197, a few years after he had become emperor of Rome and the ultimate embodiment of everything that Rome stood for, he made a state visit to his birthplace at Leptis Magna where in a formal ceremony he re-affirmed the links with the mother city: not with Rome but with *Tyre*. He also made a particular point of lavishing attention on the city of Tyre itself, making sure that it rose from the ashes of Alexander's holocaust to be once again one of the most magnificent cities of the Levantine coast (Pl. 2). Furthermore, whilst on campaign in the East against the Parthians, Septimius Severus made a point of seeking out an obscure hillside in Bithynia, just inland from the Sea of Marmara. Here at last he found the goal of his pilgrimage: the burial place of Hannibal himself (Pl. 12). Septimius ordered the place to be cleared and restored and a monument set up over it as befitted the burial place of a great hero—and his fellow countryman. We can imagine how Septimius, now master of a Roman world far larger than Hannibal himself or even his antagonists could have possibly dreamt of, might have whispered as he stood by Hannibal's grave (in Punic of course): 'Well, we won!'

The ghost of Hannibal was finally laid to rest, but what of his shattered city, Carthage, which the Romans had so thoroughly obliterated at the end of the Third Punic War? Despite this, its strategic location was too good to ignore, especially for such an acknowledged strategist as Julius Caesar who re-founded it as a Roman colony in the first century BC. Some 2,200 Carthaginians were resettled on the site eventually to rebuild a city once again over its ashes. By the third century AD Carthage had re-emerged as one of the great cities of the Mediterranean and one of the most important cities of the Roman Empire after Alexandria and Antioch (Pls 9, 10). When Rome became Christian, the Bishopric of Carthage was one of Christendom's most powerful seats. In the fifth and sixth centuries Carthage was the capital of a German kingdom founded by the Vandal chief Genseric, until it was taken for the second time by the Romans, now ruling from Constantinople, where Constantine had moved the Roman capital in the fourth century. And it was from Carthage that in the seventh century a new emperor of the Romans emerged. This was the Emperor Heraclius. Heraclius was one of Rome's best generals deserving greater prominence than history has granted him, for he was able to save an empire brought to within an ace of extinction by the

Iranians. Before that, however, on arriving in Constantinople from Carthage to assume the purple, he found the Roman capital and the eastern empire in such disarray that, like Constantine before him, he contemplated moving the Roman capital once again: the new and third Rome was to be Carthage! In the end Heraclius was persuaded to keep the capital at Constantinople (thus ensuring the survival of the Roman Empire for another eight centuries), but it would have been one of history's greatest ironies if the capital of Rome had ended up in the city of its greatest foe.

THE LEGACY TO EUROPE

In general Tyre's western colonisation did not seem to be a result of deliberate policy: it was not governed by a single set of rules or theoretical framework, but more haphazard and diverse—it was never a centrally ruled colonial empire. Nevertheless, the Phoenicians enjoyed a monopoly of the Mediterranean for five centuries, from 1100 to 600 BC, until the Greeks emerged as serious challengers. Even then, the Phoenicians of Carthage were to remain the main Mediterranean naval power for a further four centuries until Rome finally triumphed in the Second Punic War. For the best part of a thousand years, the Mediterranean was a Phoenician lake.

The Phoenicians, therefore, were the world's very first overseas colonial empire and were the first Asiatic power to penetrate Europe, a contact that was both fundamental and over an immensely long period of time. But what of its legacy? This may at first be difficult to perceive, looking back over two and a half millennia at a civilisation that appears ancient, remote and irrelevant. We have already seen how much the rise of Rome, perhaps the main root of our own European identity, was a response to the Phoenician challenge. But more than Rome, the Phoenicians' effect on Spain was fundamental, for Spain was a Phoenician sphere of influence for 500 years. Hence, when the Romans expanded into Spain it was not a rustic backwater that they found, as Gaul or Britain were, but a society already grown sophisticated from its contact with Phoenician civilisation. Small wonder that some of Rome's most gifted early emperors, such as Trajan and Hadrian, hailed from here.* But more important, it is no coincidence that Spain itself, in turn, was to inherit the mantle of the Phoenicians' outward

---

* As well as, in the fourth century, the Emperor Theodosius, all three emperors from the comparatively minor town of Italica outside Seville.

drive and become Europe's greatest overseas colonial power after the Middle Ages. We will have occasion to return to this aspect of Spain's heritage when we discuss the Arab world expansion later.

With so few material remains of the Phoenicians it is difficult to see what legacy they bequeathed, if any. Writing in 1942, Emil Ludwig could write off the Phoenicians merely as 'peddlers and swindlers' before launching into a full-scale panegyric of the Greeks as the true instigators of civilisation in the Mediterranean.[6] After all, there are no pyramids, no great temples, or cities littered with standing ruins, and our buildings for the past two millennia have adhered very firmly to Greek and Roman architectural principles; there is no hint of anything Phoenician. The Phoenician is one of the haziest of all early civilisations.

Perhaps, therefore, it is appropriate to begin with their architectural legacy. This has been one of the largest (in scale) and most obvious: planned cities. The grid system of town planning is often referred to as the 'Hippodamian' town plan after Hippodamus of Miletus, who used it in his rebuilding of the city of Miletus in 479 BC, and is generally regarded as a Greek—hence 'European'—innovation (never mind that Miletus is in Asia and that Hippodamus himself was a citizen of the Persian Empire, not of Greece). The origins of Greek town planning are seen to go back further to the ordered (rather than truly planned) layouts of Old Smyrna and pre-Hippodamian Miletus in the eighth-seventh centuries BC. The first truly planned towns of the Graeco-Roman world, however, are in southern Italy and Sicily rather than around the Aegean. The first laid-out gridded plan in Europe was probably Paestum in Italy in the sixth century BC, possibly the first properly planned town in the western Mediterranean, and several more followed.

All of these early examples of the gridded town plan are Greek colonies in Sicily and Southern Italy of the sixth-fifth centuries BC. This is in striking contrast to the lack of such plans on the Greek peninsula, the origin of the colonies themselves. The origins of such plans are presumed to be Old Smyrna and Miletus in Ionia, but Ionian colonies were usually around the Black Sea and eastern Mediterranean, not in the western Mediterranean (and are not generally characterised by gridded layouts). The evidence suggests that the origins of this system, therefore, lie in southern Italy and Sicily, rather than the Greeks of either the Balkan peninsula or Asia Minor.

It is significant that southern Italy and Sicily saw colonisation by the Phoenicians before the arrival of the Greeks. In this context it is worth noting that the only extensively excavated Phoenician city in North Africa not obscured by later overburden is Kerkouane in Tunisia (Pls 13-14). Founded probably in the sixth century, 'the urban plan shows a well-designed checkerboard pattern with regular crossing streets, but the city blocks *(insulae)* have varying dimensions and adjacent components.'[7] The earliest layout of Carthage itself also appears to be planned (although too much lies buried to be certain).

In the Phoenician homeland in the Levant, there is evidence of city planning in the layout of Byblos as early as 2800 BC. Here, 'precautions had been taken in laying out the streets so that access to the city walls from the centre of the city and the residential area would be easy and rapid in the case of attack.'[8] This would put it well within the Near Eastern tradition of planned layouts going back many thousands of years. The Phoenicians, therefore, may have brought town planning from the East long before the Greeks and Romans made it their own.

In assessing the Phoenicians and the transference of urbanisation to the west via their colonies in North Africa, it is worth contrasting the density of Roman towns in Tunisia and Algeria—the so-called 'six hundred cities'—with the lack in Cyrenaica, known in Roman times as the 'Pentapolis'—just five cities. The difference is pre-Roman: virtually all of the 'Roman towns' in Tunisia and Algeria were older Phoenician foundations, but there was no Phoenician colonisation in Cyrenaica, which remained exclusively Greek. It was the Phoenicians who bequeathed urbanisation to the west.

Perhaps the greatest legacy of Phoenician civilisation, however, was intellectual rather than material: in the fields of religion, literature and law. The religious legacy we will examine in Chapter 6, but for now we will examine some of the intellectual.

THE PHOENICIAN RENAISSANCE

The conquests of the Phoenician homeland by, at first, Alexander of Macedon in the fourth century BC and subsequently by Rome in the first century BC, appear at first sight to have extinguished ancient Phoenician civilisation for good—particularly that by Alexander, whose campaign down the Phoenician coast was conducted with a brutal savagery and destruction rarely matched at the time. But indirectly, it brought about a renaissance. The immediate result of Alexander's conquest in the Near East was the foundation and rapid rise of Alexandria, creating a direct Hellenistic challenge to the Phoenician maritime and commercial supremacy in the Mediterranean. To some extent this was off-set during the Hellenistic period by the north-south division of the eastern Mediterranean into the two rival Macedonian dynasties: the Seleucids of Antioch in Syria protecting the Phoenicians' older supremacy against the Ptolemies encouraging Alexandria's rise. But the destruction of Carthage by Rome further exacerbated the position, a Phoenician loss that was Alexandria's gain. With Alexandria and all of the Phoenician city states passing to the Romans in the first century BC, Alexandria's supremacy of the seas was assured.

Ultimately, perhaps the Phoenicians gained the most. For the Phoenician creative energies and intellectual talents, hitherto absorbed by trade, could be redirected elsewhere. Hence, the Phoenicians enjoyed a renaissance under the Romans. Historiography figured prominently, and Philo of Byblos (probably late second century AD) made available the ancient Phoenician historical works to the world of Classical learning. Chief of these were the writings of Sanchuniathon, who lived in the seventh century BC or earlier and whose work is now lost apart from later references to it. That there was an extensive Phoenician literature is known from references in later sources: historiography figured highly, but so too did geography, agriculture, law and possibly other forms such as myth and narrative literature. In this context it must be emphasised that Phoenician literature would have been written on papyrus, because of its close links with Egypt (the word 'bible' derived from the Phoenician port of Byblos, because of the huge transhipment of papyrus that passed through), unlike, say, Mesopotamian literature written on more permanent clay tablets. Papyrus is a notoriously perishable material outside its native Egypt—and one recalls too that both Tyre and Carthage, probably the greatest repositories of Phoenician culture, were razed with a deliberate and malignant thoroughness (by Alexander of Macedon and by the Romans respectively) when no documents would have survived. Josephus, although a Judaean, together with Eusebius and Procopius from Caesarea as well as Herodian, Ammianus Marcellinus, Libanius, John Malalas and other historians of the Antioch 'school', must ultimately be considered a part of this Levantine historiographical tradition.

The historian John Headley opens his discussion of the Renaissance with the European rediscovery in the fifteenth century of Ptolemy, thus firmly anchoring the Renaissance in Classical—i.e., Western—roots, and his *Geography* is described as 'the most significant single work among the classical texts recovered by the Italian Renaissance.'⁹ This may be true (although some might claim Plato) and there is little doubt that the Renaissance was a rediscovery of Classical learning, but to state that it was a solely Western inspired phenomenon is to miss the point. Leaving aside the fact that much of the Renaissance rediscovery of the Classics came via Muslim Spain and Byzantium, Ptolemy himself acknowledges Phoenician geographical science as his source and furthermore developed and practised his ideas in Africa, not Greece. Of course, to say he was an 'African' would be facile, he was Graeco-Macedonian, but equally to say he was Greek would be like describing an Australian as English. Furthermore, it was Islam that took Ptolemaic geography further: his main work is best known under its Arabic title, the *Almagest*, and it was al-Khwarazmi in the eleventh century who most fully developed his ideas. If the Renaissance rediscovery of its 'European' roots began through Ptolemy, it was a rediscovery of Phoenicia through an Islamic filter.

For in geography the Phoenician achievement in the Roman period was no less impressive. Marinus of Tyre (early second century AD) drew upon ancient Phoenician traditions of navigation, not to mention their nautical charts and other geographical records, to lay the foundations scientific geography. He was the first to allocate localities to specific latitude and longitude using mathematically based maps rather than merely descriptive itineraries. His work forms the foundation of Ptolemy's geography. Other areas where Phoenician intellectual activity excelled included philosophy, such as the Neo-Platonists Porphyry of Tyre and Iamblichus of Chalcis.

But perhaps it was in the field of law that the Phoenician renaissance was to have its greatest effect. At the beginning of the third century the Emperor Septimius Severus—of Phoenician origin as we have seen—founded an entirely new institution in Beirut that was to become world famous. This was the Law School, the first such institution in the Roman world (Pl. 15). It was enthusiastically supported by Septimius' successors. The Beirut Law School was to have a profound effect on Roman civilisation, for it represents the birth of Roman—hence European—jurisprudence, of which Justinian's monumental *Digest* was the first great achievement. It attracted many prominent legal minds, mostly drawn from the Phoenician population of the Levant itself (by this time increasingly called 'Arabs' by the Romans). The most famous were Papinian, a native of Emesa (modern Homs in Syria), and his contemporary Ulpian, a native of Tyre. Both were patronised by the Severan dynasty (although Caracalla had Papinian murdered) and both are acknowledged in Justinian's *Digest* as forming the basis of Roman Law. This subsequently formed the basis of legal systems throughout Europe. As a 'European' export, Roman Law became the basis of much of North and South America as well, and ultimately even influenced countries not colonised by Europe. The Ottoman Empire also adopted much of the Justinianic law code, thus ensuring its continuity in the Near East as well. Thus, the Phoenician legacy became world-wide.

Beirut and its justly famous law school, and with it its profound legacy, was founded and promoted by emperors whose origins and destinies were intimately bound to Phoenician culture. Above all, it must be emphasised that, Roman enclave though Beirut may have been, the environment of its law school is the Near East, not Italy. Many of the great scholars who dominated it were natives of the Near East, however Romanised, such as Papinian and Ulpian. It drew upon literary traditions that stretched back to Sanchuniathon of Beirut in the seventh century BC and legal traditions that stretched back even further to the Judaic traditions of the early first millennium and the Mesopotamian law codes of the early second millennium.

A FINAL WORD

Perhaps the greatest debt that Europe and the world owes to Phoenician civilisation lies before our very eyes every single day. For it was the Phoenicians who bequeathed the first alphabet to the world. Up until about 1600 BC all languages had been written using a complex and clumsy system of signs—hieroglyphs—often numbering many hundreds or even thousands of characters. The shortcomings of such a cumbersome system are obvious.* Hence, Phoenician scribes in Ugarit decided to simplify the

---

* Although it is interesting to observe how we are now coming full circle as, in an increasingly international world, we turn more to signs—hieroglyphs—to communicate. Compare the dashboard of a car of the fifties with one now: gone are words for 'lights', 'brakes', 'fuel', etc.; instead we have (often baffling!) symbols of flashing lights or whatever. A lavatory at an airport or other public place is no longer labelled 'ladies' or 'gents' in English or any language, but simply has a symbol of a lady or man (or top hat or high heel—hieroglyphs too can be euphemisms!). The computer on which I am writing this communicates to me more by a vast array of symbols—icons—than by words. We are, in other words, reverting to cuneiform and hieroglyphics. The Chinese, who use a similar system of writing by signs rather than an alphabet, having been disadvantaged by their writing system for so long, perhaps will end up having the greatest advantage in communication after all.

entire process: instead of using many hundreds of symbols, each meaning a different syllable, word or idea, they narrowed it down to just twenty-two signs, each representing a different sound that could be applied to all words. The world's first alphabet was born.

This invention was itself a result of the Phoenicians' commercial propensities: after all, what is trade without the ability to keep accurate records of who owes what to whom? It is impossible to overestimate the importance of this revolution. The Greeks, of course, borrowed and adapted the Phoenician alphabet for their own purposes, supposedly brought to Greece by Cadmus of Tyre, according to Greek myth. This is probably a mythical reflection of widespread early Phoenician penetration of the Greek world, as Herodotus and others cite Phoenician colonisation of Boeotia and the coasts of Asia Minor, along with various religious borrowings from the Near East (such as some aspects of the cult of Dionysus). The alphabet was a part of this cultural interchange, and Homer's great epics are the direct result of the Greek language adopting the Phoenician alphabet. It is important to remember that virtually all the world's alphabets, from Viking runes in the far west to Thai in the Far East are based upon this single Phoenician invention. In one fell swoop the Phoenicians democratised the entire literary process: from being the preserve of a small number of scribes who required many years' training to remember thousands of symbols and their meanings, writing suddenly became available to anyone who simply had to remember twenty-two (or twenty-six) simple signs and their sounds. This was probably the Phoenicians' greatest gift to mankind.

It comes as no surprise to learn that of all people, it is the Phoenicians' direct descendants—the Arabs—who perhaps honour the written word most, both in their reverence of Qur'an as being the literal written word of God and their celebration of writing in the calligraphic arts. With the Phoenicians merging imperceptibly into the Arabs of the Levantine coast during the time of their greatest legacy in the Roman period—or at least forming an essential background to their rise and eventual expansion—we turn next to the Arabs before Islam.

Chapter 3

GLITTERING KINGDOMS
Arab States before Islam

They serve as a pre-view of the gigantic show soon to come.
Philip K Hitti[1]

History gives the impression of the Arabs bursting out of the deserts and onto the world stage virtually unannounced for the first time in the seventh century with the beginning of Islam. Hence, Arab civilisation is often viewed solely through Islamic spectacles. Such an impression is misleading on two accounts. First, whilst Islamic civilisation is arguably the Arabs' greatest achievement, it can nonetheless obscure the long history of Arab civilisation in the Near East and the Mediterranean *before* Islam—not to mention an ongoing history of Arab Christianity. And second, the image of the desert background obscures the far greater Arab urban traditions, occupying centre stage of ancient Near Eastern history. The thousand years or so before Islam was a period of both increasing assertion by the Arabs and expanding influences upon the West: the great Arab empires of early Islam were as much a culmination of an earlier history as the launching of the new. This lesser known earlier history was to have as profound an effect on Europe as Islamic civilisation later did on the rest of the world.

History's attitudes to the Bedouin Arab range from uncivilised barbarians of the desert fringes—the perpetual conflict between 'the desert and sown'—to the European Romantic era's adulation of the Bedouin as the ultimate embodiment of nobility and environmental harmony. Neither view is entirely true. Near Eastern history demonstrates more than anything else the constant inter-dependence of nomad and sedentary: Near Eastern civilisation was a product of both. The Bedouin Arabs were hardly less literate than the settled Graeco-Roman-Aramaic population, graphically demonstrated by the vast number of inscriptions they have left in the desert. Hence, epigraphist Michael MacDonald writes of these inscriptions, 'We are thus faced with the curious paradox of a non-literate society in which large numbers of people could read and write. A society in which literacy, having apparently no useful place, seems largely to have been used as a pastime.'[2] Small wonder that when these desert Arabs finally did achieve power, after Islam, the importance of the written word was one of their greatest achievements, and the beauty of the written word for its own sake remains one of the Arabs' greatest contributions to civilisation.

It is not intended here to give a complete history of the Arabs before Islam, but merely to highlight some aspects of this history for their effect upon the West. According to the Muslim Arabs' own traditions, their origin lay in south Arabia when a final rupture of the great dam at Ma'rib in Yemen in the late first millennium resulted in a mass emigration of tribes out of Yemen to all areas of Arabia. Whilst the ancient Semitic peoples of south Arabia—Minnaeans, Sabaeans, Himyarites and others—also cannot be described as 'Arab',[*] they are equally one of the roots of Arab identity. It is fitting, therefore, to begin with an overview of the south Arabian kingdoms.

SOUTH ARABIA (MAP 2)

South Arabia boasts some of the most extraordinary civilisations of the ancient world, a civilisation that controlled international trade routes between India, Africa and the Middle East and evolved highly sophisticated technologies nearly three thousand years ago. The Queen of Sheba, one of the most legendary figures in the Bible, is part of this story. But apart from the 1950s King Vidor epic film starring Gina Lollobrigida and Yul Brynner (memorable more for the slaughter of horses in the filming than for any resemblance to either the Bible, history or Arabia) few people have heard of the fabled Kingdom of Sheba itself: a desert kingdom between the highlands of Yemen and the Empty Quarter of Arabia. A legendary kingdom of frankincense and perfumes, of great cities and market places, oases and caravans, today the remains of Sheba's desert kingdom hold some of the strangest ruins that can be seen in the Middle East (Pls 17-19).

South Arabia can be compared more to a desert island than a continental country in the normal sense. Surrounded on two sides by the Red Sea and Indian Ocean, it is cut off on the third, landward side by the notorious Rub' al-Khali—the Empty Quarter—one of the most formidable

---

[*] Indeed, the ancient south Arabian languages belong to a separate, albeit Semitic, group as opposed to the north-western ones to which modern Arabic belongs.

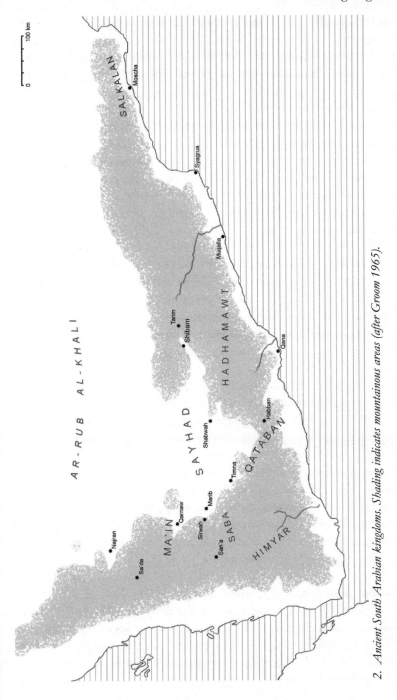

2. Ancient South Arabian kingdoms. Shading indicates mountainous areas (after Groom 1965).

and impenetrable deserts in the world. The desert effectively isolates the south from the rest of the Arabian peninsular: lying at its southern tip, Yemen turns its back upon the Middle East and faces Africa and the Indian Ocean. Hence, its people often have more in common with the highlanders of Ethiopia than the Bedouin of Central Arabia—and their role in Indian Ocean trade has been crucial (see Chapter 11). The isolation from the rest of Arabia ensured that Yemen remained largely isolated from the rest of the world until the 1960s.

Sea and sand are the main geographical elements that contribute to South Arabia's uniqueness; the mountains are a third element. South Arabia lies on the edge of the great Afro-Asian Rift Valley system, and nowhere on this remarkable rift is the scenery more impressive. It is a landscape of staggering contrasts: massive tectonic forces have thrown up mountains over 10,000 feet that have eroded into razor-edged spurs, plunging chasms and precipitous cliffs; extinct volcanic craters rising thousands of feet and spectacular black basalt lava flows. Yet its cool, airy heights, watered by the monsoons off the sea (the only part of the Middle East reached by the monsoons) have sheltered a lifestyle unimaginable in the harsh deserts below: ancient villages and even older cities, while the lush, highly fertile terraced fields that descend the slopes gave the region its ancient name of Arabia Felix—'Happy Arabia'.

In the Middle Ages, this complex agricultural system supported one of the world's most important cash crops: coffee. Although originating in Ethiopia, it is from Yemen where this important beverage first spread, and up until the time when the European sea traders recognised the potential of this plant and transferred its cultivation to other parts of the world at the end of the eighteenth century, Yemen held a world-wide monopoly. But coffee was not the only luxury commodity originating here. In the ancient past the region held a monopoly of an even more precious crop: frankincense. This highly aromatic resin—together with the closely related myrrh—from trees grown only in South Arabia, was used in embalming, perfumes and religious ritual throughout the ancient world. The ancient south Arabian kingdoms grew immensely rich on the incense trade, and a sophisticated civilisation flourished on the fringes of the Empty Quarter. The rise of the Roman Empire in the West created an almost insatiable market for this precious commodity with its demand for vast quantities of frankincense in the obligatory sacrifice to the official Roman cults. With such pagan sacrifice being outlawed when the Roman state became Christian, the incense trade collapsed virtually overnight. Both incense and coffee monopolies were lessons in over-dependence on single luxury commodities for all ages.

The earliest sites that have been recorded in Yemen are mainly in the interior, facing the Empty Quarter, rather than in the cooler highlands. This is partly because it is closer to the land routes connecting to the rest of Arabia, but mainly because the run-off from the highlands created a series of fertile alluvial fans where crops could be cultivated. This gave the interior of Yemen a lead in the development of civilisation which it was to retain throughout early antiquity.

The first major kingdoms were those of Saba' (Biblical Sheba) and Ma'in which, during a considerable part of their history, were contemporary. Both kingdoms began as theocracies and ended as secular kingships. The Kingdom of Saba' was the most distinguished branch of the South Arabian family. The Sabaean kingdom lasted from about 750 to 115 BC; the Minaean from about 700 BC to the third century BC. The title of the priest-king was *Mukarrib*, and two *Mukarribs* are mentioned in the Assyrian annals of the late eighth century BC. In their heyday the Sabaeans extended their hegemony over all South Arabia reducing their neighbour, the Minaeans, to vassalage. Sirwah, west of Ma'rib, was the first capital of Saba'. Its principal building was the temple of Almaqah, the moon-good, which has an inscription recording the victory in about 450 BC of Kariba-il Watar, the first 'King' (as opposed to *Mukarrib*) of Sheba, over the Minaeans (Pl. 18).

In the second period of the Sabaean kingdom (610-115 BC) the ruler appears shorn of his priestly character and Ma'rib has become the capital. It was the meeting place of trade routes connecting the frankincense lands with the Mediterranean. The construction for which the city was particularly famous was the Great Dam. This remarkable engineering feat reveals to us a highly advanced society in both commerce and technical achievement. The older portions of the dam were constructed in the mid-seventh century BC, and inscriptions on the dam record subsequent restorations (Pl. 19).

The Minaean kingdom Ma'in north of Ma'rib flourished in northern Yemen and in its heyday included most of South Arabia. The name Ma'in survives in present day Ma'an near Petra in Jordan, an important colony on the Minaean trade network. The capital was Qarnaw, modern Ma'in in northern Yemen. The religious capital was Yathil, modern Barraqish northwest of Ma'rib (Pl. 20). Two other important kingdoms rose in South Arabia: Qataban and Hadhramaut. Hadhramaut occupied the position of the Wadi Hadhramaut today, and Qataban lay roughly between Saba' and Hadhramaut. The Qataban kingdom, whose capital was at Timnah (modern Kuhlan) in southern Yemen, lasted from about 400 to 50 BC; Hadhramaut, whose capital was Shabwa (near the head of the Wadi Hadhramaut), lasted from the mid-fifth century BC to the mid-first AD. At times, these kingdoms were under Sabaean and Minaean hegemony.

From about 115 BC onwards the entire area falls under new masters who stemmed from the south-western highlands, the Himyarites (although the royal title retained 'king of Saba'). This marks the beginning of the Himyarite kingdom (referred to in Classical sources as the 'Homeritae'), which lasted, apart from a brief interval of Ethiopian rule between about 40 and 378 AD, until about 525 AD. The Himyarites were close kinsmen of the Sabaeans and became the heirs of the Minaeo-Sabaean culture and trade. Zafar, in the highlands between Ta'iz and San'a', was the capital of the Himyarite dynasty, although Ma'rib remained a second capital. This move of South Arabia's centre of gravity away from the lowlands of the interior around Ma'rib and up to the highlands probably corresponds to a change in trade emphasis: the rise of the Red Sea routes as improvements in navigation and sea technology (not to mention the rise of Alexandria) made sea trade less costly than the overland trade, subject as it is to the rigours of desert travel and the depredations of hostile tribes.

San'a' also rose to importance in this period. It was during the Himyarite period that the ill-fated Roman campaign under Aelius Gallus in 25-24 BC penetrated as far as Yemen to try to gain control of the fabulously rich frankincense trade. But the Romans failed across such extended lines of communication, and by about 300 AD the Himyarites had extended their rule through most of the highlands of Yemen and into the Hadhramaut as well, becoming undisputed masters of South Arabia.

Christianity penetrated into Yemen along the trade routes from Syria very early—probably earlier than its spread into the Mediterranean. Following the destruction of Jerusalem by Titus in AD 70 Judaism also spread into Yemen (if not earlier, if the story of Solomon and Sheba has any factual base), becoming widespread over the ensuing centuries. Hence, in the early sixth century the last Himyarite king, Dhu Nuwas, converted to Judaism. This resulted in a number of pogroms against the Christians of Yemen, culminating in the famous massacre of Najran in 523. The Christians of Yemen appealed to their co-religionist, the Christian emperor of Ethiopia, who sent an army of 70,000 across the Red Sea to crush Dhu

Nuwas. This ushered in a period of Ethiopian rule which lasted from 525 to 575. San'a' was made the capital of Ethiopian Yemen. The Ethiopian viceroy, Abrahah, built one of the most magnificent cathedrals of early Christianity there, and Ethiopian raids extended as far north as Mecca and penetrated deep into Arabia. It was also during this period that the great dam at Ma'rib collapsed for the final time, leading to the drying up of the Ma'rib oasis and the diaspora of its people throughout the Middle East.

But Ethiopian rule in Yemen was considered very harsh, prompting a descendant of the Himyarite royal house, Sayf ibn Dhi Yazan, to call in another outside power to oust them. He appealed to the Byzantines, but Constantinople considered their co-religionists of Ethiopia as allies, so rejected the Himyar call. Turning then to the other great power of the time, Sayf then appealed to the Sasanian empire of Persia, and in 575 the Persian emperor sent an army which defeated the Ethiopians. There followed a brief period of joint administration of Yemen, ruled from San'a', but very soon Yemen came under more direct Persian rule, governed by a satrap appointed by the emperor, and the Yemenis found that they had only changed one master for another.

By this time, however, a new power was rising in Arabia that was soon to dominate all: the Arabs under Islam in 622. In 628—only the sixth year of the Islamic era—the fifth Persian Satrap of Yemen converted to Islam, and Yemen passed peacefully under Islamic rule—the first country in what was soon to become a massive empire. Thus, with Roman, Byzantine, Persian, Ethiopian and Arab interests all playing a part, events in South Arabia very much formed a microcosm for the history of late antiquity as a whole.

NORTH ARABIAN KINGDOMS (MAP 3)

Whilst there might be some ambiguity as to the 'Arab' character of the early South Arabian kingdoms, the northern kingdoms in the Near East—Emesa, Nabatea and Palmyra, for example—were described by contemporaries unambiguously as 'Arab'. Of course, the term must not be viewed in its modern nationalistic sense, but it does nonetheless indicate a distinct cultural identity. It is often not appreciated, therefore (by Arabs themselves, as well as by Europeans), that the spectacular ruins of Petra or Palmyra, for example, or much of the early history of Christianity, or even some of the pagan religions that reached the west in antiquity, are as much a part of Arab civilisation as Islamic Cairo or Baghdad are.

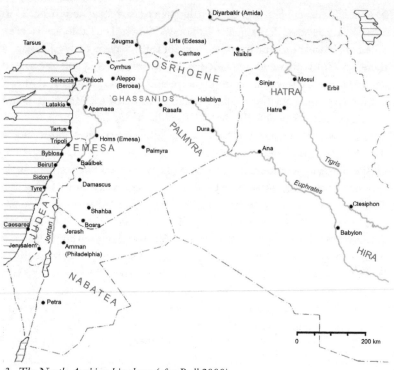

3. The North Arabian kingdoms (after Ball 2000).

The origins of most of the north Arabian kingdoms lay in the Hellenistic period. After the collapse of the Achaemenid Empire at the hands of Alexander of Macedon, the rival armies of Alexander's successors passed back and forth across the Near Eastern stage as they battled for the spoils, and the stability that the region had enjoyed under Persian rule was shattered. Some equilibrium was restored by the second century when most of Syria came under the Seleucid dynasty, ruled from Antioch, although the area of Jordan still remained a bone of contention with their arch rivals, the Ptolemaic dynasty of Egypt. But the contact between the Hellenes—Macedonians and Greeks—and the native peoples of the Near East (increasingly being referred to as Arabs in the Greek sources) was to prove crucial to both. The earlier period of chaos meant, first, that the Arabs were a useful source of manpower to incorporate into the rival armies. And second, it meant that the Arabs were forced to rely more upon themselves for their security. This was followed in the subsequent period of stability, when increasing numbers of incomers from Greece

1 *The excavations at the Phoenician port of Tyre in Lebanon. Mainly Roman remains are on the surface.*

2 *The huge hippodrome dating from the time of Septimius Severus' rebuilding of Tyre, built on the mole constructed by Alexander of Macedon to connect the island to the mainland.*

3 *The harbour at Sidon. Although partially obscured by the medieval castle on the mole and the modern Lebanese port facilities, the harbour still preserves its original Phoenician form.*

4 *The Phoenician temple of Eshmoun inland from Sidon. The square sanctuary is in the foreground, the terrace wall in the background is from the Persian period. Note the cubic form of the sanctuary.*

5 *The excavated remains of the Phoenician city of Ugarit in Syria.*

6 *The excavated Phoenician port of Byblos in Lebanon. The city ramparts are on the right; a later Roman colonnade is in the background.*

7 *The Phoenician temple at Amrit in Syria. Note the cubic form of the central sanctuary.*

8 *Phoenician tombs at Amrit.*

9 *The remains of Carthage outside Tunis. The large pillars are the supports for the forum which the Romans built over the ancient Carthaginian remains deliberately to obscure them. In the background is the 19th-century French Cathedral of St Louis.*

10 *Excavated Punic slipways at the naval harbour at Carthage.*

11 Stele representing child sacrifice at the Carthage tophet.

12 The site of Hannibal's burial place in Bithynia in Turkey.

13 The excavated Punic site of Kerkouane in Tunisia.

14 Punic Kerkouane. Note the bathroom in the foreground and the ordered layout in the background.

15 *Newly excavated remains of ancient Roman Beirut, possibly the site of its famous law school.*

16 *The Arab delegation on the Persepolis reliefs—the clothing, not to mention the camel, still characterise the Arabs today.*

17 *The line of monoliths forming the propyleum of the Temple of Awwam at Ma'rib in Yemen.*

18 *Monoliths of the Temple of 'Almaqah at Ma'rib. Note the 'cubic' form of the capitals.*

19 The great dam at Ma'rib. The overflow is in the foreground and in the background is one of the sluice gates.

20 The ancient Minnaean city of Yathil, modern Barraqish in Yemen.

21 *A stylised ibex frieze at Sirwah near Ma'rib.*

22 *The great temple complex at Baalbek in Lebanon. The huge colonnade in the background is part of the Temple of Jupiter Heliopolitanus, and the temple to the right is the so-called Temple of Bacchus.*

23 The dedicatory inscription to the Emesene 'Great King Samsigeramus' at Baalbek.

24 The elaborately decorated courtyard of the Temple of Jupiter at Baalbek.

25 The courtyard of the Temple of Jupiter at Baalbek. The single standing column is one of originally a pair of dedicatory columns, possibly relating to ancient Phoenician practice. The inscription in the foreground reads IOMH: 'Iupiter Optimus Magnus Heliopolitanus'.

26 The city of Petra in Jordan, with the great royal facades in the distance.

27 The older style of tomb facades at Petra.

28 The baetyl *in the Siq at Petra
representing Dushares and his consorts
al-Uzza and Allat.*

29 The so-called 'god blocks' at the entrance to Petra.

30 The new Nabatean capital at Bosra in Syria. Although ostensibly a Roman style of monumental arch, the capitals are Nabatean.

31 The twin pillars standing on the citadel overlooking the modern city of Urfa in Turkey, ancient Edessa.

32 The 'Fish-pools of Abraham' with their sacred carp at Urfa, probably originally part of the cult of Atargatis.

lived alongside the indigenous inhabitants. This is usually (and, in its own terms, correctly) referred to as the Hellenisation of the Near East—and one only need glance at the Graeco-Roman architecture that adorned all Near Eastern cities after that to leave little doubt (albeit a thin veneer). But the fertilisation went both ways: the period equally saw Near Eastern cultural influences eventually transforming the incomers—and one only need glance at the subsequent Christianisation of all Europe to remove any doubt of that.

The next stage in the emergence of separate Arab states was when the Seleucid Empire started to collapse, when more and more former subjects asserted their independence. Some were little more than city states or tribal enclaves, but others were to emerge as wealthy kingdoms in their own right. The main ones were Emesa, Judaea, Nabatea, Palmyra and Edessa, with numerous minor states—probably more than twenty—such as Chalcis or Anthemusia, often just principalities or even small towns or tribal enclaves.* Hence, when the Romans arrived in the East they came into direct contact with kings: a patchwork of small but glittering princely states. The contact was a heady one for these unsophisticated republican Romans arriving from the fringes of the west: with little or no experience of royalty, they were blinded and seduced by kings (and queens—literally so in Egypt). Kings, furthermore, who dazzled the Romans with opulent displays of wealth and luxury. The contact was a heady and ultimately addictive one, a contact which Republican Rome could not withstand: Rome thereafter became a monarchy.

The kingdoms were eventually swallowed up by the Roman Empire, but there was a re-emergence of at least semi-independent kingdoms with the rise of the Arab tribal confederations throughout the third to sixth centuries, such as the Lakhmid, Tanukhid and Ghassanid confederations. With the exception of Judaea, all these states were to a greater or lesser extent 'Arab'.[3]

EMESA AND THE SUN KINGS

Emesa, corresponding to modern Homs in Syria and the surrounding area on the middle Orontes River, emerged as a distinct kingdom in the first century

---

* There were also Arab kingdoms further east coming under the Iranian sphere of influence: for example, Hatra in northern Iraq, Hira in southern Iraq, Gerrha on the Gulf coast, to name the most prominent. These were often very important and produced highly distinctive characteristics of their own—spectacular remains in the case of Hatra—but are not included here as their relationship with the West was peripheral.

BC, becoming vassals to the Romans in 64 BC. By the fourth century AD, the city of Emesa had grown to rank with Tyre, Sidon, Beirut and Damascus, probably exceeding them in splendour due to its famous Temple of the Sun.

The Homs Basin of the middle Orontes region is a natural centre of communications between the Syrian desert and the sea, as well as between Arabia and northern Syria. The Emesene kingdom extended southwards to Yabrud near Damascus and into the Beq'a Valley as far as Heliopolis (modern Baalbek), and northwards down the central Orontes Basin towards Apamaea. To the west, the so-called 'Homs Gap'—later dominated by the immense Crusader castle of Krak des Chevaliers—provided access to the Mediterranean at modern Tartus. To the east, it extended deep into the desert where a boundary stone marks its 'border' with the territory of Palmyra.

The first mention of the Emesenes occurs in the mid-second century BC, with Seleucid references to a sheikh of the Emesene tribe, Iamblichus,[*] near Apamaea. It is implied that the Emesenes were a nomadic Arab tribe in the region, rather than the inhabitants of a city called Emesa, which only emerges in the first century BC. The most important of the tribal sheikhs was Samsigeramus, who became embroiled in the rival claims to the Seleucid throne between Philip II and Antiochus XIII in 69 BC. On Pompey's incorporation of the Seleucid state into the Roman Empire in 64 BC, the Emesenes were made vassals to the Romans as a way of exerting indirect control over the desert tribes of the interior. Pompey confirmed their chief Samsigeramus as King of the Emesenes, with their capital at Arethusa, a town on the Orontes just to the north of Emesa. Samsigeramus I is thus usually credited with being the founder of the dynasty. As soon as they became settled the Emesenes began to accumulate riches from their control of the trading caravans (a more profitable business than merely raiding them). Presumably as result of this new-found wealth Samsigeramus I founded Emesa as a new capital that would carry their name.

The Augustan Peace was a golden age for Emesa under the stable rule of Iamblichus II (20 BC-AD 14) and his successor Samsigeramus II (AD 14-48). A prince of the family, Sohaemus, ruled the principality of Chalcis ad Libanum in the Baq'a Valley from 20 BC to AD 14 as vassals of Iamblichus. Chalcis has been located at the modern town of Anjar, to the

---

* We know only the Graeco-Latin forms of the Emesene names Iamblichus, Samsigeramus and Sohaemus, and their original Arabic forms of Yamlikel, Shamshigeram and Suhaym are not always certain. See Shahid 1984a: 41-2; Baldus 1996: 374.

south of Baalbek, although the remains there are Umayyad. The Chalcidian princes are described as 'Arabs' in the sources and, like the Emesene kings, occupied the dual function of king and high-priest. The two branches of the Emesene royal house came together, for it was the son of Sohaemus of Chalcis, Samsigeramus II, who became Emesa's greatest king after the death of Iamblichus II in AD 14. Inscriptions at both Baalbek and Palmyra commemorate Samsigeramus as 'the great king' (Pl. 23). Samsigeramus was succeeded by his son King Azizus.

The family also consolidated its position amongst Rome's other client kingdoms in the Near East by marriage alliances with the royal houses of both Commagene and Judaea. A Sohaemus is recorded as King of Armenia for a while in 163. Under King Sohaemus of Emesa, who succeeded Azizus, relations with Rome became very close, with Emesa supplying a regular levy of archers as auxiliaries. For reasons that are not entirely clear, Sohaemus and the independence of Emesa disappeared in about 75, when it was incorporated directly into the Roman Empire.

The kings of Emesa had a dual function: they were, first of all, rulers, a role they had inherited from their days as tribal sheikhs. But they were also high priests, guardians of the great temple of the Emesene Sun-god, or the 'Baal of the Emesenes'. After Rome incorporated the kingdom directly and the dynasty no longer ruled as kings, they remained as hereditary high priests of this temple. This temple was associated with the cult of Elah Gabal, later to achieve fame when one of the Temple priests, the Emperor Elagabalus, tried to enforce it upon an unwilling Rome. The religious impact of this cult is discussed further in Chapter 6. The Temple of the Emesene Sun-god was one of the greatest in the East rivalling those at Jerusalem, Palmyra and Damascus. Contemporaries described it as a huge building, lavishly decorated with gold, silver and gemstones, richly endowed both by the Emesene and other Near Eastern kings, and illustrations on coins confirm it to have been one of the greatest of the East.

It is also one of the East's greatest mysteries, for no trace survives in or around modern Homs. For reasons I have argued elsewhere, this temple is not in Emesa itself but is to be identified with the great temple of Baalbek in the Beq'a Valley (Pls 22-25).[4] Baalbek was the site of a minor Roman veteran colony, Heliopolis ('city of the sun') established by Augustus. But despite this modest background it boasted the only temple that matches the ancient descriptions of the Temple of the Emesene Baal; it also has an inscription to Samsigeramus as we have observed. The main planning and early construction of Baalbek moreover corresponds with the main period of the Sun Kings of Emesa, enriched by the lucrative caravan traffic they controlled, while the second spurt of construction corresponds with the descendants of those kings, the Severan emperors (see Chapter 5). But perhaps the main point that needs emphasising is the sheer scale of the temple complex. The scale is certainly overwhelming, and must have been even more so in antiquity: the greatest temple in the East, indeed one of the most ambitious building works ever undertaken in the Roman world. Money was no object: dozens of colossal monolithic columns of pink Egyptian granite were imported all the way from Egypt; stones weighing up to a thousand tons—the largest monoliths in the world—were cut and dragged into place to construct the immense platforms; the raking cornices of the entablature alone, standing over a hundred feet up in the air, weighed over 75 tons. Nothing was too good, too big, or too expensive: it pushes both engineering and cost to their extreme limits. What is certain, is that Baalbek is one gigantic architectural boast. What is equally certain is that descendants of a small group of Roman veterans living off army pensions could not have built this.

Emesa was thus one of the more obscure Arab kingdoms, particularly in comparison to famous neighbours. Indeed, the history of Emesa and its kings would form little more than a footnote were it not for two important factors, both related. The first is the religion that was practised at Emesa, the sun cult. And the second was the Emesene family who became one of Rome's imperial dynasties. Both were to have major ramifications for Europe's history. The religion is discussed further in Chapter 6, and the dynasty forms the subject of Chapter 5.

THE NABATEAN KINGDOM

The Nabateans are known as early as the seventh century BC in Hebrew and Assyrian sources as a nomadic tribe inhabiting the desert regions of north-western Arabia. Their language was a dialect akin to modern Arabic—indeed, the Arabic script evolved from the Nabatean. Hence, the Nabateans form as much a part of the broader spectrum of Arab civilisation as, say, the Umayyads, 'Abbasids or Fatimids do.

The Nabatean advance into southern Jordan was no sudden invasion, but was a long process of usually peaceful infiltration between the sixth and

the fourth centuries BC, assimilating and absorbing much of the population.*
By the end of the fourth century they had established a base at Petra which
gradually grew in wealth from its location alongside several important trade
routes. The incense trade from south Arabia—reviewed above—was the
main source of this prosperity, but it also controlled the important land route
between the two great Hellenistic powers of Ptolemaic Egypt and Seleucid
Syria. The rise of Imperial Rome created a huge demand for incense to be
burnt throughout the empire as a part of the imperial cult. The Nabateans
were in a unique position to supply this demand, and Petra became one of
the most richly endowed cities of the ancient Near East (Pls 26-29).

The Nabatean Kingdom gradually expanded over much of southern
Palestine and most of Jordan, reaching as far as Damascus. In 8 BC King
Aretas IV, surnamed 'the lover of his people', ascended the throne, reigning
until 40 AD. During this long reign the kingdom reached the height of its
prosperity. It also reached its greatest extent, covering all of Sinai and the
southern Negev with a Mediterranean outlet at Gaza, as well as all of Jordan,
the Hauran in southern Syria, the Wadi Sirhan down through Arabia as far
as Jawf, and the Red Sea coast as far as modern Jeddah.

The capital was transferred from Petra to Bosra in 93 AD, possibly
to be closer to trade increasingly channelled through Antioch after its
incorporation into the Roman Empire and its consequent rise to become the
third city of the empire. Rabbel II continued the expansion of the kingdom's
activities that were begun by Aretas IV, and his equally long reign saw
increased irrigation, agriculture and urbanisation, as well as the construction
and embellishment of Bosra, the new capital (Pl. 30). The shift of focus from
Petra and the south, in the heart of Arabia, to Bosra in the more Hellenised
climate of Syria certainly ensured the importance of Bosra as an urban and
religious centre for many centuries after. Hitherto, the Nabatean kingdom
had been an essentially Arabian power, looking to the east. With this shift
of focus, the Nabateans seemed poised to become more of a power in the
mainstream of the Near East and the eastern Mediterranean. Whether the
kingdom's rise was perceived as a potential threat by the Romans we cannot
say, but for whatever reason, Trajan annexed the kingdom on the death of
King Rabbel in 106 and the area of the Nabatean state became the new
Roman Province of Arabia with its capital at Bosra.

---

* The material culture—particularly the pottery—of the Edomites and Nabateans show a
remarkable degree of continuity that would simply not be apparent from the literary sources
alone, which imply cultural displacement.

It had been over a hundred years of unbroken growth, prosperity and stability, despite occasional minor wars with Judaea. For it was a period which saw unusually long reigns of just three kings: Aretas IV ruled for 48 years and the reigns of Malek II and Rabbel II were an impressive 30 and 46 years respectively. Furthermore, the transition from one reign to the other appears to have been entirely smooth—impressive achievements in view of the civil strife that was more a characteristic of successions. Hence, Strabo's words that the kingdom was 'exceedingly well-governed ..., that none of the natives prosecuted one another, and that they in every way kept peace with one another'[5] ring true. This stability allowed for an astonishing upsurge in building activity and creativity. Nabatean skills in water management and rock cutting were already famous by the fourth century BC, and by the first century AD areas of the desert which had never before seen cultivation flourished, water resources were conserved and harnessed with an efficiency that anticipated our own era's environmental revolution, and one of the most magnificent cities of the ancient world was built whose fame today has become a byword for all that is exotic and spectacular (Pls 26, 27). Impressive achievements for a kingdom that was, after all, on the sidelines of the great civilisations of the ancient Near East.

As well as being impressive monuments, the buildings at Petra have an eclecticism rare amongst ancient civilisations, combining elements of Hellenistic, Roman, Egyptian, Assyrian and Persian architecture bonded by the strong cement of their own Arabian forms. In addition to reflecting its own achievement, therefore, Petra reflects much of the ancient Near Eastern and Mediterranean achievement as a whole.

THE KINGDOM OF EDESSA

Strictly speaking, the name 'Edessa' refers just to the city (modern Urfa in south-eastern Turkey) rather than the kingdom. The name of the kingdom, of which Edessa was the capital, was Osrhoene. The name Edessa, however, is more conventionally used for both the city and the kingdom (Pls 31, 32). Geographically the Kingdom of Edessa straddles the Mesopotamian plains and the Anatolian foothills, and the city is located at the point where the foothills meet the plains. Its geography has thus marked Edessa as both a meeting place and a buffer state throughout its history.

The Edessans identified their city with Biblical Erech, founded by the mythical Nimrod and associated with Abraham of Ur. It became one of several military colonies founded by Seleucus Nicator in 303/2, renaming it Edessa after the capital of Macedonia. With the decline of the Seleucids in second century BC, Edessa became the seat of an Arab dynasty allied to the Parthians. The other main cities in the kingdom were Nisibis to the southeast (indeed Nisibis may have been the capital of the kingdom before Edessa itself) and Carrhae (modern Harran) on the plains just to the south. Osrhoene became a client kingdom of Rome in 166 AD.

The region has always occupied a singular place in Near Eastern political history. Harran saw the last stand of both the Assyrian and Babylonian Empires: a rump Assyrian kingdom under Ashur-uballit managed to hold out against the Medes and Babylonians for a further seven years after the sack of Nineveh in 612 BC. It was also in Harran that the aged King Nabu-na'id (Nabonidus), last of the Babylonians, succumbed in 546 BC to the new Persian conquests of Cyrus the Great. Edessa, along with Harran and Nisibis, became some of the most important cities on the ancient thoroughfare linking Syria with Mesopotamia. There were particularly close trading links with Palmyra as well, and Palmyrene-type tomb towers and inscriptions have been found in and around Edessa.

The first Edessan king to achieve prominence was Abgar V (4 BC-AD 7). He established the kingdom on a strong footing, sending an army abroad on one occasion to aid the Nabateans in their war against Judea, but Abgar V is most remembered for the events supposedly associated with Jesus (discussed in Chapter 6). Abgar VIII, the Great (177-212), is considered the greatest of the kings of Edessa: a cultured king, a wise administrator, and a patron of learning that made Edessa one of the main intellectual centres of the East. Following a devastating flood Abgar ordered a massive new building programme to begin immediately, with remission of taxes for all those affected by the flood. Many new monuments were built including the magnificent Cathedral of St Sophia, but nothing of these is left today apart from the famous 'Fish pools of Abraham', possibly a part of Abgar the Great's summer palace (Pl. 32). The two columns on the citadel also formed a part of Abgar's rebuilding (Pl. 31), perhaps a part of his winter palace. Otherwise, the only remains of Abgar's today are about a hundred pagan, Jewish and Christian cave tombs—some decorated with fine mosaics—in the hills surrounding Edessa.

As well as rebuilding Edessa, Abgar built up relations with Emperor Septimius Severus to such an extent that his state visit to Rome in 204 was the most lavish that even Rome had witnessed in 150 years. But Abgar the Great is remembered not so much for his lavishness nor even his ambitious building programme, but for his reputed conversion to Christianity in about 200. If true, this makes his kingdom the world's first Christian state. This and Abgar V's earlier experiment are discussed more in Chapter 6.

PALMYRA AND WORLD TRADE

In the vacuum left by the decline of Seleucid power when many Arab principalities emerged as we have seen, Palmyra remained little more than a desert sheikhdom until two events occurred that were to change its fortunes. The first was the decline of Emesa, which had previously controlled the desert routes. But the main wealth lay in the routes controlled by the Nabateans rather than the Emesenes. The second, therefore, was the incorporation of the Nabatean kingdom into the Roman Empire and decline of the Nabatean control of the trade routes at the end of the first century AD, when Palmyra's geographical position gave it a major advantage. The trade routes moved further north, a move dictated as much by the increasing importance of Roman Antioch as by the decline of trade controlled by Petra. Parallel to these events was the rise of the new Parthian Empire of Iran in the east. Between the two, Rome and Iran, lay Palmyra, acting both as middleman and buffer state. The Palmyrenes were able to exploit the situation to the fullest.

It would be a mistake, however, to overstate Palmyra's geographical advantage in controlling trade routes. A glance at the map shows that the logical trade route from the east by-passes Palmyra, following the Euphrates to just east of Aleppo before crossing directly to Antioch through relatively well watered country: crossing the desert via Palmyra makes little sense. The point that needs emphasising is that the Palmyrenes created this trade route artificially: Palmyrene agents were planted from Dura Europos and Babylon on the Euphrates through to the Persian Gulf and mouth of the Indus to ensure that the trade went their way. Nor was the Palmyrene trade route a link in any supposed trans-Asian caravan network—the largely spurious 'Silk Route'—but formed virtually as much a part of the sea network as any sea port did. Merchants travelled directly across the desert to the Euphrates, whence they would sail down to the Persian Gulf. From there, the trade became a part of the sea routes to India, with Palmyrene agents established in ports of call on the way. Today, evidence for Palmyrene merchant houses have been found as far apart as Bahrain, the Indus Delta, Merv, Egypt, Rome and Newcastle-upon-Tyne in England.

Palmyra became a part of the Roman Empire by AD 75 or earlier, but the Romans were satisfied with merely installing a garrison to counter Parthian influence. This left the Palmyrenes free to concentrate on trade. Whilst not extending its territories much outside the Syrian desert, the Palmyrenes organised a trade network spanning much of western Asia, and the revenues invested either in further trade ventures or city embellishments. Indeed, the latter was given high priority: by the second century AD many of the monuments were privately endowed by merchants with a lavishness verging on the ostentatious as befitted an architecture of private trade— the merchants had statues of themselves on the columns lining the city's thoroughfares (Pl. 36).

Palmyra was not a 'kingdom' in the conventional sense, as the other Arab states were. Before Udaynath and Zenobia, there does not appear to have been a monarchy or a royal family like those at Emesa or Edessa or even Judaea: the first titles of Udaynath and members of his family are Roman ones awarded for good service to the empire, and are not necessarily 'royal' ones. There has not been any royal palace definitely recognised in the ruins.* Palmyra always seems to have been ruled by a council of elders, either tribal or mercantile or both. In other words, it was a traditional form of Arabian tribal government entirely in keeping with its cultural environment, a form of rule that existed more or less unchanged in the region until recently. There is no evidence that this was a 'Senate' in the Graeco-Roman sense, hence evidence for any Greek 'character' of Palmyra. The Western terms 'republic' or 'oligarchy' do not fit: 'Palmyra plc' is probably closest!

A Western visitor to Palmyra today is immediately confronted not so much with the strange, but the familiar. Here, in the heart of an eastern desert in a foreign country, one finds a civilisation with which it is immediately possible to relate: long lines of columns, arches and other forms of Classical architecture that have been the basis of Western building for over two thousand years (Pls 33-36). I have argued elsewhere[6] that much of this architecture is a veneer which disguises underlying native Arabian elements in the architecture. Indeed, the deeper one looks, the less Classical it

---

* The arguments for either the Camp or Baths of Diocletian being on the site of a royal palace are inconclusive.

becomes—not a single street in any Greek or Roman city in Europe was lined with colonnades, to give an example of Palmyra's most distinctive feature.

It is easy to forget, therefore, that the Palmyrenes and their city were Arab first and only Roman second. Arab historical sources, for example, write of the destruction of Palmyra as an entirely Arab tribal affair: the Emperor Aurelian and the Romans are not even mentioned. But both Udaynath and Zenobia are specifically described in the Classical sources as 'Saracens', i.e., Arabs. There was also a considerable Iranian element: Palmyra's art depicts Palmyrene dress to be Iranian. Palmyrene religion also reflect diverse traditions. The two main deities, Baal-Shamin and Bel, belong to two different religious traditions which may reflect two ethnic groups in the foundation of Palmyra. Baal-Shamin was Syro-Phoenician in origin, while Bel was Mesopotamian, related to Bel Marduk, the supreme deity of the Babylonian pantheon. The Mesopotamian connection is further reinforced by the cult of Nebo or Nabu at Palmyra, also Babylonian in origin, closely associated with Marduk. Little in the religion of Palmyra displays Graeco-Roman influence, despite the Corinthian and other orders which embellished the temples or the 'off-the-hook' Athena statue brought in to personify Allat.

ZENOBIA AND THE REVOLT OF PALMYRA

How did an obscure desert kingdom like Palmyra affect the West? This came about in the events surrounding the tragic end of the city in the third century. The rise of Udaynath to prominence during the third century forms the background to Palmyra's supposed revolt against Rome. Up until then, Palmyra had been ruled by a tribal council as we have seen, but after about 250 Udaynath became the supreme chief over the others. Presumably the increasing unreliability of the Pax Romana forced the Palmyrenes to be more self-reliant for their defence. This would necessitate both the raising of an army and the election from their elite of somebody to command it. Udaynath's marriage to Zenobia, head of one of the most powerful of the desert tribes, undoubtedly strengthened his position. In the aftermath of Emperor Valerian's humiliating defeat at the hands of Sasanian Persia at the Battle of Edessa in 260, it was Udaynath who rallied against the threat from Iran recapturing much of the Near East and supposedly defeated a Sasanian force. In gratitude the Emperor Gallienus bestowed the titles 'Commander-in-chief of the East' and 'Augustus' on Udaynath.

In 267, however, at the height of his glory Udaynath was murdered. His ambitious wife Zenobia was quick to take up the reins of power as regent for her son, Wahballath. History can never resist a warrior queen. Since ancient times the names of Semiramis, Cleopatra and Boadicea have been favourite heroines. Invariably beautiful, warlike yet nubile, and usually tragic, they are written about by both contemporary and later writers with a lasciviousness equal only to their disregard for truth. Attempts in the Classical sources to trace Zenobia's ancestry back to Cleopatra appear as apocryphal as the Arab tradition which link her with the Queen of Sheba. But Cleopatra was certainly a role model, as was Julia Domna, both of whom Zenobia claimed to emulate. Both Classical and Arabic sources concur that she carried herself as a man, riding, hunting and drinking on occasions with her officers.

Zenobia's initial campaign in 269 was not directed against Rome but against Palmyra's tribal enemies, the Bani Tanukh, who had been responsible for the death of her father. The campaign was unexpectedly successful when the Roman provincial capital of Bosra fell, along with a Roman force. This resulted in much of Roman Syria and Arabia falling under Palmyrene control. It added fuel to Zenobia's ambitions and she set her sights beyond Syria. Accordingly, the following year an army said to number 70,000 invaded Egypt, possibly accompanied by Zenobia herself. A battle against the Roman garrison resulted in victory for the Palmyrenes. Thus, Zenobia became Egypt's first queen since Cleopatra. Another Palmyrene force advanced into Asia Minor as far as Ankara. This was destined to be the furthest limits of Zenobia's army, for in 271 the empire struck back under Emperor Aurelian.

Aurelian pursued the Palmyrene army back to Syria, then advanced across the desert and laid siege to Zenobia's city. Zenobia, seeing the inevitability of Roman triumph, tried to escape eastwards but was captured whilst attempting to cross the Euphrates. The citizens of Palmyra continued resistance for a short while, but soon capitulated. Aurelian accordingly spared the city, taking Zenobia and her son to Rome.* A year later, however, Palmyra revolted. Aurelian was quick to return, and after a brief siege Palmyra fell and Aurelian turned the city, one of the most splendid in the entire Empire, over to his troops. After a few days, Zenobia's lovely city lay shattered.

Zenobia's revolt is often regarded as some form of 'Arab revolt', an

---

* Opinion differs as to Zenobia's fate. She probably died soon afterwards, either from illness or by fasting. According to other versions, however, she was first displayed in Antioch and Rome as 'Queen of the barbarian Saracens', then beheaded, although other sources refer to her being married off and living in retirement outside Rome.

independence movement from Rome. Zenobia's self-conscious emulation of Cleopatra is cited in support of this. But the Cleopatra analogy can be stretched too far: it must be remembered that Cleopatra wanted to be Queen of *Rome* rather than of Egypt (and was a Macedonian in any case, not an Egyptian). Hers was no Palmyrene Empire, for Zenobia was not splitting the empire but aimed as much as Aurelian did to unify it. Palmyra had no history of revolt or resentment against Rome. Quite the contrary: Palmyra did extremely well indeed out of belonging to the Roman club, and the Palmyrenes were far too astute as businessmen to be bothered with any nonsense about independence, let alone ideas of nationalism. In other words, Palmyra had not the slightest reasons for revolt.

Consequently, the rise of Udaynath represented no challenge to Rome. On the contrary, whilst his rise to strong local power may have been a response to the weakness of Roman central rule, his subsequent use of that power was entirely in Rome's interests: he fought Roman enemies, he restored Roman borders, he remained a loyal servant of Rome to the end. The aim of Udaynath was to restore Roman power and prestige, as any good servant of Rome would, not to challenge it. As a result, Rome itself rewarded him with Roman titles: he was made an 'Augustus'. The subsequent aim of Zenobia was much the same: to restore Rome. However, the stakes had simply changed: the far more ambitious Zenobia sought instead to restore Rome by making her own family's claim for the imperial purple. Her success would have meant a united empire—not an independent 'Palmyrene Empire' nor a divided Roman one.

Aurelian's aims were identical to Zenobia's: to restore the empire. Merely his methods were different. The Iranian and Gothic invasions had brought Rome to the brink of collapse, and a succession of weak emperors had dissipated its funds. Aurelian had done more than most of his immediate predecessors to restore the Empire's fortunes, but these efforts had to be paid for. Faced with empty coffers back home, a large standing army in the field, and mercenaries from all over the Empire demanding the fulfilment of promises, the rich plum of Palmyra offered Aurelian at one stroke the only short-term solution that seemed possible. Nobody realised more than Aurelian that a fickle army that supported an emperor one day might turn against him the next. So, Aurelian gave Palmyra and its citizens to his army to do with as they pleased.

Alas, Aurelian's master-stroke and Palmyra's agony saved neither the empire nor its emperor. Aurelian went the same way after all as so many other emperors of the third century when a group of officers murdered him in Thrace just a few years later. But more than that, in destroying Palmyra Aurelian had unwittingly done more than most emperors to destroy the very empire he tried to restore. Palmyra's commercial empire had brought wealth into Rome. After its sack Palmyra's commercial empire rapidly declined, and with it went the wealth its trade had brought to Rome. The real tragedy of Aurelian is that in doing so much to restore Rome's greatness, he simply did more than most to hasten its decline.

THE ARAB TRIBAL CONFEDERATIONS AND QUEEN MAWIYYA

With the collapse of Palmyra in the third century the history of independent Arab states in the Near East comes to an end: all had been absorbed directly into either the Roman or the Persian Empires. However, there was a revival of a different kind in the fourth to sixth centuries with the creation of powerful Arab tribal confederations by both Rome* and Persia, both to act as buffers in the desert border zones between the rival empires and to be used on occasion in proxy wars against each other. These confederations were designated *foederati*, or allies, by the Romans. The system of allied tribes consisted of one main confederation, whose sheikh would be recognised as *Phylarch*, or 'king', and provided with subsidies to defend the frontier, both against the Iranians and against raids by non-allied tribes. The main confederations were the Tanukhids and the Ghassanids on the Roman side of the border and the Lakhmids on the Persian side. It is the former two which mainly concern us here.

The role of the desert tribes as allies of Rome began under the early empire. At first, this just involved establishing relations with the desert Arabs and incorporating nomad auxiliaries into the army. More specifically, their role was to contribute highly mobile professional cavalry units to the Roman army. In contrast to the sedentary Arabs, these semi-nomadic Arabs were professional fighters whose techniques were based on the tradition of the raid. As such, the *foederati* comprised a mobile defence, as opposed to the static defensive line of the Roman frontier.

---

* In conventional usage, 'Rome' and the 'Roman Empire' had by now become 'Byzantium' and the 'Byzantine Empire' with the move of the capital of the empire from Rome to Constantinople by Emperor Constantine in 323. However, it was still officially known as the 'Roman Empire' with all emperors 'Roman emperors' right down until its end in 1453. In the present context, therefore, of the Near East in the last centuries before Islam, the term 'Rome' is preferred to imply continuity.

Several tribal confederations were formed which entered into more formal relations with Rome. The Emesenes was probably the first, before it evolved into the more sedentary Emesene Kingdom. The first on the desert fringes was the Thamud confederation, whose temple inscription in Nabatean, dated 167-9 at Ruwwafa in the Hijaz, honours Marcus Aurelius and Lucius Verus. Although beyond the actual boundary of the Roman Empire, it is the first evidence of a form of alliance with the Bedouin Arabs.

The third and early fourth century saw the rise of far more powerful confederations of Arab tribes in northern Arabia. These were the Lakhmid and Tanukhid confederations. Both were closely inter-related. At first, both Rome and Iran tried to woo the desert tribes to use them as pawns against each other. The Syrian branch of the Tanukh around Aleppo were allied to the Romans, and after the collapse of Palmyra the Tanukh stepped into the vacuum as Rome's main desert shield against the Persian Empire. The Tanukh confederation in Syria remained firm allies of the Romans throughout the later third and early fourth centuries, while the Lakhmids of Hira became vassals of Sasanian Iran. The Tanukh settled in northern Syria centred on Chalcis (Qinnesrin), south of Aleppo. Their leader, 'Imru'l-Qays, was one of the greatest of pre-Islamic Arab kings, celebrated in Arabic romance. He campaigned widely, reaching as far as Najran in south Arabia. When 'Imru'l-Qays died in 328 the inscription on his tomb at Namara in the Syrian desert proclaimed 'This is the tomb of 'Imru'l-Qays, the son of 'Amr, king of all the Arabs.'

Matters began to deteriorate later in the century when one of the Tanukh kings (possibly a grandson of 'Imru'l-Qays) died in about 375 leaving no heir. With no male leader with whom to treat, the Emperor Valens abrogated Rome's agreement with the Tanukh. The result was open revolt by the Arabs. To some extent this was prompted by religion: Valens attempted to impose Arian Christianity upon the Arabs who were staunch Monophysite Christian. The revolt was led by the extraordinary Queen Mawiyya, the Tanukh king's widow, who took over the leadership of the confederation on her husband's death.

Mawiyya's raids extended deep into Palestine and even Egypt as far as the Nile. They had a devastating effect upon the Romans, who had little defence against the guerrilla warfare of Mawiyya's highly mobile units. She was able to withdraw from the Tanukh settled positions around Aleppo and use only the desert as both her base and her strength: Roman units were left with no target to attack. After centuries of dependence upon the Arabs for their desert defence, the Romans found that without them they were entirely lost in a desert war which could be fought entirely on Mawiyya's terms.

It was not only in desert warfare that Mawiyya's forces were able to excel. Centuries of fighting alongside the Romans as allies had proved the Arabs good students as well, and an initial force sent against them, commanded by the Roman governor of Phoenicia and Palestine, was defeated. Victorious in the desert and in open battle, Mawiyya met success in the towns as well. For in a war fought along religious lines, Mawiyya's cause against an Arian emperor aroused sympathy amongst the Monophysite townspeople, smarting from Valens' insensitive attempt at imposing Arianism. It was beginning to look as if the whole East might break away under Queen Mawiyya and her Arabs.

Accordingly, Constantinople sent another force, this time led by the supreme Roman military commander of the East: a second defeat could not be countenanced. The two forces met in battle with Queen Mawiyya taking command in person. Mawiyya proved as good a field tactician as she was a political leader. The Arabs forces, too, proved themselves masters of both Roman battle technique and their own traditional fighting methods. The combination of strong discipline, the swift manoeuvrability of their cavalry and the long lances that they wielded proved deadly. The result was a Roman defeat. Once more, Rome faced humiliation at the hands of an Arab woman. Faced with the mounting pressure of a looming Gothic war on his western borders, Valens had no alternative but to sue for peace.

The Tanukh revolted once more in 383. This time, the Romans were better prepared, and the second revolt was quickly put down within the same year. But the lesson had not been lost on the Arabs. For Mawiyya's previous victories had, for the Romans, an ominous note. They revealed first just how quickly the native populations in the towns and cities of the Roman Near East would desert the Romans and join the Arab side in time of war. But far more importantly, they demonstrated just how effective a disciplined, well armed but highly mobile desert force of Bedouin cavalry could be against conventional Roman forces. The next time this was to happen, the Arabs would be triumphant.

With the decline of the Tanukh, a new Arab tribe was favoured by the Romans with allied status. This was the Ghassan, destined to become the most powerful of Rome's tribal allies. The Ghassan was originally a nomadic tribe from further south in Arabia. They started moving northwards in a series of tribal migrations after the end of the first century AD. They eventually arrived in the western deserts of Syria and Jordan around the end of the fifth century, using the magnificent city of Rasafa in the Syrian desert as their headquarters (Pl. 37).

The renewed emphasis on courting one of the tribal confederations was begun by Emperor Justinian in response to new threats from Iran. The eastern frontier, having been relatively peaceful for so long, was changing with the rise of a powerful—and aggressive—new Persian emperor, Khusrau I Anushirvan. Forming a strong alliance with a strong tribe was essential. The Romans used their Arabs in a surrogate war as Rome had to turn more and more to the Arabs for their eastern defence.

The Ghassanid 'kingdom' by now comprised virtually all of the eastern areas of the provinces of Arabia and Syria, and ruled with little reference to Constantinople. However, in the intensely bitter theological disputes that dominated the Christian world in late antiquity, religious hostility by the increasingly rigid Orthodoxy of Constantinople against the heterodox Monophysitism of the Ghassan and the subsequent virtual independence of the Syrian church led to open breaches with the Arabs on a number of occasions. Such breaches were usually patched up by Constantinople, for without Arab support all of the Roman Near East was vulnerable. But after 586 the power of the Ghassan was considerably reduced and the federation began to break up. Their sheikh was still accorded the title of Phylarch by Constantinople, but the remaining Ghassanid princes were left to lead a life of considerable extravagance but little real power.

There was some rapprochement with the Ghassan by Heraclius in 629 after his successful campaign against Iran. The last Ghassanid king, Jabalah ibn Ayham, was made supreme over the other tribes once more. Acccordingly, the Ghassan remained loyal to the Romans to the bitter end, joining Heraclius in resisting the Arab Muslim invasion. The Ghassan, however, fell to Muslim rule after the Battle of Yarmuk and submitted to 'Umar in 637. But they never surrendered their religion to Islam, so revolted again soon after. Jabalah and the last members of the house eventually retreated to Constantinople, where one of his descendants even became emperor in the ninth century (Nicephorus I, 802-811).*

Thus, the Ghassanids eventually disappeared, swallowed up by subsequent Byzantine and Islamic history. But their importance in history was crucial. For by the time of the Ghassanid ascendancy the Arabs had become a major factor on the Near Eastern stage and monotheism had

---

* Curiously, according to the twelfth century Andalusian geographer al-Zuhri, the Genoese were thought by some Arabs as descended from the Ghassanids. See Lewis 1982: 146-7.

become a major factor for the Arabs. In the words of the Arab historian Philip Hitti, 'they served as a pre-view of the gigantic show soon to come.'[7] When it did come, Islam was as much a new beginning for Arab civilisation as a culmination: a culmination of the gradual rise of Arab civilisation over the past seven centuries of Roman rule. 'The clients of Byzantium had become its rivals.'[8]

But before we move on to the great early years of Islam, this long and complex relationship between the Arabs and ancient Rome had an outcome that forms the most extraordinary episode of all in this relationship, when Arabs ruled the Roman Empire directly. It is to this story that we turn next.

Chapter 4

ROME'S ARAB HALF CENTURY
Arab Empresses and Emperors of Rome

> [Alexander] ruled for fourteen years without blame or bloodshed
> so far as it affected his subjects. A stranger to savagery, murder
> and illegality, he was noted for his benevolence and good deeds.
>
> Herodian[1]

The above description of Alexander might sound familiar to any reader of
ancient history and one would be forgiven for assuming it to be but one of
many panegyrics to the great Macedonian emperor. One would be wrong: it
is not referring to Alexander the Great, but to the Arab emperor, Emperor
Alexander Severus.

We have seen in the last chapter how the Roman conquest of the
Near East accelerated the rise of the Arabs onto the Mediterranean stage,
a movement that culminated in the Arab invasion of Europe in the eighth
century AD. But it is not often realised that Arabs dominated the very heart
of Rome as well, most notably with the emergence of Arab families who
married into—or became—Roman emperors. Indeed, it is true to say that
from the end of the second century until the middle of the third—fifty-six
years to be exact, from 193 to 249—the empire was dominated by Arabs:
an Arab half century.

The first of these families was—appropriately in the context of
Semitic domination of the Mediterranean—of both Phoenician and Arab
descent. The Phoenician side came from the aristocracy of Leptis Magna
in Africa. The Arab side came from the line of priest-kings who ruled the
client kingdom of Emesa in Syria.

Septimius Severus, Julia Domna and
the orientalisation of Rome

The Pergamon Museum in Berlin houses a particularly revealing painting of a Roman family group: a dark-haired, wavy-haired woman; a white-haired, white-bearded elder statesman supremely confident at the peak of his powers; a youth whose features have been savagely erased; and a pampered-looking, puffy-faced boy. Romans all of them—and in another sense none of them Romans: Empress Julia Domna and Emperors Septimius Severus, Geta and Caracalla.* The family was probably Rome's most successful imperial dynasty† since the Julio-Claudians—and as deeply flawed. But unlike the Julio-Claudians, the Severan dynasty hailed from distant corners of the empire, not from Rome itself nor even Italy. Its founder was Septimius Severus, born at Leptis Magna in North Africa in 145 (Pl. 40). Leptis in origin was, like Carthage, a Phoenician colony. Septimius Severus, despite the Latinisation of his name, was a member of the Phoenician aristocracy and a descendant of the original colonisers from the Levant, not a Latin colonial incomer. Even as late as his birth Leptis still officially looked to Tyre on the Levantine coast as its traditional mother-city, rather than to Rome, despite its becoming formally a Roman colony in 112. Indeed, as late as 197 the links with Tyre were re-affirmed at Leptis Magna by Septimius Severus himself after he became emperor. Its population remained close to its Phoenician roots—Septimius Severus was nick-named 'Punic' on a number of occasions ('Punic Sulla', 'Punic Marius' etc.) and was teased for his strong Punic accented Latin, while his sister never spoke Latin properly at all (to the emperor's considerable embarrassment). Thus, his posting to Syria in about 180 as a young officer in the Roman army was probably seen by Severus as a journey back to his Phoenician 'homeland': he travelled throughout the region, he consulted native Phoenician oracles, and after he had become emperor he revived the ancient name of 'Phoenice' for the new province he created out of Syria. It was at one of these oracles that he first heard of the Arab princess from Emesa whose horoscope forecast she would marry a king. This was Julia Domna.

For it was more the Syrian princess—and her female relatives from Syria—rather than the Punic aristocrat who dominated the dynasty. Julia

---

* Illustrated, for example, on the front cover of the Penguin Classic edition of the *Lives of the Later Caesars*.

† The term 'dynasty' is used in the strict sense of family kinship here, not in the adoptive sense as the Antonines were.

Domna was the daughter of Bassianus, a descendant of the hereditary priest-kings of Emesa. Despite the romanisation of this family, they were Syrian first and foremost. Their descendants—as well as other Syrian relatives of Julia Domna's—were to become the first ruling dynasty of Rome since the Flavians.[*]

It has been pointed out that there is no evidence for a connection between the family of the ancient kings of Emesa and that of Julia Domna—and hence, the Severan dynasty of emperors. However, the latest biography of Julia Domna assumes that they were and the evidence of the historical sources implies overwhelmingly a connection.[2] The immense wealth that Julia Domna's family was able to command on a number of occasions (the coup that elevated Elagabalus, for example, or the opulence of Leptis Magna's new embellishments) must have derived from the Emesene royal house, famous for its fabulous wealth as we have noted in the previous chapter. In addition, the Emesene royal family deliberately aligned itself with other important families through a policy of dynastic marriages: the royal houses of Judaea, Commagene and Armenia numbered amongst them.

Emesa's famous temple and its position as the seat of an important local dynasty would have merited the attention of the young Septimius, both as a young 'Phoenicophile' seeking his roots and as an important Roman officer in his own right. Doubtless Septimius met the young princess then, although he was still married to his first wife Marciana (a Phoenician from Leptis). He certainly remembered the horoscope—'the fruitful offspring either of his superstition or his policy' as Gibbon dryly puts it[3]—concerning her destiny. When Marciana—conveniently!—died during his subsequent posting to Lyon, he lost no time in sending for Julia Domna. In this way Septimius Severus consolidated his Phoenician sentiments with his marriage in about 183 into one of Syria's oldest, most aristocratic and wealthiest families.

Both her wealth and her connections certainly stood him in good stead. That Septimius Severus, a provincial, had been able to rise up through the ranks of imperial administration was thanks to Marcus Aurelius, to whose

---

[*] It is probably a mistake to read too much into the presence or lack of Roman names in Arab families: the Arabic names used by modern Iranians, for example, does not detract from their Iranian character. Herodian, for example, calls the family Phoenician, not Roman, and gives the derivation of Julia Maesa's name as 'Emesa.' The names of the Emesene women were all Arabic in origin: Domna from *Dumayna*, Maesa from *Masa*, Sohaemia from *Suhayma*, 'black', Mammaea from *Mama*, and the name Bassianus may derive from a Semitic root meaning 'priest'. See Shahid 1984: 41-2; Levick 2007: 14-15.

entourage he attached himself early on. However, the aftermath of Aurelius's death and the short but bloodthirsty reign of Commodus was a time for anybody who had been in Aurelius' administration to lie low. Septimius Severus and his bride therefore became tourists, visiting the sights on the 'grand tour' through Greece and down through Egypt. However, in the chaos following Commodus' assassination when rival claimants made bids for the imperial purple, it was the wealth and the connections that Julia Domna commanded, as much as the talents and troops that he commanded, that enabled Septimius Severus to triumph over other claimants. With Severus' victory over Niger, whose bid for power was made from a Syrian base, it would be Domna's connections and influence in Syria that healed wounds. Hence, her biographer Barbara Levick writes: 'At the side of her bearded, middle-aged, relentless military man of a husband, Domna's beauty and comparative youth, her speaking Greek ... with a lilt that belonged to the region, were thrown into higher relief. ... It was added to her appeal and authority as a mother and to the charm of her curly-headed, winsome little boys. ... It will all have made her a high card in the hands of the new master of the Greek world.'[4] Small wonder that the Punic North African emerged as master of Rome in 193. What of Scipio's great victories now? Hannibal could rest in peace.[*]

Perhaps more important than the Punic emperor was the Syrian empress. Julia Domna became a real power behind both Septimius Severus and—even more so—his son Caracalla, prompting the contemporary Roman historian Dio to proclaim her another Semiramis.[5] Under her influence, more and more people from the East were incorporated into high positions in Rome—we read of Syrian tribunes, for example, in the Praetorian guard. It was probably she rather than Caracalla who was ultimately behind Caracalla's famous decree in 212 extending Roman citizenship to all free citizens of the empire, thus abolishing all legal distinctions between Romans and provincials. Most important, Julia Domna consistently appeared alongside her husband, both in public appearances and in imperial portraiture (Pl. 39). She accompanied her husband, and after him her son when he succeeded as emperor, on all their travels, whether peaceful tours of duty or military campaigns apart from actual battle front-lines (and even then would remain not far behind).

---

[*] There is little doubt that Septimius Severus, whilst a Roman and an emperor foremost, nonetheless identified very closely with his great compatriot: in Bithynia he made a point of seeking out the tomb of Hannibal and having it restored.

No other imperial wife and mother had done this in Rome—Julia Domna resembled more the presidential 'first ladies' of our own era.

Julia Domna's assertiveness was exceptional. She is depicted on the Arch of the Argentarii in Rome as taking a prominent position at an official state sacrifice, and on the Arch of Septimius Severus at Leptis Magna as participating in a Roman triumph (Pl. 39). This was almost unheard of for a woman, even an empress. It might reflect the stronger role of women in Syria, or that she and her sister assisted their father as priestesses at the great temple of Emesa in their youth. There is certainly now an increasing body of evidence to suggest that women had higher status in ancient Arabia than in Greece and Rome.[6] Perhaps it was simply her stronger personality.

Julia Domna surrounded herself with a 'salon' of prominent literary and philosophical figures. One of her main protégés was the philosopher Philostratus, himself a disciple of the remarkable mystic Apollonius of Tyana, examined more in the next chapter. This 'salon' is now regarded as overstated, largely a nineteenth-century gloss when such circles became fashionable in Europe (and women's education generally more acceptable). That Julia Domna was highly—and unusually—educated is not in doubt. But apart from Philostratus, members of her 'salon' remain elusive: a few very obscure figures have been tentatively suggested, virtually all of whom—and their works—have sunk into history without trace, although the great philosopher-physician Galen from Pergamon is a remote possibility. At the same time it would be a mistake to go too far the other way. Just because members of her supposed salon are not still renown eighteen hundred years later does not necessarily mean that they were insignificant or nonentities. Many far greater luminaries and men of letters of more recent times have sunk into oblivion. Intellectual court circle or simply 'rent-a-guru', either way there can be little doubt that the great and the good would flock to Domna's orbit: with wealth, education, beauty and position, who would not?

In the winter of 202-3 the imperial couple made a state visit to Severus' home town of Leptis Magna: local boy made good displaying his 'trophy wife, the eastern princess won by the bourgeois from Lepcis' in the perhaps overly cynical words of Barbara Levick.[7] The visit transformed this hitherto minor provincial city, a transformation where one sees Domna's hand as much as Severus'. For the new embellishments of Leptis were *oriental* in nature: the grand triumphal arch for which both design, marbles and craftsmen were imported from the East (Pl. 38); the magnificent colonnaded avenue that led down to the showpiece of a newly enlarged harbour; the stupendous new third forum resembling the great temple enclosures of the East. All transforming the city into an eastern city, a Syrian city, where the hand of a single master architect whose eastern origins cannot be in doubt has been recognised.[8] It is not difficult to recognise Julia Domna in the transformation, depicted so prominently on her husband's arch at Leptis.

There was another aspect to Leptis Magna's transformation. It was embellished on a scale and a lavishness that was hitherto unprecedented, transforming it into one of the most magnificent cities of the empire. It was the home town of an emperor, it is true, but so too were Falacrina in Italy or Italica in Spain, the former the birthplace of Vespasian, the latter of Trajan and Hadrian, which remained small, unembellished provincial towns to the end. This reflected the immense family fortune of Julia Domna of course, but it had another dimension. No other emperor had embellished his home town on anywhere near the same scale: Septimius lavished more money on his birth place than he did on Rome itself. For his reign saw the rise of real provincials to supreme power, not only provincials from North Africa and Syria, but natives of those areas rather than descendants of Italian colonists. Hence, we see the beginning of the city of Rome itself being marginalised. Septimius spent more of his reign outside Rome than in it. Under subsequent emperors the city of Rome was to become less and less a factor in Roman affairs. In lavishing such attention on Leptis he might well have been anticipating Constantine in moving the capital.

Perhaps Julia Domna's most lasting legacy was her insistence upon dynasticism. This was so strong and so successful that after Caracalla's and her own death, the continuation of the dynasty was perceived as essential. This emphasis on dynasticism, clung to occasionally tenuously but always tenaciously (and usually by the Syrian women of the dynasty), anticipated the transformation of the Roman *Imperium* into an hereditary monarchy.

EMPERORS CARACALLA, GETA AND THE EXORCISM OF THE EAST

Septimius died in 211whilst on campaign in Britain. His eldest son was Antoninus, better known under his nick-name, Caracalla. Caracalla would probably have succeeded his father as sole emperor, but his dissolute ways and obsessive ambition—even amounting, on one famous occasion in Britain, to an attempt on the life of Septimius himself—led his father to have grave doubts about the desirability of leaving the empire to one so unsuitable.

In the end, he left it to both sons, Caracalla and his younger brother Geta, hoping that joint rule would temper the more unsavoury side of Caracalla's character. Septimius' decision in fact could not have been worse, for it simply turned Caracalla's hatred of his brother into an obsession.

Of the two sons, Caracalla at first seemed to be the better choice: his youth was exemplary while Geta was a foppish dandy. But the division of the empire into joint rule was soon to reveal Caracalla in his true colours. To end the sibling rivalry between Caracalla and Geta, a meeting was called presided over by Domna, who pleaded with her two sons:

> 'Your mother! How are you going to divide her? How am I to be
> cut up and assigned to the two of you, God help me? You had
> better kill me first, then each of you can cut me up and bury each
> part. Then I can be shared between you, like the land and the sea.'[9]

The outcome was merely further divisiveness. The empire was to be divided between the two brothers, reflecting a precedent begun by Marcus Aurelius and Lucius Verus. This time, both players in the game were of an eastern family and would look to the East. Caracalla was to get the West, Geta the East. Whilst the capital of the western Empire was to remain at Rome, Caracalla anticipated Constantine in choosing Byzantium as his headquarters. Geta's headquarters was to be Chalcedon (opposite Byzantium), with either Antioch or Alexandria as his capital. Julia implored reconciliation between her two sons, but both stormed off to sulk in their respective halves of the divided imperial palace in Rome. Whilst the events of that evening foreshadowed the momentous decisions of Diocletian and Constantine, the over-riding impression of them is of two spoilt boys squabbling over their toys. A pity the stakes were so high, the precedent so important.

The spoilt Caracalla, the good-looking darling of his mother and the Roman people, proved dissatisfied with merely a half an empire. He pursued his brother relentlessly, eventually having him killed in his mother's arms. Thus the half Punic, half Syrian* boy ended up with the lot (and even remained his mother's favourite, judging by the way Julia so quickly forgot the fratricide). But the ghost of Geta and an eastern empire remained to haunt Caracalla for the remainder of his life. Having

---

* Dio LXXVIII. 6. 1 writes 'Antoninus [Caracalla] belonged to three races; and he possessed none of their virtues at all, but combined in himself all their vices; the fickleness, cowardice, and recklessness of Gaul were his, the harshness and cruelty of Africa, and the craftiness of Syria.'

begun his reign in a blood bath Caracalla followed up Geta's murder with more butchery, and 'Geta's friends and associates were immediately butchered ... No one who had the slightest acquaintance with Geta was spared: athletes, charioteers, and singers and dancers of every type were killed. Everything that Geta kept around him to delight eye and ear were destroyed. Senators distinguished because of ancestry or wealth were put to death as friends of Geta upon the slightest unsupported charge of an unidentified accuser. ... Their bodies, after first being dragged about and subjected to every form of indignity, were placed in carts and taken out of the city; there they were piled up and burned or simply thrown into the ditch.' ... 'Indeed, if anyone so much as wrote the name Geta or even uttered it, he was immediately put to death.'[10]

Caracalla proceeded to exorcise the ghost of an eastern empire. In Rome he not only consciously aped Alexander the Great but even claimed he was a reincarnation. Then, in pathetic emulation, he set out for the East in 214. He proceeded to Alexandria, Geta's choice as capital, and wiped out half the male population of the city in an act of treachery appalling even by any standards. Dio writes 'in spite of the immense affection which he professed to cherish for Alexander, [Caracalla] all but utterly destroyed the whole population of Alexander's city.'[11] But for Caracalla, Alexandria was not so much Alexander's as Geta's city.

Having finally satiated his grudge against Geta with the blood of the Alexandrians, Caracalla set his eyes on Iran. He first grandly proposed uniting the two empires of Rome and Parthia by a marriage to the daughter of King Artabanus of Parthia—a proposal consciously harking back to Alexander's marriage to the Persian Princess Statira and the fusion of East and West. At first spurned, Caracalla's suit was finally accepted by Artabanus—obviously Caracalla's reputation had not gone before him. The groom and his vast (and heavily armed) entourage entered Mesopotamia in grand style and proceeded to Ctesiphon for the marriage of the millennium. Artabanus had prepared a huge royal wedding reception for him in the fields outside the city. Leaving their arms and their horses behind for the festivities, the Parthians were caught totally unprepared for Caracalla's ruse. The Romans massacred the unarmed Parthian warriors in their thousand, with Artabanus himself (and the doubtless relieved bride) only just managing to escape at the last minute. Caracalla left the blood-soaked wedding field and turned back westwards, claiming 'victory' of the entire East. But the East had not finished with Caracalla. On his return, Caracalla was murdered while he paused to relieve himself near Carrhae—a suitably ignominious end for one of Rome's worst tyrants.

To this day the ghost of the East still returns to haunt Caracalla, almost two millennia after his death. For the one thing more than anything else that is commonly associated with his name today is the immense baths he had built in Rome. It has in modern times been converted to the world's largest out-door opera house. As such, it is the regular venue for one of opera's greatest spectaculars: Verdi's grand epic, *Aida*, set in ancient Egypt. Ironic indeed that the country whose capital he did so much to destroy is now associated more than ever with his name.

Julia Domna had followed her son to Antioch, as much to be near as to be able to wield power through him. On receiving news of her son's death, she foresaw her own subsequent loss of power, so hastened a death already made inevitable from advanced breast cancer by fasting to death. But Julia Domna left an equally forceful woman to succeed her as the power behind the throne, her sister Julia Maesa.

Caracalla's portraits are particularly revealing. The features of the pampered brat pictured in the Berlin portrait are still easily recognisable in the adult, although the over-indulged plumpness disappears in the Hermitage bust (Pl. 41). Instead, the over-indulgence is replaced by a quick, uncontrolled temper suggested by the scowl depicted in the immensely powerful New York Metropolitan portrait, which otherwise depicts youthful good looks. But the good looks are marred by the scowl, which also suggests underlying cruelty, and the 'designer stubble' simply suggests affectation. Subsequent portraits of Caracalla growing older mark inevitable regression. By the time that the Berlin bust was made the designer stubble is replaced by a short beard, the youthful good looks have given way to coarser, heavier features, only the cruel—but by now deeply suspicious—scowl remains (Pl. 42). Finally, the University of Pennsylvania granite portrait depicts a hideous image: a coarse, thoroughly brutalised tyrant where the ever-permanent scowl has become a baleful glare, not softened even by affectation or self indulgence.

It is easy to see where Caracalla's looks came from, despite rumours that Julia Domna was not his mother: of the two boys, only the short-lived Geta appears to take after his father. Or perhaps it is just that the few surviving portraits of the youthful Geta are unmarred by the cruelty that characterises his brother, giving a superficial resemblance to the kinder features of Septimius. Most portraits of Julia Domna seem to convey an image of subtlety, suggested perhaps by a mouth which appears locked in an expression of perpetual calculation, with eyes that are never direct. Only in a bust in Munich do her features appear warmer and more relaxed. But whatever the expression, the portraits convey the impression of a far more powerful personality than either her son or her husband. No sloe-eyed, empty-headed eastern floozy here, interested only in harem intrigues. Small wonder she became the power behind the throne of two emperors, and one is left wondering whether the supposed horoscope foretelling her future greatness was simply of her own devising. Such a pity that Caracalla, who in some ways had some admirable characteristics (he was good with the army, for example), never inherited her force of personality. But both he and Julia Domna were obsessive people, obsessed with the pursuit of power as much as with each other. One wonders whether a Roman relief of the Severan period depicting Mars and Venus contains more than a hint of Caracalla and Julia Domna.[*]

EMPEROR ELAGABALUS AND THE SUPREME GOD

Apart from a brief usurpation by Macrinus, Caracalla was succeeded by his second-cousin Elagabalus (Pl. 43). Elagabalus was the grandson of Julia Domna's equally redoubtable sister Julia Maesa, the son of her daughter Julia Sohaemias (Pl. 44). In Elagabalus we have one of the most curious—and perhaps maligned—emperors ever to receive the Roman purple. His name was the same as his great-grandfather, Bassianus, and after he became emperor he adopted the name of Marcus Aurelius Antoninus. Elagabalus was his title as hereditary high-priest at the Temple of Emesene Baal. But Elagabalus—or Heliogabalus, a variation—is the name under which he has entered history.

Elagabalus was also endowed with the fatal combination of youthful good looks and a scheming, ambitious grandmother. Following the death of Caracalla and the elevation of Macrinus, Syria was flooded with disaffected troops after the humiliation of defeat at the hands of the

---

[*] Now in the Villa Albani, Rome. For this and other portraits see Kleiner 1992. There is some suggestion in the sources that Caracalla was not the son of Julia Domna but of Severus' first wife, Marcia, in explanation of a suggested incestuous relationship between mother and son (although even a stepson-stepmother relationship was regarded as incestuous under Roman law). See Levick 2007: 98-9.

Parthians. They were also smarting under the rule of Macrinus, having enjoyed greater privileges under Caracalla who had been as popular with the army as he was unpopular with civilians. Julia Maesa had two grandsons, Elagabalus and Alexander, sons of her daughters Sohaemias and Mamaea respectively, both of them born to the hereditary priesthood of the Temple. Elagabalus was the elder of the two cousins by some six years, hence high-priest. Ungallantly, his grandmother spread the rumour that Elagabalus was the illegitimate offspring of Caracalla and her daughter Sohaemias. The army accepted it and in 218 proclaimed the sixteen year old boy-priest emperor in Emesa.

Emperor Elagabalus proceeded to Rome, taking all the trappings of his cult with him. Sources describe him and his religious rites as 'frenzied orgies' and 'a frenzy of arrogance and madness', with details of his private life even more lurid. Such descriptions have all the disapproving relish of a prude in a brothel, and can be dismissed as propaganda—similar Roman descriptions of cannibalism and other such unspeakable orgies in Christian rites have, after all, long been relegated to the dustbin.* With the more lurid details stripped away, there are some details that have a ring of truth and even bring out a more endearing side to Elagabalus' character. He had a propensity for practical jokes, for example, such as his practice of seating his more pompous dinner guests on 'whoopee cushions' that let out a farting noise as they sat down, or placing his drunk dinner guests after they had fallen asleep into a room with wild, but (unknown to the guests) perfectly tamed and harmless, beasts. Frenzied depravity or mere youthfulness (he was, after all, only sixteen)? Contemporary censure and outrage at Elagabalus' giving women—his mother, Julia Sohaemias, and his grandmother, Varia—a place in the Senate, or at promoting freedmen to high office, should surely attract praise rather than be condemned as a 'disgrace [to] the acts of the senate'[12]—presumably evidence again of the higher status that Syrian women enjoyed over Roman. Indeed, even the author of the most scurrilous of the Elagabalus stories in the *Augustan History* has to concede that 'However, both these matters and some others which pass belief were, I think, invented by people who wanted to depreciate Heliogabalus to win favour with Alexander.' Contrasting with the almost universal condemnation of Elagabalus, John Malalas is alone of the Romans who wrote warmly of this emperor.[13]

---

* Indeed, it is surprising that otherwise respectable historians have been so selective in their acceptance or rejection of the more purple Roman descriptions of foreign religious rites.

It is Elagabalus' religion rather than his 'depravities' that are of real interest, and these are explored more in Chapter 6. And it is for his religion above all that he has received most censure from posterity. But one can hardly censure Elagabalus for continuing his hereditary religious rites in Rome after becoming emperor. He never plotted to become emperor, his grandmother did. Elagabalus was a priest first and, being brought up as high-priest, would have been sincere and punctilious in his beliefs and practices; the purple was thrust upon him, he never chose it. As the high priest of the cult, Elagabalus would feel bound to continue his rituals in Rome. He may, it is true, have executed 'many famous and wealthy men who were charged with ridiculing and censuring his way of life,'[14] but what high-priest and absolute emperor would not retaliate for insults to his beliefs? But Elagabalus alienated the Praetorian Guard. In the end the ever fickle Praetorian Guard—never a good judge of emperors, as history proved on numerous occasions—murdered Elagabalus and his mother, dumping the bodies in a sewer. Alexander was proclaimed emperor in his place.

We thus leave the rather sad figure of Emperor Elagabalus, a tragic enigma lost behind centuries of misalignment.* He was an unsuccessful emperor, it is true. But he was a sincere priest, which is what he was born to be. Born and brought up to the cloistered ceremonies of an eastern religion rather than cynical power games of Rome's street rabble, he was a Syrian and a priest first, and only a Roman and an emperor second. But above all he was young: from sixteen, when he first ascended the throne, to nineteen when he was finally butchered after a reign of merely 'three years, nine months and four days'[15] is surely too young for so much to be thrust upon one so young. One of his few surviving portraits, in the Capitoline Museum in Rome, shows a rather pathetic figure: a cocky youth with a wispy, pubescent moustache, but with a sense of overwhelming youth, vulnerability and uncertainty, despite the cockiness, reflected too in an unattributed bust in the Cyrene Museum (Pl. 43).[16] One is left feeling sorrow for the boy rather than condemnation for the emperor.

---

* Both the sources and the modern histories almost universally revile him, e.g., Gibbon I: 143-8, or Antony Birley, 'Introduction' to the *Lives of the Later Caesars* (Penguin Classics 1976), p. 20: 'Elagabalus, the perverted Syrian youth'. Elagabalus was no more a pervert than Hadrian with his Antinous was.

Emperor Alexander* and the end of a dynasty

Like Elagabalus, Alexander was born to the Emesene priesthood but, being six years his junior, never became high-priest. He was born at Arqa in present day northern Lebanon where a few remains mark his birthplace (in modest contrast to Leptis Magna). Coming to Rome at the age of nine in Elagabalus' entourage, he was not subject to such Syrianising influences as Elagabalus was, being brought up more as a Roman (although on his return to Syria, it is notable that 'the inhabitants of the provinces looked up to him as a god'). In contrast to his cousin, he was one of the wiser and more moderate emperors of the chaotic third century. But like all members of his family, he was dominated by his women-folk. His mother, Julia Mamaea, younger daughter of Julia Maesa, was the last of that extraordinary line of Syrian women who dominated Rome behind their men-folk. Mamaea was no exception and was on hand at all times to advise and guide her son in the ways of the imperial world, accompanying him even into the field. Like Julia Domna and Julia Maesa, she also wielded considerable power behind the throne. Indeed, Gibbon extols Mamaea's virtues above Domna's, awarding her much of the credit for Alexander's exemplary reign. Her portraits show that she inherited all the strength of character of her aunt, but without the calculation—Julia Maesa's position after all was already established by a family of emperors before her. Her face is confident but more inward looking. She was also known to be favourably disposed towards Christianity, although not Christian herself.

The other trait that Alexander shared with all other members of his family was a destiny with the East: it dominated his life—and destroyed him in the end. He returned to Syria in response to the new threat from Sasanian Persia. Despite conducting his campaign 'with such discipline and amid such respect, that you would have said that senators, not soldiers, were passing that way,'[17] his armies suffered disaster. He returned from the East discredited. His popularity with the army consequently plummeted, exacerbated by the army's resentment at being ruled by a 'mother's boy' and a woman (note that the resentment was entirely sexist, never racist: there was no hint of resentment of her being a Syrian). Matters reached a head when Alexander was commanding a campaign on the Rhine frontier. The soldiers dispatched both Mamaea and Alexander while he clung to his mother's arms,

---

* It is curious that despite the long shadow that Alexander the Great cast over the ancient world, Alexander Severus is the first emperor—or ruler of any real note—to be named after him.

proclaiming the brutish Thracian giant and former shepherd, Maximinus, as emperor. Rome's line of Phoenicio-Syrian emperors finally came to an end.

In this extraordinary line of Syrian women who dominated their husbands and sons and through them the empire, one senses a matriarchy— or at least a higher status enjoyed by Syrian women over their Roman counterparts (and one recalls Elagabalus was the first emperor to elevate women to the Senate). Apart from the emperors themselves, husbands and fathers are shadowy figures. Whenever the dynasty looked like failing it would be a female relative from Emesa who would be called upon to take over the helm at Rome, not a male. Caracalla, Elagabalus and Alexander may well have been dominated by their mothers. But they cannot stand condemned for reasons of simple lack of maturity (or masculinity). After all, Elagabalus was merely sixteen when proclaimed emperor and Alexander only thirteen, both still boys when a mother's influence is natural. Caracalla was undoubtedly a tyrant of the worst sort, but he was good with the army. This is what counted when it came to the real business of running Rome, which was protecting the borders. Even Elagabalus had sound albeit flawed intentions. And apart from the disasters in the East, Alexander's fourteen year rule was as mild and wise as his portraits depict him. Herodian's epitaph is thus a fitting one: '[Alexander] ruled for fourteen years without blame or bloodshed so far as it affected his subjects. A stranger to savagery, murder and illegality, he was noted for his benevolence and good deeds.'[18] Even the *Augustan History* writes of Alexander as the perfect prince in 'an awkward imitation of the *Cyropaedia*' according to Gibbon, who sees Alexander as the greatest and wisest of emperors since the golden age of the Antonines whose exemplary reign could serve as a model for modern princes. Aurelius Victor goes even further when he states that Alexander saved Rome from collapse.[19] This most noble 'Roman' thus formed a fitting end to Rome's most extraordinary dynasty of Phoenician emperors.

LAST BID FROM EMESA

Alexander was not quite the end of Rome's extraordinary Emesene dynasty of emperors. In about 248 during the reign of Philip the Arab (discussed below) there was a revolt in Syria led by Iotapianus, who claimed to be related to Emperor Alexander. Although proclaimed 'king of Syria' Iotapianus never made a bid for the imperial purple, but the next claim from Emesa did. In 253 Gallus, Aemilian and Valerian were contending for the imperial position in Italy. With Rome's back turned on the East, the Persians under Shapur invaded Syria and captured Antioch. In the power vacuum left by the temporary collapse of Roman rule, another priest of Emesa, Samsigeramus, supposedly inflicted a defeat on Shapur outside Emesa. As a result of its great victory, Emesa proclaimed a new emperor. This new emperor was a young Emesene called Sulpicius Antoninus who assumed the purple under the name Uranius Antoninus. It is unclear from the sources whether Samsigeramus and Uranius were the same person, or two related people. Samsigeramus was priest of the temple of Aphrodite. In the usual confusing way of Eastern syncretism, the deity Urania was equated to both the Phoenician Astarte/ Aphrodite and the Arabian Allat, so they may have been the same. At first, Uranius simply regarded himself as a younger colleague to Valerian, but it inevitably became a direct challenge. With the immense wealth of the Emesene temple treasury behind him, Uranius was for a while even able to issue his own coinage. The coinage came to an end in 255, either because the funds from the Emesene Sun-temple was exhausted or because Valerian eventually put him down. The fate of Uranius is not known.

The 'Emperor Uranius', last of the Emesene sun-kings, was seen as a champion of the Roman cause against Persia. He had everything behind him: wealth, dynastic roots, and a victory against Rome's greatest enemy. But Valerian, for all his failings, had the trump card: Rome itself. Uranius' brief two years of glory was probably the last claim by a representative of Julia Domna's family for the imperial purple. Whilst there is no conclusive evidence that Uranius did belong to this family, it seems likely that he did. A near contemporary and local source, the so-called *Sybelline Oracles* that were probably written in Emesa, in fact describe him as the 'last of all' of the priests who 'came from the Sun.'[20] Indeed, given the hereditary nature of the Emesene high priesthood, as well as his adoption of the dynastic name of Antoninus and pretensions to the purple, the implications are that he was related, however distantly.

Emesa was also the scene of another claim to the purple a short time later by Quietus, which was suppressed by Udaynath of Palmyra in about 263, but there is no evidence that he was connected to the family. There was another Uranius who claimed the Bishopric of Emesa in about 444; given the priestly tradition, he might have been a descendant. Iamblichus, a second century novelist and author of *The Babylonian History*, may also have been connected to the family, as was another Iamblichus, the Neo-Platonic philosopher born in Chalcis in the Beq'a Valley in the third century, who wrote in Aramaic. But apart from sharing the Emesene 'royal name' of Iamblichus, there is no firm evidence either way.

EMPEROR PHILIP THE ARAB

The minor episodes of 'King Iotapianus' and 'Emperor Uranius' is to anticipate events. Before that, another Arab emperor was established in Rome who had no connection to the Emesene dynasty.* This was Marcus Julius Philippus, better known as Philip the Arab, a native of the small provincial town of Shahba in southern Syria (Pls 45, 46). Philip's origins as the son of a bandit from Trachonitis, which Shahba formed a part of, has been rejected as later Roman propaganda. One country's 'bandit' is in any case another country's aristocrat, the two terms usually amounting to the same thing, depending upon viewpoint. In 243 Philip became the praetorian prefect of Gordian III, who was then fighting a campaign in the East against Persia. When Gordian was killed on this campaign, Philip was proclaimed emperor by the troops in the East in 244. He then swiftly negotiated a peace treaty with Shapur—Sasanian rock reliefs depict him on bended knee before the mounted figure of Shapur—and returned to Rome. Philip's reign was short—just five years—but it was a stable one in the unstable third century: Rome enjoyed a respite. It came to an end only too soon when he and his son (prematurely proclaimed as Philip II) were eliminated in 249 in a revolt by Decius.

Although relatively brief it was also a particularly important reign in the annals of Rome. This was for a number of reasons. First, the year 248, four years after he had assumed the purple, was the year of the Millennium. Rome celebrated a thousand years of its existence, a thousand years from its origins as a minor city to its becoming the greatest empire of the world. The secular games to mark this event were remarkable even by Roman standards: games and gifts were endowed by a munificent emperor on a lavish scale. Certainly a thousand years is reason enough for the event to be remarkable, but what made it even more remarkable was that the Roman emperor who presided over the games, as the ultimate Roman and embodiment of Roman civilisation, was from Syria. A country that the founders of the city would

---

* Although the name of Philip's wife, Ocatilia Severa, also an Arab, implies that some favours at least had been granted her family by the Severan dynasty. See Bowersock 1983: 123.

never have heard about, let alone dreamt that they would one day be ruled by someone from there—and ruled as one of their own, not as a foreign conqueror. In some ways this makes Philip's reign a greater one than Trajan's or Hadrian's, for nothing else demonstrated just how far in every way Rome had come by the middle of the third century.

The second reason is more controversial. For it was Philip—not Constantine—who was Rome's first Christian emperor. This is discussed further in Chapter 6. If Philip's reign was important for anticipating Christianity, it was also important for anticipating the rise of the Arabs. Portraits depict Philip with the features that characterise many Syrians even today (Pl. 45). Whether Philip in fact felt in any way 'Arab' in the modern sense is unlikely: Philip was a Roman above all. Of more importance is what Philip meant to the Arabs themselves: that one of their own could aspire to the world's highest office and succeed. This signified more than anything else that the Arabs were no mere barbaric nomads of little account on the fringes of the civilised world, but were becoming an increasing factor on the world stage. The accession of Philip the Arab is one of the more important in the chain of events that culminated in the eventual triumph of the Arabs in the seventh century when the Near East ceased to be Roman and became Arab.*

THE ARABS IN THE FAR WEST

Near Eastern penetration and colonisation of Europe has a long history—certainly far longer than European colonisation of the East—as we have seen with the Phoenician outward expansion in the second millennium BC. The eventual defeat of Carthage at the hands of Rome and the collapse of its colonial empire did not bring about an end to this expansion. Quite the contrary, for the unification of the Mediterranean world under Rome brought Near Eastern communities in the wake of Rome's conquests in Europe. The Jewish Diaspora, for example (which actually started before the destruction of Jerusalem by Titus in 66), and the establishment of Jewish communities

---

* For a thought-provoking new biography of Philip from the Arab perspective, see Zahran 2001. Philip was not quite the last Roman emperor who was Arab. The Emperor Nicephorus I (802-811), or Niqfur in the Arabic sources, although heavily Romanised was a descendant of the Ghassanid king Jabalah. The Isaurian or Syrian dynasty of emperors (717-802) whom Nicephorus displaced, whilst perhaps not Arab in the strict sense, were at least closely related to them—Emperor Leo III spoke Arabic as his first language, and their fanatic iconoclasm has been seen by some authorities to be derived from Islam.

in every major city of the Mediterranean was a part of this broad pattern. As early as the reign of Trajan much of the new monumentalisation of the city of Rome itself was carried out by architects from Syria (Pl. 48). Under the patronage of the Syrian families and emperors reviewed above, a steady stream of people from the Near East continued to arrive and settle in the western Mediterranean. But the influence of these emperors and patronage of people from the 'home country' should not be over-stated, as it was more the continuation of a process that had began a thousand years before.

Substantial Arab minorities are recorded in most of the ports of southern Spain from the first few centuries AD, especially in Malaga, Cartagena, Seville and Cordoba. These locations are significant, the first two being major centres of earlier Phoenician settlement, the last two major Arab settlement under Islam, indication of a continuity of immigration over thousands of years. Wealthy Near Eastern merchant colonies—usually Syro-Phoenicians—lived in Puteoli and Ostia in the second century AD. Indeed, the cults of Tyrian Melqart, Egyptian Isis, Anatolian Cybele, Syrian Atargatis, Iranian Mithras, Nabatean Dushara, Jupiter Heliopolitanus, Jupiter Damascenus (Hadad), Jupiter Dolichenus and numerous other eastern cults are known to have flourished in Puteoli—it must have resembled an oriental city in the first few centuries AD. Apamaean, Palmyrene and Nabatean communities in Italy are also known, and there is Palmyrene dedicatory inscription to Malakbel and a Nabatean dedicatory inscription to the Sun God in Rome. Safaitic inscriptions have also been recorded at Pompeii. Other Syrian merchant communities have been recorded in Pannonia, Lyon, Grenoble, Arles, Trier and elsewhere. In Lyon, for example, a bilingual inscription by Thayn ibn Sa'd from Qanawat had been left by one of these Syrian merchant families. Such Syrian merchant communities became more influential after the adoption of Christianity, particularly in encouraging eastern forms of monasticism and the adoption of the crucifix as the Christian symbol. Salvian (who died in about 484) wrote of Syrian merchants in Marseilles, and there was still a Syrian merchant community in Narbonne as late as 589. After the fourth century Ravenna was noted for its Syrian influence, both in its mosaics and its religion, with a number of Syrian bishops recorded there. There was a Syrian bishop of Paris in the fifth century, and Aramaic was still being spoken in Orleans and Narbonne in the fifth and sixth centuries. Marseilles and Bordeaux still had a substantial Syrian population in the fifth century, mainly mercantile. In the first hundred years after the Muslim invasion, no less than six popes were Syrian. One of these, Pope Sergius I (687-701), was particularly instrumental in introducing elements of Syrian liturgy and Christian belief into the Church of Rome. Theodore, the Archbishop of Canterbury from 669-690, was from Tarsus.

After Emperor Alexander's Persian war in 230-3, many 'Moorish', Arab and Iranian troops, mainly archers, were brought back and stationed in Germany. Syrian elements have been recorded in Roman army camps in Europe, particularly along the Danube frontier, where the Syrian cults of Aziz, Hadad and al-'Uzza are known. On the British frontier, shrines to the Syrian Jupiter Dolichenus have been found at Caerleon, and shrines to Phoenician Astarte and Melqart have been found at Corbridge and Jupiter Heliopolitanus at Magnae, both near Hadrian's Wall. Near the end of the wall, at South Shields, a Palmyrene funerary memorial has been found associated with a Syrian community in Northumberland. The ancient name of the South Shields fort was Arbeia (Pl. 47), a corruption of 'Arabs', and the control of the river traffic at the mouth of the Tyne at that time was in the hands of an Arab community known as the 'Tigris boatmen'.

The above survey, although brief, is enough to underline the interchange. Against this background, the Arab conquest of Spain under Islam in the early eighth century and the subsequent expansion into Sicily, Italy, southern France and even Switzerland is not so much the first act in Islam's expansion but the last in a tradition of Near Eastern expansion into Europe. It is to this expansion that we must turn next. But before entering the era of the new religion to come out of Arabia, we must take a last look at the older religions and how they paved the way—for Christianity as much as for Islam.

Chapter 5

IMPACT OF THE ABSTRACT
Ancient Arabian Religion and the Christian West

No statue made by man in the likeness of the god stands in this
temple, as in Greek and Roman temples.

Herodian[1]

Christianity's origins in the ancient Near East have never been in doubt.
However, these origins are almost invariably viewed as rooted exclusively
in Judaism. I do not propose to doubt the Judaic origins of Christianity
here, but wish to emphasise the part that the pagan Arabian religions played
in the development of Christianity.* This was a twofold role. First, there
were elements in ancient Arabian religions—outside Judaism—that found
their way into Christianity. And second, the Arabs were instrumental—
fundamental even—in that greatest step of all: the transmission of this
strange oriental religion to the very different West. But before that, it is
necessary to stress just how much Europe's identity has come to be defined
in terms of Christianity in order to demonstrate just how successfully these
Arabian influences paved the way.

EUROPE AND CHRISTENDOM

The increasingly blurred terms of 'Europe' and 'the West' have for many
centuries been defined in terms of Christendom. The world historian J M
Roberts, for example, writes: 'most of the story of world Christianity is the
story of a western success in spreading its ideas ... Christianity had been
the original and defining matrix of western civilisation.'[2] Following the

---

* The part played by Iranian Zoroastrianism was also huge and now largely ignored. I will be
discussing this further in Volume 2, *Towards One World*.

fall of Constantinople in 1453, Pope Pius II defined Europe in terms of a Christian fortress in opposition to Islam generally and the Turks specifically (but at the same time could not help but admire the achievement of Mehmet the Conqueror, bemoaning that if he were only to convert to Christianity he personally would crown him 'king of the world'), and King George of Bohemia proposed a political union of Europe as a front against the Turks.[3]

'Europe' then becomes a 'them and us' construct (ignoring that the Turks by then were a major European power and Islam a European religion), a narrow definition that is essentially medieval Latin Christendom—it excluded Byzantine Christendom—but on the other hand hijacks anything from outside this exclusion zone that might help prop up this narrow self image. Historian Charles Le Goff, for example, in a book entitled *The Birth of Europe* in a series itself entitled *The Making of Europe* emphasises this when he writes 'Latin Christian Europe ... lies at the origin of present-day Europe.'[4]

I do not wish to imply criticism of any of the above cited works here. I am simply stressing the fact that 'our' religion, the religion which defines Europe, European civilisation and our very European identity more than *anything* else is not European. This cannot be emphasised too strongly—or too often—not because it reveals such a European definition as essentially questionable, but because it has been Christianity more than anything else that has been used to proclaim European superiority over the rest of the world: it has been used as a stick to beat Muslims, Africans, American Indians, Asians.

Of course, the importance of Christianity to European civilisation cannot be denied: European atheists or even Buddhist, Muslim or Druid converts are still 'Christian' in cultural terms.[5] But its use as a definition has limitations, and it would be a grave mistake to confuse 'Christian country' with 'European country'. One country that is both Christian and in the 'East' is a good example. The rear cover of a recent book, *The Armenians*, in a series entitled 'Peoples of Europe' begins: 'There is a 3000 year history of one of *Europe's* most fascinating and ancient peoples. Situated *south* of the Caucasus mountains, historical Armenia has been a pivotal point between the forces of the east and of the west over much of its long history'(the italics are mine). The book subsequently begins with the words 'A generally accepted definition of the extent of Europe ... does include the present day Republic of Armenia, the boundary between Asia and Europe being regarded as running along the Caucasus.'[6] Armenia and Georgia are routinely defined as European, 'honorary' members of the European club *solely* on the grounds of Christianity;[7] Azerbaijan or Turkey, also south of the Caucasus, never are. 'Europe' and 'Christian' have become virtually interchangeable, and the definition has become a self-evident fact that need not even be questioned. This is even applied retrospectively: Armenia has been Europe for '3,000 years', long before Christianity. But even if one were to define Europe and European identity in terms of Christianity, the inescapable fact would remain: Europe would be defined in terms of a religion from the Near East.

It is not often appreciated just how revolutionary a step the adoption of Christianity was for a European people. So closely is Christianity now associated with European civilisation that it is simply taken for granted. But to begin with, Christianity for the West was a radical, revolutionary idea, far more revolutionary than Communism or other nineteenth-century radical movements in Europe in our own era. For unlike Communism, which was rooted in European political and philosophical ideas, Christianity in antiquity was completely alien to the Western mind with no counterparts and few points of contact in European religion or philosophy. In the transition from European paganism to Christianity, the question of how such an alien, non-European idea became so implanted on such infertile soil that it has become one of the fundamental definitions of European identity, is one of the most important questions in history, and perhaps the most important historical process in the development of European civilisation.

ANTICIPATING THE ABSTRACT

Many of the elements of Christianity were long a part of Near Eastern religion quite outside Judaism. Cities throughout the ancient Near East were usually dominated by single, large temple complexes dedicated to their patron god. Religion and holy cities were a major part of the entire urban fabric. Jerusalem, of course, was—and is—the archetypal such holy city, with its Temple appropriate to such a status. But it is important to remember that before circumstances made Jerusalem pre-eminent, the East had many such holy cities, sacred to specific cults, all jostling for pre-eminence. Mambij was sacred to Atargatis, Byblos 'the holy' to Baalat-Gabal, Emesa to the Sun god Elagabal, Damascus to Hadad, Sebaste to a rival Jehovah, to name but some of the main 'Jerusalems' of the ancient Near East. This is essentially a part of a broader ancient Arabian tradition of the holy city and place of pilgrimage or *haram*: Mecca, Najran, Yathil, Ma'rib and San'a' were the main ones in southern Arabia before Islam made Mecca pre-eminent. When a city had more than one temple, there would always be the one to the patron god that outshone all others. It would dwarf the city around it, providing the main focal point around which all of the city's life revolved. It would be built on a massive—one could almost say monolithic—scale, usually much larger than those in the West. Incipient monotheism was never far away in the East.

A major contribution to Christianity that is reflected in these temples was the idea of congregation—probably the most revolutionary concept that Christianity brought to the West after the concept of monotheism. The idea that all members of a community meet on specific regular days to participate in communal worship was completely alien to Western pagan practice: the public cults demanded participation only from the few officials, while the private religions of the majority were practised individually in the home or the neighbourhood shrines. There was no concept of religious congregation. In the East, however, the idea was almost universal.

This concept was expressed architecturally in the East in the vast temple compounds built to accommodate huge congregations, temples which had no counterpart in the West. The congregation was the single reason for the massive scale of Eastern temples. In many ways, it was the enclosure itself, rather than the sanctuary building inside it, that was the main element of these great temples. The sanctuary was merely the residence of the deity, while outside in the enclosure was where the sacrifices to the god's honour took place and where mass worship was performed. Hence, the enclosure was more than just a perimeter wall between the city (or country) and the temple: it *was* the temple. It was also an arena, a theatre which provided a setting for elaborate and gorgeous religious spectacle involving mass participation by thousands—'performances' far more sumptuous than the most ambitious of theatrical productions. There was always an element of theatricality in Eastern temple architecture. Hence, like a stage back-drop, the walls would be lavishly embellished commensurate to the status of the deity itself. The great temple compounds at Palmyra, Baalbek, Damascus, Jerash, Petra and elsewhere in the East reflect this universal emphasis on congregation in pagan Arabian usage (Pls 24, 25, 33, 35 and 49). The idea continued with the great mosque courtyards of Islam.

Central to most Arabian religion was the abstract concept of deity. This was expressed by the *baetyl*, or stone cult object, the focal point of many temples. Many deities were represented in abstract—and often cubic—forms.

Such were the ubiquitous 'god-blocks' of Nabataean religious architecture, or the black stone of the Temple of Elagabal of Emesa, or similar black stones of Phoenician temples to Melqart. Indeed, the *baetyls*, usually the stone blocks symbolising their gods, were a feature of ancient temples of the Near East, even after the influence of Greek and Roman art had personified the gods into shadows of Western likenesses. When the prosaic Romans first entered these temples they were often baffled by the absence of images, the abstract concept of deity being at that time alien to the Western mind, for 'no statue made by man in the likeness of the god stands in this temple, as in Greek and Roman temples.'[9]

The idea of the abstract is expressed architecturally throughout ancient Arabia by a preference for bold, abstract, cuboid forms. These elements are seen at their purest in the ancient South Arabian architecture of the early first millennium BC. Here, temples entrances are typically marked by rows of square monoliths, such as at the Moon Temples at Sirwah and Ma'rib (Pls 17, 18). Even capitals, which are incorporated into the shafts, are entirely 'cubist', consisting of a series of smaller squares. Altars usually take the form of a cube and are decorated in repeated rows of squares; columns are either square or polygonal, surmounted by capitals in the form of faceted squares. At Sirwah, even a frieze consisting of a row of ibex is reduced to abstract, cubist form (Pl. 21). The predominantly 'cuboid' appearance of ancient South Arabian architecture gives it a strangely elemental, almost modern—or, indeed, futuristic—appearance.

Such a 'cuboid' theme is a constantly recurring one at Petra. The severely rectilinear smaller facades, for example, resemble almost abstract, cubist sculpture: the rows of regularly repeated square facades, divided by bold horizontal and vertical lines, capped by equally square crow-step gables and merlons (Pl. 27). Such tomb facades belong to an older Arabian tradition rather than Classical—all of the Nabataean facades at Medain Saleh in Saudi Arabia belong to this category. Elsewhere at Petra carved squares and the cubic motif abound. The enigmatic 'god-blocks,' for example (Pl. 28), or the *baetyl* in the Siq consisting of a cube with two squares carved into the face of one side and two further squares carved onto the larger one (Pl 29). Such rectangular carvings of squares or blocks at Petra are interpreted as abstract representations of Dushara, the main Nabataean deity.

The Phoenicians took the concept westwards with them in their expansion in the first half of the first millennium BC. The Carthaginian *tophet* or sacrificial memorial, for example, is marked by a *baetyl* or cube or cubic stele (Pl. 11). We have observed how this motif translated into architecture at Petra, but it occurred elsewhere as well. At the Phoenician site of Amrit on the Syrian coast, for example, the central temple consists of a courtyard surrounded by a colonnade of simple, square upright stone slabs resembling stelae with a small cella in the centre raised on a high, rock-cut cube surmounted by a crow-step frieze (Pl. 7). The cube motif also occurs at the funerary monuments at Amrit, consisting of cubes, sometimes superimposed on each other and occasionally rock-cut, often surmounted by cylinders, pyramids or obelisks (Pl. 8). The ancient Semitic idea of the sacred cube reaches its culmination in the centre of Arabian worship today: the Ka'ba (which is simply Arabic for 'cube') at Mecca.

Another belief common to many ancient Semitic religions was the concept of rebirth and resurrection. This was particularly prevalent in Phoenician religion, where it was a part of the cult of Melqart. Melqart was often Hellenised as Adonis, and was related to the ancient Sumerian Dummuzi, Biblical Tammuz, where rebirth and resurrection figured highly. In this context it is worth noting that Bethlehem was originally sacred to Tammuz. When Phoenician colonists took the cult of Melqart to the West it was equated by the Romans with Hercules.

Many other religious practices in the Arab Near East anticipated Christianity. A cult practised initially at Edessa, which became fairly commonly practised all over northern Syria before Christianity, was that of the virgin mother and child. Women in fact traditionally held a high position at Edessa. Another popular Semitic cult throughout the East was the Sun God. This went under various guises—including Elagabal of Emesa and Heliopolitanus of Baalbek—but was adopted by the Greeks and Romans under the name Helios. With the advent of Christianity the cult of the prophet Elias easily replaced the cult of the Sun God in the East simply because of the similarity in names. (The sun cult is examined in more detail below.) Thus, long before Christianity had supplanted paganism in the Semitic Near East, many of the elements of Christian belief were already in place.

EASTERN RELIGIONS AT THE HEART OF ROME

Religions from the Arab Near East certainly came to Rome long before Roman emperors began toying with Christianity: indeed, to the imperial families themselves at a time when Christianity was still an underground religion. These mainly came, as would be expected, through the Syro-Phoenician dynasty founded by Septimius Severus and Julia Domna that we have reviewed above in Chapter 4. For Julia Domna's family were not only royalty in Emesa long before they became royalty in Rome: they were priests first, and priests they remained.

Whilst the family no longer ruled as kings after its incorporation into the Roman Empire, they remained hereditary high priests of the temple of the Emesene Sun-god, or the 'Baal of the Emesenes'. This temple was associated with the cult of Elah Gabal, later to achieve fame when one of the Temple priests, the Emperor Elagabalus, tried to enforce it upon an unwilling Rome. The emperor's name is actually the name of the deity itself, a Latinised form of *Elah Gabal*, which literally means 'God of the Mountain' (the modern Arabic words *Allah*, 'God', and *jabal*, 'mountain', are the same). The cult object was a large black stone or *baetyl*, presumably volcanic or meteoric, a relatively common type of cult object amongst the pre-Islamic Arabs as we have seen. The huge temple to this deity was one of the greatest and most lavish in the East according to contemporary obeservers, being amply endowed by neighbouring rulers with sumptuous gold, silver and precious stone ornamentation, so that Emesa became 'the Jerusalem of the Sun God', richly endowed both by the Emesene and other Near Eastern kings.

For reasons I have argued elsewhere, the only temple answering such a description in Emesene territory is Baalbek, ancient Heliopolis (Pl. 22), a building that otherwise defies a satisfactory explanation.[8] For any visitor today the scale is certainly overwhelming, and must have been even more so in antiquity: the greatest temple in the East, indeed one of the most ambitious building works ever undertaken in the Roman world. Although founded by Augustus as a minor veteran colony, there is no way that a settlement of pensioners on half pay could have undertaken such a building. But the fabulously wealthy family could: it is notable that the temple has an inscription honouring the Emesene 'great king' Sohaemus, son of 'the great king' Samsigeramus of Emesa, and that the two main periods of construction correspond exactly to the height of the Emesene kingdom and of the Severan dynasty.

With such a background, it would be surprising indeed if Julia Domna and her family did not make religion a prime concern when they came to Rome as rulers. One of the main figures in Julia Domna's 'salon' was the philosopher Philostratus, himself a disciple of the mystic Apollonius of Tyana. The religion of Apollonius interested Julia Domna, and she commissioned Philostratus to write a life of him so that his teachings could be more widely disseminated. Apollonius was born in Tyana in Cappadocia sometime in the first century AD, and his life spanned the era of the Flavian emperors. Apollonius espoused an extreme form of mysticism and asceticism, whose beliefs appear to combine elements of Pythagoreanism and perhaps even Brahmanism. Renouncing the drinking of alcohol, the eating of meat, the wearing of wool, and hot baths, Apollonius maintained a severe abstinence from all luxuries throughout his life. He believed in reincarnation and claimed to speak all languages, including those of birds and animals which he venerated and advocated their complete protection (anticipating St Francis of Assisi). Apollonius supposedly undertook a major journey to the East in 43-44 AD, travelling through Iran to India, where he held conversations with the Magi and the Brahmans, as well as several secular rulers such as the Parthian King Vardanes. On his return he attracted a wide following throughout the East, and his teaching and following was seen as a rival to that of Christ. Indeed, in many ways Philostratus' *Life of Apollonius* was a pagan answer to the Gospels. As late as the beginning of the fourth century, Apollonius was being held by pagans as a viable alternative to Christ with his philosophy contrasted with Christianity. Whether or not this is so, Julia Domna's patronage of the cult certainly prepared the ground for Christianity.

This was not the only oriental cult that was patronised under Julia Domna and her husband. The cult of Mithras from Iran, although widespread long before, became more popular, as did the cult of Libyan Liber Pater or Bacchus. Whilst Liber Pater-Bacchus might be viewed as Graeco-Roman, under its specifically Libyan version it was a Punic cult thinly disguised: Liber Pater was Punic Shadrapa, and it is easy to see Septimius' influence here. Julia Domna herself was associated in Rome with the new cult of Dea Celaestis, as was her niece Julia Sohaemias, mother of Emperor Elagabalus. In Rome this cult was assimilated with Juno, but in its Punic guise it was Astarte. Originally the cult of Dea Celaestis was a Syrian cult known simply as the 'Syrian Goddess' and incorporated many Near Eastern fertility and mother goddess cults, in addition to Astarte. Thus, in Rome the Syrian princess became the Syrian empress linked with the Syrian goddess.*

---

* One of the main temples overlooking the old forum in Septimius' home town was a Temple to Liber Pater, equated to Roman Bacchus, Greek Dionysus. In the Near East the cult of Dionysus was equated with Nabatean Dushara. Temples to Liber Pater/Bacchus/Dushares are common throughout Punic North Africa, as are temples to Dea Celaestis/Astarte, such as the impressive

But it was her Syrian grand-nephew, Elagabalus, who first brought an Eastern religion to Rome in a major way. Elagabalus was born and brought up as hereditary high-priest in the great temple of Elagabal, the Sun God, in Emesa as we have seen. Hence, as high-priest it was only natural that he brought his religion when the imperial purple was thrust upon him—there is no reason why one should doubt his religious sincerity. Equally, as emperor it was only natural that he should attempt to make his religion the official one of the empire. Through the welter of conservative Roman prejudice that invariably characterised their views of any alien religion (Christian cannibalistic rites, for example), some interesting details are apparent. There are references, for example, to 'dancing', a commonly accepted religious rite in many Eastern cults, surviving in some cases to this day (dervishes in Islam or the ceremonies in the Ethiopian Church spring to mind). Elagabalus carried a parasol, a common symbol of oriental kingship from earliest times until the Islamic Middle Ages. Elagabalus' ritual procession demanded that he and his doubtless embarrassed senators follow the black stone cult object of Elah-Gabal placed in a chariot for religious procession. Such processions were important rites common to many Eastern religions, and were to be adopted into Christianity (where ritual processions of cult objects are a frequent practice in Catholic countries). He also attempted to associate other cults with his own: Trojan Pallas, and Carthaginian Urania, not to mention the Jews, Samaritans and Christians (a refreshing and often overlooked fact, compared to other emperors who persecuted them). However, his religion simply alienated the conservative establishment. Elagabalus slowly but inevitably lost popularity to his younger cousin, Alexander, and the ever-powerful Praetorian Guard despatched him, his mother and his religion.

It is for his religion that Elagabalus has been most condemned, as much by modern historians as by the Praetorian Guard, but it is for his religion that we must remember him. To begin with his religion might not have been as one-sided as is thought, and the sun cult a genuine effort to attract support through a cult that might prove widely popular in a tricky political climate. For Elagabalus might well have been responding to ground roots' dissatisfaction to the official Roman cults, and that his offering of the sun cult as an alternative might prove popular. For in the end, it did. The

---

one at Dougga in Tunisia. The way that Graeco-Roman cults were assimilated with various oriental cults often seems baffling: see Turcan 1996. For Julia Domna's religious associations see Levick 2007: 133-7.

cult may have proved unpopular with the senatorial class when Elagabalus tried to impose it, but the Emperor Aurelian resurrected the Sun God cult later in the third century as part of a great Eastern victory, when it gained in respectability. This was because Aurelian attributed his victory against Zenobia outside Emesa in 272 to divine intervention from the Emesene Sun-god. As a result, he paid his respects at the Temple immediately after the battle and afterwards built a magnificent temple to the Sun God in Rome, decorating it with the trophies looted from Palmyra. The Sun God cult then achieved wide popularity in the Western Roman world, a prime adherent being Constantine before he adopted Christianity. Elagabalus' Sun cult, therefore, not only paved the way for Christianity, it was later actually grafted on to Christianity to make it more palatable: churches faced east to the rising sun, the day of worship was changed from the Sabbath to the day of the Sun and the birthday of the sun on 25 December became one of the most important dates in the Christian calendar.

Elagabalus' and Aurelian's actions were important precedents for Constantine's, but there was another emperor who made a far greater precedent. For it was Philip the Arab—not Constantine—who was Rome's first Christian emperor. Philip's Christianity has always been subject to considerable controversy, not least because of the ambivalence amongst the sources, although Eusebius, the main source, leaves little doubt. Modern scholarship ranges from complete rejection to complete affirmation, with most taking the middle road conceding that Philip at least 'dabbled' in Christianity. Why, therefore, does Constantine take precedence over Philip? Later Christian propagandists have tried to down-play Philip's Christianity in order to emphasise Constantine's, but more important, it was Constantine who 'came out' and publicly supported Christianity (and did not, in fact, formally become a Christian until his death-bed). Philip, on the other hand, did no such thing: paganism remained Rome's official 'religion', while a Roman citizen's private beliefs—even the emperor's—were of little concern so long as they remained private. Philip's position, it must be remembered, was insecure: a local boy made good who, furthermore, had to go far to secure his position in an unstable age. He was hardly going to publicise some obscure Eastern belief in the heart of Rome, particularly so soon after Elagabalus' debacle, but would have kept quiet about it and made even more scrupulous care to follow Roman public ceremonial to the letter. The Christian persecutions of his successor, Decius, has been viewed as a reaction to Philip's support of Christianity.

Philip may have been the first Christian emperor, but he was not the first Christian king. This is usually regarded to have been King Tiridates III of Armenia, whose adoption of Christianity in 301 (or 314) makes Armenia the world's oldest Christian state. But there was an Arab king with older—albeit more controversial—claims. This was King Abgar VIII of Edessa a century before Tiridates. Religion had always been central to Edessan civilisation, and Edessa was one of the main religious melting pots of the ancient Near East. Bel and Nebo were the main cults, the former from Palmyra and the latter from Babylon. The cult of Nebo became quite popular in the Near East: it was from a Mt Nebo that Moses looked out over the promised land. Many more flourished at Edessa. There was the cult of the Moon and Sun of Harran—known as the Sabian religion—as well as the rather gruesome cult of Atargatis of Mambij. An important ritual of the latter centred around two wooden columns at the entrance to the temple, which a holy man would ascend twice a year to spend seven days in contemplation (Pl. 31). This anticipates the Christian stylite practice which became particularly popular through northern Syria, most famously with St Simeon Stylites. The father of St Simeon from Edessa, and the golden emblem that stood between the two deities in the Temple of Atargatis, was known as a 'Simeion.' From further away came the Nabataean cult of Dushara, as well as Ishtar from Mesopotamia, who was equated with Venus or Astarte. Both found their circuitous way to Rome as we have seen, the former as Liber Pater and the latter as Dea Celaestis. In Syria the latter was the cult the 'great Syrian Goddess', which originated at Edessa. Another important variant of the Syrian Goddess cult at Edessa was that of the virgin mother and child, which became widespread all over northern Syria before Christianity—with obvious implications for the development of Christianity.

Judaism was also very strong, and one of the largest Jewish communities in the Near East was at Nisibis. The rapid progress made by Christianity at Edessa was probably through the Jewish community. To this medley may be later added Marcionites, Gnostics and Manichaeans, in addition to the Edessan home-grown religions of the Bardaisanites and the Elkasaites. Their beliefs we need not enter into here, but they incorporated monotheistic elements and all made a ready home for another cult when it arrived: Christianity.

King Abgar V, who reigned at the time of the birth of Christ, is remembered for his supposed correspondence with Christ. After the crucifixion, the Apostle Addai (St Thaddeus) was accordingly sent to Edessa by the Apostle Thomas and, on converting Abgar through a miraculous cure, was encouraged to preach throughout the kingdom. The story is undoubtedly apocryphal (although the supposed correspondence was preserved in Edessa for centuries as a talisman). But further events in the development of Edessan Christianity occurred almost two centuries later in the era of Abgar VIII (the Great, 177-212) who displayed a liberal attitude to religion and converted to Christianity. The conversion is, of course, controversial, and there are axes to grind by all sides in the controversy. But whether or not he became a Christian, Abgar had the wisdom to recognise the inherent order and stability in Christianity a century before Constantine did, and did establish Edessa as one of the more important centres for early Christendom. This resulted in the establishment of a line of bishops in the early fourth century lasting a thousand years, which included such major theologians as St Ephraim in the later fourth century. By the fifth century Edessa had become one of the main centres of Christian learning in the East.

PHOENICIAN RELIGION AND THE BEGINNINGS OF CHRISTIAN EUROPE

The Phoenicians brought their religion with them and the Roman towns of North Africa are littered with the remains of temples to Shadrapa, Melqart, Astarte, Baal, Hathor and other deities, thinly disguised under tenuous Roman equivalents. Central to much of Phoenician religious belief was the very Semitic abstract concept of deity, as well as the concept of rebirth and resurrection, already noted above. Cadiz, for example, had a famous temple dedicated to Phoenician Melqart. This temple preserved its Semitic characteristics until long after it had been absorbed into the Roman cult of Hercules: the absence of figural representation puzzled the Classical authors, and the central feature of the Melqart cult, both in Cadiz and elsewhere in Phoenician Spain, was the spring cycle of annual resurrection. This has obvious implications for paving the way for Christianity, with its emphasis on resurrection and the Easter festival every spring.

Tyrian Melqart was originally an aspect of Baal. Tyre was founded according to legend by Usoos, who dedicated two pillars on the island, one to fire and one to wind. According to Herodotus, one of these pillars was supposedly of gold, the other of emerald (presumably glass, for which Phoenicia was famous). The twin pillars then became a central feature of the cult of Melqart. It was transferred to Jerusalem when the Temple of Solomon was built with the aid of architects from Tyre, where twin pillars also featured. The Phoenicians brought the cult west with them, naming the straits of Gibraltar after the twin pillars of Melqart: the 'Pillars of Hercules' (whom the Romans equated with Melqart; Pl. 51). The twin pillars became a fairly common feature in religious architecture of the east, featuring at Edessa, Mambij, Baalbek, Jerusalem and elsewhere, as well as in Phoenician temples west, such as at Kerkouane (Pls 25, 31).

In the Melqart cult we once again see myth and reality being intertwined. Elissa's murdered husband, Acherbas, was a priest at the Temple of Melqart at Tyre. The cult of Melqart was thus taken to Carthage by Elissa where it was implanted as the new city's patron deity. The cult of Melqart was later superseded at Carthage by Tanit and Baal Hammon, but every year an official delegation would leave Carthage to worship in the Temple of Melqart at Tyre, thus retaining the link with both Melqart and the mother city. The matter is an important one, for however great and distinctive the Carthaginians became, they never forgot their Near Eastern roots. Even as late at the mid-second century AD, the Carthaginian colony of Leptis Magna still looked to Tyre as its mother city rather than to Rome, despite it ostensibly having been an entirely Romanised city for a century or more.

Baal-Hammon and his consort Tanit became the chief deities of the Carthaginians. This cult is almost wholly Carthaginian, although there is some slight evidence for the cult in the Phoenician homeland. Although these gods had figural representations in the Graeco-Roman manner, like Melqart the concept was essentially abstract, often represented by a *baetyl* ('house of god') or simple square slab of stone. Another central fact of Punic religious practice was the *tophet* (Pl. 11). This gruesome rite, associated with the cult of Baal-Hammon, consisted of the sacrifice of young children, infants and babies to the god by fire. In the earliest periods there is some evidence for substitution, but in the later periods in the fourth-second centuries, the sacrifices were almost wholly of babies and young infants. It was by no means a universal Phoenician practice, but confined mainly to the Phoenicians of North Africa, most notably at Carthage. The sacrifices were usually of high born children, preferably the first born. As many as 500 children were recorded as being immolated in a single ritual at Carthage. Because of the horrific nature of the *tophet* it has come under considerable and sceptical scrutiny by archaeology in recent years, particularly in the recent US excavations at Carthage. Here it has been confirmed that the ages ranged from a few days to a few years old. In the earlier period they were often new born or still-born babies, but later at the height of Carthage's power, the majority of the child sacrifices were between one and two years old. The number of victims between about 400 and 200 BC have been estimated as at least 20,000 in the Carthage *tophet* alone. Most of them were from the wealthier classes judging by the inscriptions: traders, priests and magistrates. The question that one must ask—but dreads to—is whether the babies were dead before they were sacrificed in the fire-pit? At present archaeology cannot answer that question. All one can say is that all evidence confirms the sacrifice by fire of large numbers of high-born babies and infants as an incontrovertible fact of Phoenician society.

Modern scholarship has attempted to explain the *tophet* as a form of Phoenician upper-class birth control. Such an explanation is, of course, nonsense, an attempt to rationalise an ancient and distasteful practice in entirely modern-day terms. The *tophet* was simply a sacrifice, a very personal self-sacrifice of a possession greater than life itself to one's profoundest beliefs. In ancient terms it makes sense, as an expression of sheer, unquestioning faith that is inconceivable now; in modern terms it is a superstition that defies explanation. But the *tophet* was fact.

The Phoenician *tophet* in North Africa was to have a profound effect on early Christianity, even though the practice had long been suppressed by the Romans. For in the population of North Africa, the concept of self-sacrifice—the Christian cult of martyrdom—was already firmly implanted long before Christianity arrived. Sacrifice, an abstract god, resurrection, all the elements were there. The Semitic Phoenicians of Carthage must have welcomed this new Semitic religion with relief as a return to their ancient ways and most treasured beliefs, a renaissance after centuries of Romanisation. It comes as very little surprise, therefore, to learn that the greatest spread of early Christianity outside the East was in Carthage and the North African provinces. North Africa was probably the first area in the West to have a majority Christian population. Many prominent early Christian martyrs were from North Africa: St Perpetua and St Felicity spring to mind, St Cyprian of Carthage was probably the most prominent Christian martyrdom after St Paul, and there were many others. Carthage rapidly became the most important bishopric in the western empire after Rome itself. It was in North Africa that the first major schism in Christendom occurred, with the Donatist movement in the early fourth century. In the following century there emerged from North Africa the father of Western Christendom, St Augustine of Hippo. Phoenician Africa was the most Christian of all provinces, and with good reason.

As well as being Phoenician and Christian, North Africa was *Roman*. After the Phoenician influence, the North African provinces were subject to more Romanisation than any other part of the Empire outside Italy, with the possible exception of Gaul. The hundreds of Roman towns there, unlike the Roman cities of the East, were virtually identical to their counterparts in Italy. North Africa in Roman times was culturally an extension of Europe: before Islam imposed a north-south division on the Mediterranean, the cultural step from Africa to Europe did not exist. From this contact between Roman and Phoenician, the movement of Christianity to Europe was unbroken and logical.

Chapter 6

MUHAMMAD, CHARLEMAGNE AND ROME
The Effect of the first Islamic Empires
on Europe

> Without Mohammed, Charlemagne would indeed have been
> inconceivable.
>
> Richard Hodges and David Whitehouse[1]

It is commonplace in the West to associate Arab history solely with Islam—
and conventional histories would have, at most, merely a brief summary of
pre-Islamic history by way of a preface. Few would doubt, of course, that
Islam is one of the Arabs' greatest achievements, but as the above chapters
have demonstrated, Islam represents less than half of their history in purely
chronological terms—and the Islamic achievement is far from exclusively
Arab in any case (in purely demographic terms, Islam is now mainly a Far
Eastern religion). Furthermore, most in the West think of Islam solely as an
'eastern' religion—as characterising the East, reinforcing a 'them and us' idea
of Islam versus Europe. Again, this is only partly true. The first movement
of Islam out of Arabia was towards the west, not the east, fundamentally
influencing Europe in many different ways. Even after Islam later turned
eastwards, it continued to expand in Europe and to influence Europe in a
number of surprising ways. The fact the Islam is perceived now as essentially
non-European is nothing to do with either its nature or its early history,
merely historical circumstance.

Islam in Europe is only partly an Arab legacy, and is as much Berber,
Turkish and Mongol, the latter two to be examined in later volumes. Before
we turn to the role that the Arabs played in this, it is necessary first, to look
at the religion itself and the part it played, and then to examine why the early
years of Islam looked westwards and how it affected Europe.

The Worshippers of Allah

One cannot, of course, discuss the rise of the first Arab empires under the Caliphate without discussing their religion. Indeed, many would regard the rise of the Arabs and the rise of Islam as one single movement, and perhaps rightly so. This is not the place to discuss the religious origins of Islam or the revelations of the Prophet Muhammad, and Islamic civilisation's contribution to universalism is discussed in Chapter 12. But we may offer several general observations if only as a background to the Arab expansion under Islam.

Islam did not arrive suddenly out of nowhere; it was not even solely a product of the deserts of Arabia. Of course, most are familiar with its roots in Judaism and Christianity, and the overwhelming similarities between these three religions is all too easily forgotten, or at least overlooked. Islam and Christianity are far closer in every way than, say, Christianity and Buddhism— if Hindu-Buddhism is viewed as a single unit as Huntingdon or others would have it, then Judaism, Christianity and Islam is another unit, not clashing fault-lines.* More importantly, Islam was born out of an extraordinarily rich and productive ferment of religious and philosophical experimentation in the world of Near Eastern late antiquity. Both state religions, the old Iranian Zoroastrianism and the new Roman Christianity, developed enormously during this period, both confronting each other but at the same time feeding off each other. New religious ideas emerged out of this ferment—Gnostic and Neo-Platonic ideas, for example—and new movements emerged from the older religions: Nestorians and Monophysites from Christianity, Manichaeans and Mazdakites from Zoroastrianism, to cite just the main ones, as well as Elkasaites, Bardaisanites, Sabians, Neo-Pythagoreans, Marcionites, Montanists, Paulicians, hermetics, heretics, mystics, cenobites, stylites and a host of others. Alexandria in Egypt, Antioch, Nisibis and Edessa in Syria, and Jund-i Shapur in Iran all formed major centres, but there were many others—indeed, many such groups and sects retired to the remotest areas in order to escape persecution (or at least interference) from the major religions. Arabia in general and Mecca in particular was never isolated from this, but formed an integral part of this intellectual network, contributing native elements of its own (the ideas of sanctuary and sacred places, for example), and there were numerous prophets prior to Muhammad (as well

---

* Samuel Huntingdon's now notorious *Clash of Civilizations*—and even here the divisions were never neat, but subject to cross-fertilisation and overlaps throughout.

as a few claimants after). Islam emerged from this background—and did not stop there, but continued to develop, first in the cosmopolitan climate of Damascus and then in Baghdad, the former where it became receptive to Hellenistic influence, the latter where it became open to more Iranian and Eastern influences. This is important: Islam was a product of both Western and Eastern ideas right from the beginning, it was born out of change and has been subject to change and modification ever since, and it is still changing; there has never been a static or 'fundamental' Islam.

At the risk perhaps of glibness, I would like to make two further points from personal anecdote. I once profoundly shocked a devout Christian by saying that she worshipped Allah. 'But I am a Christian!' was the astonished retort. 'Precisely why you worship Allah,' I pointed out. A pedantic and perhaps a simplistic point, but a very important one. Christian Arabs—of which there are many millions—pray to Allah. To underline the point, one need only visit Malta (and there are few more devoutly Catholic countries in Christendom) where the Maltese—whose language is Semitic—worship Allah in their churches: *Allah* simply being the Maltese for 'God'. But the idea that somehow 'Christians worship God' and 'Muslims worship Allah' has a strong hold in both religions. Apart from making about as much sense as saying that 'the English worship God, but the French worship *Dieu* and the Iranians *Khoda*', the Prophet Muhammad himself made the point that the God of the Christians and the Jews was the one single god. Of course, most educated Christians and Muslims might realise this, that *Allah* is merely the Arabic translation of 'God' and vice-versa. Nevertheless, when used in an Islamic context, the word *Allah* is rarely translated, but is used to underline the difference between Islam and Christianity, 'them' and 'us': there is implicit prejudice in the use of the term 'Allah' instead of 'God'. When visiting a Muslim country, for example, a Western visitor on experiencing a delay or minor frustration might say rather condescendingly, 'it is the will of Allah', meaning it in a slightly mocking, patronising way; to say 'it is the will of God' would sound mildly shocking, almost blasphemous—as if to say *they* do not worship 'God', a term reserved solely for oneself. The implication is admittedly often unintentional, but even in so overtly pro-Arab and pro-Islamic a history as David Levering Lewis' *God's Crucible*, the distinction is still made: Muslims do not worship 'God'.[2]

Muslims themselves often too fall into the same trap in their frequent reluctance to translate *Allah* into English. Written over the entrance to the Birmingham Central Mosque, for example, are the words 'There is no

God but Allah' in a deliberate—and confrontational—*mistranslation* of the Qur'an and distortion of the words of their own prophet. The same applies to the unfortunately frequent reference to Christians by many Muslims as 'infidels': Christians, according to the definition in the Qur'an, are expressly not infidels. For many Muslims too, not only the difference in religion but the difference in deities worshipped must be underlined, even at the risk of distorting their own sacred book.

My next point relates to travel. At any time from about 1990 onwards, a visit to virtually anywhere in the Middle East, would elicit the almost invariable response of an odd look and the remark, 'But isn't it dangerous out there!'* Never mind if one was just visiting, say, Turkey when there was a war in Iraq, or visiting Iran when there was a flare-up in, say, Lebanon, the response would be the same. Tourism in the Middle East certainly suffered accordingly. But a skiing holiday, for example, in Austria or a seaside holiday in Greece during the time of the war in former Yugoslavia would never have elicited the same response: few if any cancelled holidays to Austria or Greece or other countries in the vicinity of war-torn Yugoslavia. In practice, a visit to, say, Iran was just as safe as (or probably safer than) a visit to Greece. In fact it is true to say that one generally experiences more overt warmth, friendliness, genuine hospitality—and less 'danger'—in the Islamic world than almost anywhere else, media impressions notwithstanding. The difference, however, is purely one of prejudice: Muslim Middle Eastern countries are perceived as self-evidently 'dangerous', European countries are not, regardless of whether there is or is not a war.

The two points, worshipping 'Allah' and perceived threat by Muslims, might be very minor ones. But they are symptomatic of deep-seated prejudices (on both sides). Islam is commonly viewed as innately aggressive, as the very antithesis of Christianity's neighbour-loving message of peace and as opposed to Islam having been 'spread by the sword:' that subject peoples were routinely given the choice of death or conversion.

To begin with, the word *Islam/Muslim* is related to the Arabic *salam*, which means 'peace'. Of course, Islam like any religion has had its fair share of bloodshed. Even a supposed pacifistic religion such as Buddhism is not

---

* Or another frequent response would be the only half-joking 'Oh, I don't suppose I will ever see you again!' This at a time when arguably the most dangerous place for the British tourist was Florida, but nevertheless the perception of the Muslim Middle East was dominated by the almost nineteenth- (or fifteenth-!) century preconception of wild-eyed fanatic mad-mullahs whose only desire was to cut honest white Christian throats.

without its periods of aggression, whilst Christianity was repeatedly spread by force of arms. The Christianisation of much of Europe and even the rest of the Christian world was carried out by enforced conversion by the sword. Charlemagne, the 'father of Europe', in his ultimatum to the Kingdom of Saxony (effectively most of the modern area of Germany and not just the area of present day Saxony) specified a choice between conversion or the sword, and his subsequent invasion was overtly forcible conversion to Christianity (a policy begun by his grandfather Charles Martel) culminating in 782 in the massacre of 4,500 Saxon hostages who had been voluntarily handed over to Charlemagne.[3] The enforced conversion of the Cathars during the Albigensian Crusade in the thirteenth century is one of the bloodiest episodes in European history, matched by the enforced conversion of much of eastern Europe—Prussia, Livonia, Lithuania and much else of the Baltic—by the Teutonic Knights in various northern Crusades. The conquest and conversion of the Americas by the Spanish conquistadors was effected at the cost of an astounding seventy million or so lives. The Christianisation of much of present Christendom in other words—Europe and the Americas—was the direct result of the sword.

Of course, few religions are without their horrific acts of blood-letting and Islam certainly has its fair share: it would be as much a mistake to view Islam through rose-tinted spectacles as blood-tinted. But the frequent claim by Christendom that Islam was spread by the sword does not stand analysis. In the early years of Islam's most rapid expansion, enforced conversion of 'fellow believers' was forbidden. Indeed, the Qur'an (2:256) specifically forbids intolerance and forcible conversion: 'There shall be no compulsion in religion.' Fellow believers were defined as fellow 'people of the book', i.e., Jews and Christians, and this exemption was later extended to Zoroastrians as well. Naturally not every Muslim soldier was exactly angelic in this regard, but the fact remains that early conversion was by persuasion rather than enforcement (and in the light of this, historians are still debating the almost total disappearance of Zoroastrianism in Iran to this day), and doubtless most conversions were neither persuasion nor enforcement, but simple convenience. The greatest single conversion in early Islam was that of the Turks of Central Asia, and this was carried out entirely by pacific means, through missionaries and—most of all—traders. The Turks themselves by and large continued this tradition: the overwhelming majority of the populations in their European possessions remained Christian throughout Ottoman history. Of course, the sword spread Muslim empires, but no more nor less than it spread Christian or Buddhist empires. Today, the demographic centre of Islam is no longer the Middle East but South-east Asia, a region where no Arab army has ever penetrated, but became Muslim solely through peaceable means, whilst the most rapid expanse of Islam is being made in sub-Saharan Africa—again, through peaceable means.

Unhappily, many Muslims too suffer from similar misconceptions, especially now when arguing the case for 'traditional Islam'. 'Traditional' Islam, by which is usually meant the great ages of Islamic civilisation (largely pre-thirteenth century, but also later, for example, Ottoman), was never conservative, but adapted and embraced change without losing the central message. Islam was never a 'citadel' to ward off everything from the outside, but was always in a state of flux, forward moving and all-embracing. The great ages of Islam were never backward-looking as many Islamist movements today wish to be; to become bogged down into such irrelevancies as cutting off the hand of a thief or flogging an adulterer is to miss the point of Islam. Real *traditional* Islam was characterised by its ability to embrace ideas and cultures from outside and to absorb them, without losing sight of the central message which, at heart, is a simple one and so can easily embrace and absorb. Modern Islam, whether 'traditionalist' or 'fundamentalist', often becomes side-tracked with issues such as how to cope with/combat 'the West'. There is no reason why Islam cannot absorb much of the 'West', just as traditional Islam embraced and absorbed Greek civilisation as well as Jewish, pre-Islamic Iranian, Central Asian and Indian—Descartes, Marx and Adam Smith can become a part of Islamic tradition as Aristotle and Plato have become. Only in this way were the great 'sages' of Islamic civilisation, such as Avicenna or Ibn Khaldun, universalist. The argument that Western ideas are to be taught only to 'confront' and 'refute' them is to miss the point.* Attempts by traditionalists or fundamentalists to 'return' to some form of perceived traditional or 'primitive' Islam is to not only risk turning Islam into an irrelevant fossil, of little more than antiquarian interest, but is to miss one of the central messages of Islam, which is universal. Otherwise, Islam would be condemned to becoming like the Amish or the Hasidim: righteous perhaps, even prosperous and happy, but essentially irrelevant. The point for both Muslims and non-Muslims is neatly made by a Pakistani writer:

---

* Even a liberal, non-fundamentalist Islamic thinker like Seyyed Hosein Nasr, who lives in the West, sees Islamic and Western philosophy solely in terms of confrontation: a Muslim must learn both his own and Western culture in order to 'confront' and 'refute' the West. Nasr 1987: Chapter 12.

'Many Western commentators do not particularize the Taliban, but condemn Islam wholesale for being intolerant and anti-modern. The Taliban, like so many Islamic fundamentalist groups today, divest Islam of all its legacies except theology—Islamic philosophy, science, arts, aesthetics and mysticism are ignored. Thus the rich diversity of Islam and the essential message of the Koran—to build a civil society that is just and equitable in which rulers are responsible for their citizens—is forgotten.'[4]

There is a common tendency to see all of the history of the relationship between Islam and Christendom in terms of a perpetual holy war, viewed by both Christians and Muslims in almost Manichean terms as the perpetual struggle between good and evil, godly versus infidel—and from both perspectives. But whilst one should not forget the great wars and even greater misunderstandings, the history of Christian-Muslim relations has equally been characterised by long periods when the two sides rubbed well enough along together, co-existing more or less amicably, even during the Crusades or the wars of the sixteenth century. In the long perspective, the history of the two cultures is as much one of cross-fertilisation as struggle, and it is important to remember this during comparatively brief periods when mutual hatred and prejudice dominate just a small minority in both camps for relatively brief periods of time.

In fact at the lower level, everyday contacts and fraternisation between Christian and Muslim—even conversions both ways—belies the impression of impermeable barriers given by political histories; 'Between the two religions, it would be unrealistic to imagine a water-tight barrier. Men passed to and fro, indifferent to frontiers, states and creeds. They were more aware of the necessities of shipping and trade, the hazards of war and piracy, the opportunities for complicity or betrayal provided by circumstances.'[5]

THE UMAYYADS, THE WEST AND A 'THIRD ROME' (MAP 4)

Syria was the Muslims' first conquest outside Arabia and after the Battle of Yarmouk in 636 all of Syria fell to the Arabs. From Alexander's conquest in 333 BC it had been nearly a thousand years of rule by Macedonians and Romans; from Pompey's conquest in 64 BC to Heraclius' loss at Yarmuk in 636 exactly seven hundred years of that millennium was Roman alone. All went virtually overnight. The centre of early Islam moved

4. The Umayyad Caliphate. Shaded area shows its greatest extent.

from Arabia to Syria. Damascus, successively an Aramaean, Hellenistic and Roman centre, appropriately became the universal capital of a new universal order. The Muslims were largely welcomed by the majority Monophysite Christians, liberating them from the persecution by the Orthodox court in Constantinople. Soon, Sasanian Persia too crumbled as easily as the Byzantine east, and the Arabs with their new message to the world appeared irresistible.

The seemingly invincible Roman arms in the West had all but been inundated under barbarian invasions, while the might of the Roman army in the Near East crumbled virtually overnight. The ancient civilisations of the Near East, dormant for so long, were re-awoken. Syria became the centre of a new world, with Damascus as its capital under the Umayyad dynasty of caliphs (Pls 49, 50). The world saw the most spectacular series of conquests since the days of Alexander. By the beginning of the eighth century, Umayyad rule extended far into Central Asia almost to the borders of China, while to the west all of North Africa and most of Spain were conquered. Such an empire was far greater than even Rome had been at its greatest; Rome's own power base, the Mediterranean became divided and the power of Islam appeared invincible.

The Umayyads rapidly became a sea as well as a land power, and as early as the latter half of seventh century had built a strong navy and began raids into Byzantine territory, both land campaigns into Anatolia and by sea. In 655 an Arab fleet under Mu'awiyah, the governor of Syria under 'Uthman, met the Roman navy led by Emperor Constans II (son of Heraclius) off the Lycian coast at the Battle of Finike. Arab commanders took the novel step of lashing their vessels to the Byzantine fleet, and Byzantine forces were totally destroyed. Constantinople lay open but was given a reprieve by the murder of 'Uthman.

Early Islam is often viewed as a religion of the desert and the early Arab expansion as a movement from the deserts of Arabia—Arab conquests are traditionally associated with the camel rather than the oar. Arab navigation is examined more in Chapter 12, but for the moment it is worth emphasising that it was entirely natural that they would become a maritime power as easily as they had become a land one. Unlike the Romans in the beginnings of their expansion, who had to learn seafaring in their wars against Carthage, the Arabs became heirs to seafaring traditions even older than those of the Greeks whom they fought when they inherited the Phoenician legacy of the Levant.

In all there were three sieges of Constantinople by the Umayyads. The first was in 669 by Yazid, then between 674 and 680 the Island of Cyzicus (presumably Marmara) was used as a base by the Arabs in a mainly naval war. Constantinople itself was saved—mainly by Byzantine flame-throwers (the legendary 'Greek fire')—but Rhodes and Crete were occupied by the Arabs. The third siege in 716-7 under Maslamah, brother of Caliph Sulaiman, was almost successful. Constantinople was defended by Emperor Leo the Isaurian (himself an Arabic speaker—Isauria in southern Anatolia was on the borders of Muslim Syria), forcing the Arabs to withdraw, with Maslamah subsequently losing much of the fleet in a storm. This emphasis on Constantinople right from the beginning of Islam is important. Constantinople was the ultimate goal, not so much because it was the capital of a rival empire but because it was the ultimate symbol: it was Rome, *the* city. The first Rome had been pagan, the second Christian: the third Rome was to be Muslim.

Rome was not built in a day and her empire took several centuries. But the Umayyad Empire seemed to happen virtually overnight. What were the reasons behind its astonishingly rapid expansion? The power of the message of course was a part of the story, not for any facile 'god on their side' reasons but merely because any new idea, particularly religious, motivates powerful bursts of energy. But religion did play another role, albeit less directly. The previous centuries had witnessed increasing dissensions within the Christian Church, mainly relating to the nature of Christ: human, divine, a combination, and if so, the degrees of combination. Such theological disputes today appear abstruse, hair-splitting and largely irrelevant. But in the early days of Christianity the issues were hugely important and discussed in every walk of society, from emperor and bishop to butcher and baker. For it must be remembered that the Christian religion had been made a part of the Roman state: not only did this produce the need for it to be defined, it had to be made subordinate, just as any other state institution—such as the army—had to be subordinate. Dissension in the Church could no more be tolerated than dissension in the army. Heresy was not so much an act against God but quite simply an act of disloyalty against the Roman state.

Furthermore, although Christianity was born out of the philosophical and religious background of the Semitic East, it soon came to be dominated by a people from a totally different intellectual tradition: the Greeks. To the Greek mind, heirs as they were to a thousand years of Greek philosophy and logic, everything had to be explained, ordered and measured. But the contradictory human and divine natures of Christ could not be explained so easily in terms of Greek logic. To the Semitic mind which produced Christianity, it was simply a divine mystery beyond human comprehension—indeed, to question it as the Greeks did was considered blasphemous. Open breaches occurred after the Council of Chalcedon in 451, called in order to settle the question of exactly who or what the Christ figure was. Most of the Semitic East led by Egypt broke openly with Orthodox Constantinople, and were hence labelled 'Monophysite' by the Greeks in the mistaken belief that the Eastern Churches believed in just a single (divine) nature of Christ. This led to open persecution by Constantinople against the Arab Christians of the East: long before Islam, the Arabs regarded the Byzantine court as heterodox, as persecutors, as the enemy. Hence, the Muslims with their tolerance (indeed, open veneration) of Christianity were regarded as liberators.

There was much more. To begin with the Arab expansion was not so much a first act as a final one: the last act of the gradual rise of the Arabs to centre stage that we have reviewed in the above chapters. In this sense their Empire was also not made in a day, but was a part of a far older historical process. In addition, the previous century before Islam had seen the two ancient super-powers, the Roman and Persian Empires, fight an increasingly bitter and ultimately debilitating war out of which neither side emerged victor. This war has been dubbed 'the last great war of antiquity' by one historian and will be discussed in more detail in a later volume.* In fighting each other into exhaustion, it only needed the Arab straw to break both empires' backs.

The rapid rise of the Arab empire under Islam also represented the last act of the ancient world. Their conquests and advance were so rapid and successful because they were directed against the *ancient* powers, Rome and Iran, powers that had been in existence for a thousand years (albeit under different incarnations). The first set-backs and the eventual decline of the Caliphate was caused not by ancient powers but by the first of the medieval ones: northern Europeans in one direction, Turks in the other.

The establishment of the Umayyad Caliphate and the Muslim Arab empire extending through the Near East and North Africa to some extent contributed to the rise of Roman papal authority and the emergence of Rome as the centre of the Christian Church. For with the loss of the three apostolic patriarchates of Antioch, Jerusalem and Alexandria to Muslim rule

---

* Volume 2, *One World*, where I have dubbed it 'the greatest war in the history of the world.' 'The last great war of antiquity' was coined by James Howard-Johnston 2006.

(long largely *de facto*, with the Orthodox-Monophysite split discussed above), Rome was the only other apostolic patriarchate that remained independent. The loss of the bishopric of Carthage also exacerbated this; whilst not of apostolic foundation, Carthage, up until the Muslim conquest, was one of the most important bishoprics in Christendom. The Constantinople patriarchate, although politically supreme as the seat of the Roman Emperor, never gained the religious authority of the apostolic patriarchates. This was exacerbated by the Monothelite controversy, creating further disagreements between Rome and Constantinople, culminating in the Lateran Synod of 649 under Pope Martin, the first open breach between Rome and Constantinople, resulting in the exile of Martin to Cherson in the Crimea.

The split between Rome and Constantinople was political more than theological: iconoclasm was mainly just an excuse in the eighth century, just as Monthelitism had been in the seventh. The split was caused more by the division of the Mediterranean by Islam in the seventh century, and then by Constantinople's turning its back on Italy in the eighth century, resulting in the loss of Ravenna. The pope henceforth had to look to the Franks for support, resulting in the emergence of the papacy as an independent force and supreme bishopric. One of the ironic indirect consequences of the Muslim conquests, therefore, was that it contributed to the rise of the medieval papacy and the Franks, culminating in the establishment of the revived Roman Empire under the Carolingians.

THE 'ABBASID AND CAROLINGIAN 'REVOLUTIONS'

Christianity held no monopoly of religious dissension. As with any religion, Islam was also characterised from the beginning as much by internal conflict as by external conquest. Internal dissensions were revealed as early as 661, less than thirty years after the death of the Prophet, when his cousin and son-in-law, 'Ali, died at the hands of a fellow Muslim in Iraq. The issue was the succession of the leadership of Islam—the Caliphate—after Muhammad. One party, the Sunni, favoured an essentially elected succession whilst the other, the Shi'a, favoured an hereditary succession of leaders through the descendants of 'Ali and ultimately the Prophet himself. Other conflicts emerged during the course of the seventh and eighth centuries, such as discrimination of new converts—particularly Iranians—by the older Arab Muslims, as well as other religious dissent. All of these issues finally came to a head in the mid-eighth century when a coalition of Shi'ites and other disaffected elements in Islam, mainly from the eastern parts of the empire, gathered under the leadership of Abu'l 'Abbas, a rival claimant to the Caliphate. The Umayyads of Syria were overthrown and members of the Umayyad family ruthlessly exterminated. A new Caliphate was proclaimed under the 'Abbasid family, with its capital first at Kufa in Iraq. Subsequently, the Caliph al-Mansur created an entirely new Islamic capital at Baghdad.

The overthrow of the Umayyads and the move of the capital of Islam away from Damascus to Iraq had huge consequences: for Islam, for Europe and for the world at large. In creating a new city at Baghdad, al-Mansur was to some extent emulating Constantine's momentous move of the Roman capital to Byzantium: a wholly Islamic city untainted by a Christian or pagan past as Damascus was. Baghdad was Islam's 'Second Rome'. It was a way of completely separating Islam from both its Arabian pagan and its Judaeo-Christian roots. More important, it turned Islam's back upon the West. Islam under the Umayyads had been westward-oriented: the Syrians still retained much of their Hellenism, and much of the thrust of the Umayyads was towards the West, with the ultimate goal of overthrowing Constantinople and becoming the 'new Roman Empire'. Europe received a reprieve and raids upon Byzantine territory largely stopped. Damascus itself was reduced to provincial status and the 'Abbasid dynasty in its new capital in Iraq came to be dominated more and more by the older civilisation of Iran next door: both the empire and the religion itself became Iranised. Although there were naturally still campaigns in the west, it looked increasingly eastwards as its natural areas of expansion, a move reinforced by the gradual domination of the 'Abbasid court by powerful Persian vizirial families. Syria and the west became backwaters to the 'Abbasids: Egypt, followed by other North African possessions were the first to break away from direct 'Abbasid rule. Islam's early victories in the west lay forgotten and ignored as it looked eastwards. From now on, Islam's natural outward expansion and consolidation was to be eastwards. At first no more 'eastern' than Christianity initially was, this move more than anything else imparted to Islam the 'eastern' character that it is perceived as today. The movement eastwards did not stop: today, the demographic centre of Islam is no longer the central Islamic lands of the Middle East, but South-east Asia.

At the same time that Islam was beginning to be defined as 'eastern', a definition of 'Europe' was beginning to emerge in the West. The end of the eighth century sees the emergence of the Carolingian Empire under

33 The great Temple of Bel at Palmyra in the Syrian desert.

34 The start of the great colonnade at Palmyra, with the tomb towers and the desert beyond.

35 The courtyard of the Temple of Bel at Palmyra.

36 The distinctive statue brackets on the Palmyra street colonnades.

37 *The city of Rasafa, ancient Sergiopolis, in northern Syria, used by the Ghassanids as their headquarters.*

38 *The Arch of Septimius Severus at Leptis Magna in Libya, marking the emperor's massive new embellishments at his home town.*

39 *The Severan imperial family depicted on the Arch of Septimius Severus at Leptis. The bearded Septimius Severus with his two sons, Caracalla and Geta, are in the centre; Julia Domna looks on at the left.*

40 *Bust of the Emperor Septimius Severus at Djemila in Algeria.*

41 Bust of the youthful Caracalla in the Hermitage, St Petersburg.

42 Bust of the older Emperor Caracalla in the Pergamon Museum, Berlin.

43 *Unattributed bust of the Emperor Elagabalus in the Cyrene Museum in Libya.*

44 *Bust of Empress Julia Sohaemias in the Antalya Museum in Turkey.*

45 *Bust of Emperor Philip the Arab in the Hermitage, St Petersburg.*

46 *Philip the Arab's home town of Shahba in Syria, showing the 'Philippeaum' honouring his father.*

47 *Remains of the Roman fort of Arbeia, 'Arabs', named after the ancient Arab community on the Tyne at South Shields outside Newcastle.*

48 *Trajan's Forum in Rome, built by the architect Apollodorus from Damascus.*

49 *The courtyard of the Umayyad Mosque Damascus.*

50 *The citadel of Damascus.*

51 *The Pillars of Hercules, the modern Straits of Gibraltar, looking across to Morocco from Spain.*

52 *The 10th century Qasba or fortress of Tarifa, marking the first Moorish landing in Spain by Tarif ibn Malik, after whom it is named.*

53 *The mountain of Gibraltar or Jabal al-Tariq, named after Tariq ibn Ziyad, the conqueror of Andalusia.*

*54 South side of the Great
Mosque of Cordoba overlooking
the Guadalquivir River, with a
noria or Syrian waterwheel in
the foreground.*

55 Exterior of the Great Mosque of Cordoba.

56 Interior of the Great Mosque of Cordoba.

57 Madinat al-Zahra, the vast palatial complex built by Caliph Abd al-Rahman III *outside Cordoba.*

58 *The Giralda in Seville, originally the minaret of the Almohad Friday Mosque, now forming the bell tower of the cathedral.*

59 *The Almohad city walls of Seville.*

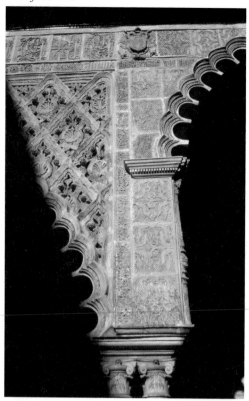

60 Detail of the Alcazar of
Pedro the Cruel at Seville, probably
incorporating parts of the former
Almohad palace but rebuilt using
Muslim craftsmen from Nasrid
Granada.

61 Ceiling in the Alcazar in Seville.

62 The city of Granada, last Muslim Emirate in Andalusia.

63 A garden pavilion in the Alhambra Palace at Granada.

64 The 'Myrtle Court' in the Alhambra at Granada.

65 The 'Court of the Lions' in the Alhambra at Granada.

Charlemagne, the first recovery since the barbarian invasions, culminating in the coronation in Rome of Charlemagne by the pope in 800 as Roman Emperor. This was more than the resurrection of the Roman Empire: it was the creation of Europe. 'Europe' was used by Charlemagne's contemporaries as the equivalent of Charlemagne's empire and Charlemagne himself was known as *Europae Pater*, the 'Father of Europe'.

Charlemagne's coronation also represented a deliberate effort by the papacy at seizing both leadership of Christendom and the Roman legacy back from Byzantium. For Charlemagne never sought to become Roman Emperor, it was a unilateral move by Pope Leo, as far as we know taking Charlemagne himself unawares. Rome was just one of the four ancient patriarchates as we have already observed (and even Antioch claimed St Peter before Rome), so in one move Leo elevated the papacy to king-maker. More than king-maker, a maker of emperors, hence above imperial authority. And in specifying Charlemagne as *Roman* Emperor, Leo was issuing a direct challenge to Byzantium, whose emperors were still officially Roman in a direct unbroken institutional line going back to Augustus.

To some extent, Pope Leo's move was also indirectly the result of the challenge from Islam. As well as Byzantium, the only other rival empire was Baghdad and for Europe and Christendom to be perceived as the viable alternative it had to be a viable empire, an empire moreover that, like Baghdad, combined secular and religious authority. For up until this period Christendom had no supreme religious leader: there was no equivalent of the papacy in primitive Christianity, only patriarchates. The first religion to produce such a single leader above all other priests was Islam. Christianity had to follow suit. Although the papacy is an older institution, in its medieval transformation the pope became effectively the Christian Caliph.

Hence, the Carolingian Empire is viewed as the 'scaffolding of the Middle Ages,' a sort of proto-renaissance that underpinned the foundation of Europe. But what underpinned the Carolingians? In a now famous thesis, *Mohammed and Charlemagne* published in the 1930s, the Belgian historian Henri Pirenne related their rise and fall directly to the 'Abbasid Caliphate in Baghdad. The foundation of Baghdad after 762 resulted in a sudden increase in the Indian Ocean trade channelled through port cities such as Siraf and Basra on the Gulf. Massive wealth from this trade poured into Baghdad making it one of the wealthiest cities of the world in this period. The 'Abbasid economy was extremely strong. The early 'Abbasid gold dinars were of exceptionally high quality, usually 96-98 percent pure, and were depended upon for their purity, accuracy and weight. Large numbers were in circulation, and this led to low inflation and low interest rates. For example, interest was usually 20 percent in wealthy western European towns, but as low as 4 percent in the Near East. At the same time, there was huge 'Abbasid trade to the north, mainly to Russia and the Baltic, where furs were the main commodity. 'Abbasid silver dirhems poured into Scandinavia and Russia eventually to find their way to western Europe. Thus, the Caliphate in Baghdad provided the silver that underpinned the Carolingian renaissance.

The reigns of Harun al-Rashid (786-809) and Charlemagne (768-814) corresponded almost exactly. It also corresponded to an economic boom throughout the Middle East brought about by the Indian Ocean trade, as well as the high point in the silver exports to north-western Europe: Baghdad lay at the centre of—and largely controlled—a world system.[*] After the ninth century the 'Abbasid state began to decline, leading to the drying up of the supply of silver to the north-west. The eventual collapse of the 'Abbasids contributed to a general collapse: the Khazar state in southern Russia, the collapse of the Carolingian renaissance, and economic recession in Europe. In examining the archaeological evidence to test Pirenne's thesis, archaeologists Richard Hodges and David Whitehouse were forced to conclude that 'without Mohammed, Charlemagne would indeed have been inconceivable.'[6]

Thus, even with its back turned upon Europe after the move to Baghdad, Islam continued indirectly to influence Europe. It is often recognised that the rise of Islam did much to define Europe, albeit negatively, i.e., Europe came to be defined in terms of a Christian response to Islam. Historian Norman Davies writes:

> Most importantly, perhaps, Islam cut Christianity off from the rest of the world. Before Islam, the Christian gospels had reached both Ceylon and Abyssinia; after Islam they were definitively excluded for centuries from further expansion into Asia or Africa. Most Christians never saw a Muslim during their lifetime; but all of them lived in Islam's shade. Islam, in fact, provided the solid, external shield within which Christendom could consolidate and be defined. In a sense, it provided the single greatest stimulus to what was eventually called 'Europe'.

---

[*] Although to claim that the Islamic Middle East wove a 'global economy' that incorporated all of Eurasia, Africa, Polynesia 'and perhaps Aboriginal Australia' as Hobson (2005: 36) does is overstating the case!

But such a definition misses the point right from the beginning, for European civilisation is also Islamic: in the Balkans, in eastern Europe and—above all—in Spain. It is significant that the only member of the Umayyad house to survive the 'Abbasid massacre escaped to Spain to found a neo-Umayyad Caliphate in Europe. Hence, with Islam and the 'Abbasid Caliphate becoming 'eastern', it is noteworthy that there appeared two rival Caliphates in the West: the Fatimid of Egypt and the neo-Umayyad of Andalusia. It is to here, therefore, where we turn next.

Chapter 7

CALIPHS IN EUROPE
Caliphs, Emirs and Sayyids in Spain

Perhaps the interpretation of the Koran would now be taught in the schools of Oxford, and her pulpits might demonstrate to a circumcised people the sanctity and truth of the revelation of Mahomet.

Edward Gibbon[1]

The main city square of one the greatest cities of Europe has an Arabic name: Taraf al-Ghar. One of Europe's and Christendom's most iconic heroes has an Arabic title: al-Sayyid. The former is London's Trafalgar Square, the latter is Spain's El Cid. Perhaps these examples might be a little facile, but it nonetheless underlines an important point. In emphasising the Greek, Roman, Viking, Norman, Germanic and Slavic backgrounds of Europe, we neglect the Arab.

Arabs ruled in Spain for nearly 800 years—a period longer than the Romans ruled there. In one way it was even longer. When writing of Muslim Spain, historian Ian Almond observed that to the Arabs, Spain was 'a strange, alien land' at the time of the conquest.[2] This was not so. Spain had been Romanised for many centuries, just as the lands of North Africa and the Near East whence came the Arabs had been, so Spain would have been familiar. It is an important point: too often the Muslim conquests are viewed as a break from the past, a new era. This is only partly true, for it equally represented continuity. More important, Arabs had been coming to Spain throughout the Roman period, and had in any case been heavily colonised by peoples from the Near East for many centuries before that as we have seen.

Traces of the Phoenicians in Spain are elusive outside museums. Muslim remains, however, are everywhere, some of them the most famous in the world. Indeed, the deeper one looks in Andalusia the more one sees of its Islamic heritage: every church belfry, it seems, hides a minaret, every castle has a Moorish history, and hammams, caravanserais, madrasas and other Muslim buildings are hidden away in back streets (Pls 52-72). As well as the castles, mosques and palaces, the oriental presence lingers on in the very place names themselves. Cadiz and Malaga are Phoenician Gades and Malaka; Gibraltar, Guadalquivir and Alcazar are Arabic Jabal al-Tariq, Wadi al-Kabir and al-Qasr. Even the title of the greatest of all Spanish heroes, El Cid, is the Arabic Al-Sayyid. And that most Spanish of all expressions, 'Olé Olé,' is perhaps Arabic 'Allah Allah.' Against this background, the Arab conquest of Spain in the early eighth century is not so much the first act in Islam's expansion but the last in a tradition of Near Eastern expansion into Western Europe.

ADVANCE TO POITIERS: WHOSE VICTORY, WHOSE LOSS? (MAP 5)

The first Muslim that we know of to set foot in Europe was Tarif ibn Talib, who led a raid with some four hundred Berbers across the Straits of Gibraltar in 710. This was little more than a raid for booty lasting only a few weeks and leaving no mark apart from the name of their landfall, still called Tarifa today (Pl. 52). Then in 711 the young Berber adventurer Tariq ibn Ziyad—said to be barely in his twenties at the time—crossed from North Africa to southern Spain with seven hundred men, mostly Berbers. Islam was still less than a century old: the old empires of Rome and Persia had been rolled back, all of the Near East, Iran and Central Asia in one direction and all of Egypt and North Africa in the other had been quickly occupied; the same year as Tariq's raid saw another Arab army invading India; less than forty years later Arab armies would be defeating a Chinese army at one end of the world and capturing Avignon at the other. Islam under the Arabs appeared irresistible.

Tariq's first European landfall was named Jabal al-Tariq—'Mount Tariq'—after him. Still called Gibraltar today, the Arabs' first outpost in Europe was to become a modern imperial power's (Britain's) last outpost in the Mediterranean (Pl. 53). The Visigothic armies under King Roderick were routed and most of Spain fell easily to Tariq, with the Visigothic capital of Toledo falling in the same year. This was followed up between 712 and 715 by Musa, the Arab viceroy of North Africa, with further conquests and consolidation in Spain—or al-Andalus as the Arabs called it—and its Visigothic rulers were taken in chains to Damascus. By 714—only three years after Tariq's initial landfall—virtually all of Spain and most of Portugal was directly or

117

indirectly ruled by the Arabs. 'Islam has rolled across Iberia like a tsunami, gathering up the old order like flotsam and jetsam swept into the sea of history,' writes David Levering Lewis.[3] The Viceroy Musa celebrated his victory by striking the first Andalusian gold coin with an inscription proclaiming to his new European subjects the Islamic message that 'There is no God but God and Muhammad is the Prophet of God' in Arabic—and in Latin. This culminated in 715 with a great 'Roman' Triumph in Damascus, when dozens of European royalty, thousands of captives and boundless treasures were paraded and paid homage to the Caliph al-Walid. Damascus had indeed become the new Rome. Spain was made a province of the Umayyad Caliphate ruled from Damascus. The first European reawakening from the Dark Ages was ignited. Latter day descendants of the Phoenicians, history it seemed had come full circle with the Roman Empire in Constantinople defeated, the Caliph assuming the mantle of both Prophet and Caesar, European princes taken captive, and Spain colonised from the Near East once again.

Tariq's initial force was tiny—less than a thousand men—and the ensuing conquest of Spain by both him and Musa was accomplished with little more force against vastly superior numbers, not only Visigothic but also native Iberians and descendants of Roman colonists. That it was accomplished with relative ease was due partly to the unpopularity of the Arian Visigoths (who themselves ruled the Catholic population with a tiny force). But most of all it was because the Muslims sought accommodation with the native population: there was no enforced conversion, on the contrary religious toleration was strictly adhered to. The treaty drawn up by the occupying forces with the Duke of Murcia, for example, makes a point of emphasising that 'His followers will not be killed or taken prisoner … they will not be coerced in matters of religion, their churches will not be burnt.'[4] Hence, many saw them as protectors of the Catholic Church against the heretic Visigothic Arians, and so were as often welcomed as resisted, particularly by the Jews of which Spain had a large population. Doubtless the *Realpolitik* of ruling a large population with such a tiny force played its part as well, but as in so many of their other conquests, the Muslim advance into Europe was as much collusion as conquest, a characteristic of both the initial Arab advance into the Near East in the seventh century and the initial Ottoman advance into the Balkans in the fourteenth.

The Arabs did not rest in Spain. In 717-18 'Abd al-Rahman al-Thaqafi, the Arab governor of al-Andalus, crossed the Pyrenees. Narbonne was captured 720 and in 732 'Abd al-Rahman sacked Bordeaux. This spectacular advance was briefly halted in the Battle of Poitiers, when the reputation of Arab invincibility was at last broken by the great victory of Charles Martel in 732. The Battle of Poitiers is often cited as one of the most decisive battles in history, prompting Gibbon to write one of his more memorable passages: 'A victorious line of march had been prolonged above a thousand miles from the rock of Gibraltar to the banks of the Loire; the repetition of an equal space would have carried the Saracens to the confines of Poland and the Highlands of Scotland: the Rhine is not more impassable than the Nile or Euphrates, and the Arabian fleet might have sailed without a naval combat into the mouth of the Thames. Perhaps the interpretation of the Koran would now be taught in the schools of Oxford, and her pulpits might demonstrate to a circumcised people the sanctity and truth of the revelation of Mahomet.'[5]

Wonderful words. But even had the Arabs been victorious at Poitiers, it is unlikely that Gibbon's forecasts would have transpired. To begin with, Charles Martel's arms did not check the Arab advance into Europe: two years after Poitiers the Arabs took Avignon and a year later advanced to Lyon, which they pillaged. It was not until 759 that the Arabs finally evacuated Narbonne. Even after that date the Arabs successfully invaded and occupied Provence in the late ninth century, which remained a Muslim centre for some eighty years, forming the base of substantial Arab penetration into and colonisation of south-eastern France, northern Italy and even Switzerland (see Chapter 9). More importantly, Arab lines were already long over-extended and their expansion had probably reached its natural limits. After all, the Arab victory against a Chinese army at the Talas River in Central Asia just a few years later did not result in any Arab extension into China, so a similar victory at Poitiers was unlikely to have resulted in the Qur'an being taught in Oxford and the Sorbonne. It is significant that Poitiers, one of the great decisive battles of world history from the European perspective, is barely mentioned in Arab historical writing. Not for any reasons of glossing over a defeat (Arab sources make no attempt to hide their defeats but write, for example, of their several momentous failures before Constantinople) but merely because it was not significant. 'It was the failure of the Arab army to conquer Constantinople, not the defeat of an Arab raiding party at Tours and Poitiers, which enabled both Eastern and Western Christendom to survive.'[6]

The Battle of Poitiers ever since the eighth century has been regarded as one of the most decisive battles in all history, a battle that 'saved' Europe from Islam. It could equally be argued that far from 'saving' Europe, Charles Martel's victory on the contrary retarded it: by remaining outside the civilising international world of the *Dar al-Islam* it prolonged the European Dark Ages by several centuries. For there is no doubt that the part of Europe that was incorporated into the *Dar al-Islam*, Andalusia, was incomparably in advance in every way to the rest of Western Europe throughout the ninth and tenth centuries—even Cordoba in decline was superior to Paris in the same period. Hence, recent more apologistic histories have tended to regard Poitiers as either irrelevant or a myth; indeed, a recent apologist entitled his chapter on the battle—doubtless rightly—'The Myth of Poitiers'.[7]

But however one interprets Poitiers, there is no getting away from the fact that a defeat is a defeat, the first major Muslim defeat in Europe in their hitherto almost unstoppable path westwards. And for the Christian powers of the West it demonstrated that the Muslims were not, after all, invincible. Myth it may well have been, but that is precisely its importance: myths *are* all important, regardless of their truth, and since the dawn of history we have depended upon myths for our identities, for our self-perceptions, indeed for our very histories.

Poitiers ensured that France remained outside the world of Islam and inside the Dark Ages, but one part of Europe—and an important part at that—did remain firmly a part of the Arab world for many centuries: Muslim Spain. It altered Spain beyond recognition, and was ultimately to have an indelible effect upon the rest of Europe and even the New World. When looking back at that legacy, Charles Martel's brave victory appears almost irrelevant.

Dark Age Europe's first awakening

At first, however, it looked as if the Arab occupation of Spain was to be even more short-lived than their later occupation of Switzerland, and Caliph al-Walid's triumph in Damascus as hollow as Charles Martel's in Poitiers. For in 750 the royal house of the Umayyads of Damascus was exterminated by the 'Abbasid house of Iraq. Damascus itself was reduced to provincial status and the capital of the Islamic world moved to Baghdad.

Out of the general massacre at Damascus, when the entire Umayyad house was wiped out, only one member of the family managed to escape by the skin of his teeth. This was the young Umayyad prince 'Abd al-Rahman. He fled across North Africa narrowly escaping 'Abbasid assassins, finding

5. *Muslim Spain. Shaded areas represent maximum extent of Moorish occupation; arrows represent campaigns into France.*

some refuge with Berber relatives on his mother's side. Finally, in 755, 'Abd al-Rahman reached Spain, founding a Neo-Umayyad dynasty in Europe. The following year he captured Cordoba which he made the capital of his Emirate. This was followed up with consolidation of his rule throughout Spain. In 778 a counter-attack by Charlemagne was defeated (a campaign that gave birth to the medieval romance, the *Chanson de Roland*). When 'Abd ar-Rahman I died in 788 he left behind a strong dynasty and stable kingdom that was not so much a revival of the splendours of Umayyad Damascus but a continuation of it: the very first and one of the greatest periods of Islamic civilisation, brought to a Europe that was still in the Dark Ages. His capital of Cordoba was embellished, and the Great Mosque of Cordoba was built not so much as just another splendid mosque but as a new centre of Islam, built deliberately to rival both Jerusalem and Mecca: Mecca itself had come to Europe and Islam was to be European (Pls 54-56).

The dynasty established by 'Abd al-Rahman I lasted until 1031, although it declined after 1002. It reached its height under the great prince 'Abd al-Rahman III, who reigned from 912 to 961. Receiving his blond, blue-eyed colouring from Basques and Franks on his mother's side, 'Abd al-Rahman III was a true heir of both East and West, combining elements from both as one of the most energetic and enlightened princes that Spain has ever enjoyed. He proclaimed himself Caliph, thus directly confronting the rival 'Abbasid Caliphs in Baghdad and laying claim to the spiritual and secular leadership of all Islam. As well as extending and consolidating his rule in Spain, Cordoba was massively embellished as befitted the capital of the Caliphate, making it one of the greatest cities of Islam—and easily the greatest centre of learning in Europe at the time. Much of the surviving work of the Great Mosque of Cordoba is his, and many would rate this mosque as the greatest in Islam (Pls 55, 56). Visigothic Spain had in fact preserved more of the Classics than elsewhere in the West,[8] and 'Abd al-Rahman was able to build on this by establishing a library in Cordoba that was the greatest of its time. It attracted many of the leading scholars not only of the Islamic world but of the Christian and Jewish as well: poets, scientists, doctors, astronomers, mathematicians, artists. This library incorporated all the learning of Islam, as well as the Classical works of Greece and Rome, much of it otherwise lost in the European Dark Ages.

The cultural make up of Muslim Spain was mixed from its start. To begin with, the Muslim newcomers comprised large numbers of Berbers as well as Arabs and others—indeed, one of Tariq ibn Ziyad's commanders in the very first campaign was a Greek, Mughith al-Rumi, who captured Cordoba and achieved renown by his generous treatment of the townspeople, particularly Jews. Berber immigration was accelerated after the advent of the Berber dynasties of the Almoravids and Almohads. It is thus important perhaps not to over-emphasise the Muslim character as 'Arab' (although the language used was Arabic throughout, not Berber: 'Arab Spain' perhaps not, but 'Arabic Spain' certainly). To this may be added the local populations, both indigenous Iberian and Visigothic newcomers from the fifth century invasions, as well as descendants of the Latin colonists from Roman times. Of these, most probably remained Christian—there was no policy of enforced conversion—but whilst freely allowed to practise openly their religion, many became increasingly Arabised, adopting Arabic customs and the Arabic language: we even hear of the New Testament being translated into Arabic at this time.[9] Many too went even further and became Muslim. There were considerable numbers of these converts, both through intermarriage and direct conversion. It would be a mistake to think of this as in any way enforced, although at the same time much was doubtless political expediency, for many noble Spanish families converted. The Banu Qasi, for example, were a prominent Muslim family of the eighth-tenth centuries, descendants of a Romanised Visigothic noble family the Casii who were dukes before the Muslim conquest. Conversion to Islam opened the road to political advancement. Between 1271 and 1273 a group of Spanish nobles preferred allegiance to the Marinid Sultan of Morocco rather than to Alfonso X of Castile who had recently 'liberated' them.[10] Of more note was the iconic (and over-romanticised) Spanish hero El Cid who, whilst remaining a Christian, went over to the Muslim side, eventually becoming a prince of Muslim Valencia. His title is an Arabic one: *al-Sayyid*, 'the lord.'

That the achievement of Andalusia under the Caliphs was a Muslim achievement—one of the greatest of that civilisation—is not in doubt. It was also Christian of course: Christians were not merely onlookers but active participants and contributors—and probably made up the majority of the population. The achievement of Christian Spain hardly needs reiterating here, it is well and rightly acknowledged. It was also a great Jewish achievement, one of the greatest of Judaism. This was greatly disproportionate to their size, as Jews probably made up no more than one percent of the population. Jews contributed at all levels: commercial of course—their traditional role—but also cultural, artistic, medical, intellectual and diplomatic. Their intellectual achievement was particularly rich, out of which the figure of Moses Maimonides in the twelfth century towers head and shoulders above the others, not just as a great Jewish philosopher, but as one of the greatest of the neo-Aristotleans. Although he was eventually forced to flee after the decline of the Caliphate, it was without doubt the intellectual climate of Cordoba that created Maimonides. Jews even rose to high state positions: in the tenth century Hasday ibn Shaprut became special envoy of the Caliph 'Abd al-Rahman III to no less a power than the Byzantine Empire. Interestingly, Ibn Shaprut also tried to form diplomatic relations between Andalusia and his co-religionists, the Jewish Khazar Empire of Russia. In the eleventh century another Jew, Shmuel HaNagid, became vizier to the

Emir of Granada: it took a Muslim state to create Europe's first Jewish prime minister, eight centuries before another European state would.

While on his official mission to Constantinople, the Emperor Constantine VII enquired of Ibn Shaprut an appropriate gift to send to 'Abd al-Rahman. He suggested a gift beyond price: a copy of a work to fill a gap in the shelves of Cordoba's library, already the greatest in the West. This was a lavish edition of a lost Greek classic of the first century AD, Discorides' *De Materia Medica*. In order to assist in its translation a Greek monk returned with the envoy to Cordoba, and the Greek, the Jew and several Arab scholars collaborated in its subsequent translation into Arabic. Thereafter it became one of the main works that underpinned European medical science for centuries, a perfect example of what the Spanish termed *convivencia* at its best. Historian Ian Almond sums up:

> 'Muslim Spain was a place where, quite simply, Jews, Muslims and Christians shared a wide variety of languages, arts and customs. It was a place where bishops spoke Arabic, imams spoke Ladino and Jewish viziers advised caliphs and gave dinner parties for Muslim poets in their presidential gardens.'[11]

Most of all, the fusion of Arabs, Syrians, Berbers, Numidians, Goths, Franks, Basques, Iberians and Jews into one multi-cultural society made Islamic Spain from the ninth to the eleventh century one of the greatest centres of civilisation in the world. Nobody was excluded, either by race or by creed, all were welcomed, tolerated, encouraged under its enlightened princes: intolerance, ignorance and fanaticism had no place in Cordoba. From it, Near Eastern and Islamic learning, as well as Europe's own forgotten Classical legacy, spread to Europe to launch Europe's eventual recovery with the Renaissance. That Muslim Spain was both an Arab and Islamic as well as a European civilisation—one of the greatest in its history—is not in doubt. But above all, Muslim Spain was a universal civilisation, a world culture. It is no coincidence that the first Western European nations to appear on the world-wide stage were Portugal and Spain.

Cordoba was a Mecca in another sense too, the greatest city and intellectual centre in Europe by far becoming a major goal for travellers from all over. These were not just other Islamic travellers and scholars from as far afield as Central Asia, but travellers and diplomats from Byzantium, Germany, France and England, one of whom described Cordoba as the 'jewel of the world'—and rightly so. From them, Europe first learnt of Islamic scholarship that was patronised by or studied at the court of Cordoba: towering intellectual figures such as al-Kindi, al-Farabi, al-Ghazali, and above all Avicenna (Ibn Sina) and Averroes (Ibn Rushd). Indeed, it is probably true to say that Muslim scholars such as Avicenna and Averroes underpinned the European Renaissance as much as Aristotle or Da Vinci did. This opened up the world of Islamic learning to the Europe of the Dark Ages, but more than that it re-awoke Europe to its own heritage, for Islamic learning had incorporated the work of ancient Classical learning as well, much of it lost in Europe itself. It is one of the great ironies of our Classical heritage that European scholars learnt Arabic in order to translate European Classics into Latin. Islamic literature with its poetry and images of chivalry also left its mark in a whole new genre of romantic writing in Europe, of which the *Chanson de Roland* is probably the best known.* Islamic Spain was a new dawn for Europe, without it, the Renaissance as we know it would not have happened.

THE END AND THE BEGINNING

The great Arab historian and philosopher Ibn Khaldun, writing in the fourteenth century, notes a direct correlation between the decline in scientific research in Spain and the advance of the Christian reconquest. However, in tracing the origins and development of scientific thought back to the Persians and Greeks (which was thought to have been stolen from the Persians by the Greeks at Alexander's conquest), it was seen as being preserved in libraries but not developed by the Romans, to be brought to ultimate fruition by the Muslims. Finally, despite its loss in Spain with the advance of the reconquest, he anticipates the European renaissance when he concludes his overview with: 'We further hear now that the philosophical sciences are greatly cultivated in the land of Rome and along the adjacent

---

* The *Chanson de Roland* dominated medieval European romantic writing, yet it is almost entirely a re-invention of a true historical event that took place in 778 during the era of the Arab campaigns into France. In fact the real story had nothing to do with the Muslim incursions. The actual event concerned a certain Roland, Count of the Marches of Brittany, who was ambushed at Roncevalles in the Pyrenees with his small group of followers and killed by *fellow Christians*. This minor event was transformed after Charlemagne into a great martyrdom at the hands of the Muslims, 'elevating the defeat at Roncevalles into a key moment in a centuries-long—indeed, in symbolic terms, eternal—conflict between Christendom and Islam. Roland became the key patron saint and martyr, an example for Christianity in as far as his death resembled a true Passion.' Cardini 2001: 45-6.

northern shore of the country of European Christians. They are said to be studied there again and to be taught in numerous classes. Existing systematic expositions of them are said to be comprehensive, the people who know them numerous, and the students of them very many.'[12] Thus, learning and knowledge is perceived—at least by Arab scholarship—as neither 'eastern' nor 'western', neither Muslim nor Christian, but as a single world that incorporates the Persians, Greeks, Byzantines, Muslims and north-western Europeans—as well as the ancient Babylonians and Egyptians ('Chaldeans' and 'Copts' in Ibn Khaldun).

The last Umayyad Caliph, Hisham II, died at the sack of Cordoba by the Berbers in 1013.[*] After the collapse of the Umayyads of Cordoba in the eleventh century, Spain broke up unto a number of petty Emirates, often characterised by rivalry and fighting. This break-up encouraged the rise of the Christian powers of Leon and Castile in the north. The Emirates were centred on Cordoba, Seville, Granada, Malaga, Toledo and Saragossa, and is known as the Taifa period. There was still some expansion, however. For example, Mujahid, the Emir of Denia, in the early eleventh century began to extend his emirate throughout the Balearics, Corsica and Sardinia, forming an Islamic enclave in the north-western Mediterranean, and there were still Christian setbacks. But slowly, Christian Spain managed to inch its way back, taking advantage of internal rivalry amongst the Emirates. Their first great victory was the capture of Toledo in 1091 by Alfonso VI of Castile. This campaign gave birth to one of Spain's greatest icons, the legendary warrior El Cid—a warrior, it must be emphasised, who fought *alongside* the Muslims as much as against them and whose title is an Arab one.

Equally, one must not characterise Alfonso of Castile solely in terms of 'the great Christian warrior of the re-conquest'. In his capture of Toledo he consistently refused to permit the mosque be turned into a cathedral, even threatening on one occasion to behead the bishop who wished to carry this out. He numbered several of the leading Muslim Emirs amongst his friends and received censure for his generous treatment of the Muslims who came under his rule. This is an important point: the tolerant climate of Muslim Spain worked both ways, and it is only afterwards that it turned to unmitigated hatred.

Although the Taifa period between 1009 and 1090 was one of political disintegration in Muslim Spain, it was also one of intellectual brilliance. Both

---

[*] There were subsequent Mahdist myths that Hisham II survived the sack of Cordoba, with consequent supposed rediscoveries of him. See Almond 2009: 21-2.

Christians and Muslims fell in and out of each others' beds and alliances—marital as well as political—both with and against each other, the sole motivation being one of political expedience. For example in 1073 when Pope Gregory VII instigated a new Crusade against Muslim Spain, King Sancho of Navarre immediately formed an alliance with Emir al-Muqtadir of Zaragoza *against* the pope.

Early in the twelfth century the Emirs of Spain appealed to the Almoravids of Morocco for help against Castile. The Almoravids invaded Spain putting an end to the independence of the Emirs, creating an Almoravid Empire covering both Spain and Morocco. In 1147 the Almoravids were in turn overthrown by the Berber Almohad dynasty, which ruled Spain until 1184. The Almohads were strongly religious and stand in stark contrast to the more urbane Umayyads. Their architecture, of which a great deal survives, reflects this with a severe simplicity that is both effective and impressive (Pls 70, 71). From 1147 to 1492 the last, smallest, but longest lived dynasty ruled in a remote corner of Spain at the foot of the Sierra Nevadas, surrounded and encroached upon by an increasingly resurgent Christian Spain. This was the Nasrid Sultanate of Granada. The Nasrids are one of history's footnotes, a tiny but glittering pocket of Islamic civilisation within Christendom, far from—and largely forgotten by—the rising new great centres of Islamic civilisation in Ottoman Turkey and Timurid Iran. Indeed, Granada has little history except its ending, and fortunate indeed is the state with no history: it made no conquests, it fought few battles, it did few people any harm. Muslim Granada is one of the greatest small gems of Europe, for the Nasrids loved beauty in all its forms: they patronised beauty, they appreciated beauty, they created beauty (Pls 62-67). Even great empires can rarely boast a finer epitaph.

But Granada's ending *was* history. It was captured in 1492 by Ferdinand and Isabella of Castile, finally bringing to an end the history of Muslim Spain; and its Emir, Abu 'Abdullah, the last Arab ruler in Europe, died in forgotten retirement in a small castle in the Sierra Nevadas in 1533. By that time the civilisation of Muslim Spain had given the Spanish a lead in Europe's recovery from the Dark Ages and Spain became the first of Europe's great powers in the modern era. It is no coincidence that the very year that saw the end of the Near East's expansion into Europe—1492—saw the beginning of Europe's expansion into the New World. Both an end and a beginning. For 781 years Arabs had ruled in Spain, longer than Crusaders had ruled in the Holy Land, longer than the Romans themselves had ruled in Spain (and Europe, in looking back to Rome for its identity, would do well to remember this). The fact that the Arab presence in Spain had endured for so long—nearly eight hundred years—was due to the power of traditions that stretch back into the past to the earliest Phoenician merchants.

It was not quite the end of Islam in Spain.* Muslim styles of architecture became a permanent part of Spanish civilisation surviving to this day (Pl. 73), but in the first years at least after the reconquest there is a barely perceptible difference from the styles that went before, and Islamic-derived architecture—Mudejar—remained the most popular at the courts (and even spread into neighbouring parts of France). The main difference was that mosques were no longer built, but Arabic calligraphy and even Qur'anic quotations still figured in the decoration.†

But what of the people themselves, the Muslim Arab and Berber families from peasants and small landholders to city artisans and great aristocratic families, who for many centuries had become as much a part of the land as the Iberians and Visigoths—and belonged here as much as, or more than, in North Africa or Arabia? Muslims—and Jews—were forced to either leave or convert to Christianity. Many did leave, and the civilisation of the Ottoman Levant was enriched by the influx of Jews, and of North Africa by the influx of Muslims (where they survive as distinct communities today). But many—particularly peasants—stayed, remaining with the soil they had been tied to for centuries (if not millennia, for many of the Muslims had been Iberian converts in the first place) and paying the relatively small price of token conversion to Christianity for the privilege. Christians or not, these converts—the 'Moriscos'—remained objects of suspicion, contempt, discrimination and eventually open persecution by the Spanish. This culminated in the War of Granada of 1568 to 1570, when the Moriscos of Granada revolted and reverted to Islam, attempting to re-establish Islamic rule.

The War of Granada is a useful marker. Not only on the narrower scene, as the last episode of the history of the Arabs in Europe, but on the broader international canvas as well, illustrating just how inter-connected the 'Eastern' and 'Western' worlds were by this time and is explored further

---

* In fact the Moors returned to Spain in the twentieth century, when General Franco brought in some tens of thousands of Moroccan mercenaries to fight on his side in the Spanish Civil War of 1936 to 1939.

† 'One thing is certain: Moslem civilization, supported by the remnants of Morisco population as well as by those elements of Islam which Spain had absorbed over the centuries, did not cease to contribute to the complex civilization of the peninsula.' Braudel 1973: 797.

in a later volume.* This war—the Battle of Lepanto on 7 October 1571 was the event that brought many of the strands together—was fought most immediately between Ottoman Turkey on one side and Spain and the main Catholic powers on the other, but more distantly had a ripple effect over much of the world.

The eventual suppression of the Moriscos by Spain culminated in the subsequent total expulsion—ethnic cleansing in modern terminology—of Moriscos from the European mainland. It is not possible to overstate the implacable, fanatic Christian hatred of the Muslims. Hatred of the Turks by the Greeks of the European mainland has occasionally been justified in terms of Turkish suppression, albeit with two sides to the story. But in Spain the Christian backlash not only against the Muslims but even against those who revoked Islam and adopted Christianity (the Moriscos), taking the form as it did of wholesale repression, rape, expulsion and even genocide—'a gesture of cold hatred' in the words of Braudel[13]—has not the smallest shred of justification when balanced against the Muslim rule of Spain, characterised as it was by exemplary wisdom, good government and above all tolerance for its religious minorities. The Spanish *reconquista* must surely rank, alongside with the Nazi holocaust and the Mongol genocide, for its utter irrationality, its elevation of pure hatred to an art form. Such hatred between Christian and Muslim in its blind irrationality still survives to pervert world politics.

---

* Volume 3, *Sultans of Rome: the Turkish World Expansion.*

Chapter 8

ACROSS THE ALPS
The Arabs in Sicily, Italy, France and Switzerland

The Ishmaelites [Arabs], have left their homeland in order to march into the Province of Aquitaine.

Life of Eucharius of Orleans[1]

The one event most often recalled (not to mention subject to historical re-enactment) in Hannibal's campaign against Rome during the Second Punic War was his crossing of the Alpine passes. Far less known is the latter-day descendants of the Carthaginians repeating Hannibal's epic journey when an Arab army crossed the Alps in the early tenth century and occupied much of Switzerland (although they did not use elephants!). Like Hannibal, the Arabs campaigned the length and breadth of Italy almost without restraint—and unlike Hannibal they had more success against Rome, sacking the Vatican on one occasion.

Mere raids? Much of this little known history was undoubtedly just that, leaving little trace either in the historical records or in archaeological remains. But much else was aimed at permanent occupation and colonisation, with brilliant Islamic civilisation in the heart of Western Europe second only to Andalusia—but unlike Andalusia, emulated and even continued by its Christian conquerors. Like Andalusia, once again, we see an achievement that is at once both European and Muslim.

Muslim and Norman Sicily (map 6)

After 820, the Arabs increasingly raided Crete, Sicily and southern Italy from bases in North Africa. In 827 Crete was seized from Byzantium, and between 827 and 847 the Arabs captured Sicily from Byzantium and established an Emirate there, with Malta added in 879. It would be a mistake to write this

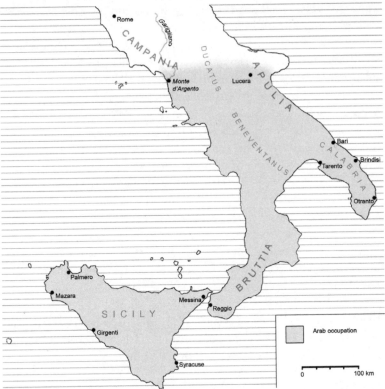

6. *Muslim Italy and Sicily. Shaded area represents maximum area of Arab occupation.*

off merely as Muslim pirate raids against the Christians, however. For the Arabs originally came by invitation: it was the Byzantine governor of Sicily, Euphemius, who requested military aid from the Aghlabite Emir of Tunis in 827 in his quarrel with Constantinople. Euphemius got more than he bargained for, and by 902 all of Sicily was under Arab rule. This was followed up when they crossed over to mainland Italy. Bari was made the capital of an independent Arab Emirate in southern Italy and was used as a base for raids throughout Italy until 915. In about 912, a huge fortified colony was established by the Arabs at Monte d'Argento on the banks of the Garigliano in southern Italy in lands formerly belonging to the Princes of Capua.* The

---

*   Excavations by La Sapienza University of Rome at Monte d'Argento have been inconclusive: later medieval material was found but nothing of the period of the North African invasion. There is a small, sheltered cove overlooked by the medieval enclosure wall, which would make a convenient spot to beach a boat. The sources point to the existence of some kind of a base at the mouth of the river, this is the ideal (only) spot, and almost certainly the site of the base—but

Arabs ran virtually free rein throughout Italy as far as Genoa during the ninth and early tenth centuries—in 846 even the Vatican was sacked.*

In 917 Sicily came under the rule of the Shi'a Fatimid dynasty of Tunisia, then in 948 Hasan al-Kalbi established Sicily as an emirate independent from the Fatimids under his own Kalbi dynasty. The Kalbis became great patrons of the arts and embellished their capital, Palermo, on an opulent scale. The dynasty came to an end in 1071 when Arab Sicily was conquered by the Norman adventurer Robert Guiscard. Again, this must not be viewed as mere Christian-Muslim confrontation, but was virtually a repetition of the events that brought the Arabs into Sicily in the first place—albeit in reverse. For in 1061 the Kalbi Emir Ibn al-Thimnah formed an alliance with Robert Giuscard (at that time carving out a kingdom in southern Italy) against two rival Sicilian emirs.

However, far from bringing about the end of Muslim Sicily, the Norman rulers remained not only tolerant of their Muslim subjects but at times openly Arabophile. Robert Guiscard himself enlisted Sicilian Muslims into his army immediately after conquering them in 1071, and Roger I's army was mainly Muslim by the end of the century. The golden age of 'Islamic' Sicily was the age of King Roger II, who oversaw a period of Arab renaissance under Christian rule and patronised Islamic scholars and artists. Ian Almond adds a note of caution when he writes:

> 'There is room for cynicism here—as the historian Abulafia points out, many second-rate poets from North Africa who couldn't earn a living from their Arab rulers fled to Sicily to compose flattering verses in Arabic to King Roger, who probably didn't understand a word they were saying.'[2]

However, the most famous scholar enjoying Roger's patronage was the great geographer and polymath al-Idrisi, whose work was dedicated to Roger and who was no mere court flatterer. Roger's grandson, William II, could certainly read and write Arabic, most of the high officials at the tolerant Norman court remained Muslims, and Muslim merchants continued to control its flourishing economy. More than anything, it was the force of Muslim arms that propped up the Norman Christian state: Roger's own

---

there does not appear to be any firm archaeological evidence. I am grateful to David Whitehouse for this information.

* Curiously, according to the twelfth-century Andalusian geographer al-Zuhri, the Genoese were thought by some Arabs as descended from the Ghassanids. See Lewis 1982: 146-7.

royal guard in 1130 consisted solely of Muslims, and the Norman attack on Muslim Alexandria in 1174 had Muslims fighting alongside Normans.

Sicily thus stands out in the otherwise intolerant world of medieval Christendom. As well as Arabs and other Muslims drawn to the court, Sicily still had a large population of Greeks, descendents of the first Greek colonists of the sixth century BC, and their Hellenism was reinforced by more recent Byzantine rule. There were also descendants of the earlier Phoenician colonists, as well as indigenous Sicilians and Latin colonists from the Roman period. Norman Palermo was therefore as cosmopolitan as it was tolerant, an Arabo-Graeco-Norman syncretic culture, on a par with (albeit on a smaller scale) the court of 'Abd al-Rahman III of Cordoba.

There is far less to see today of the Muslim influence in Sicily as there is in Andalusia with its wealth of Islamic and Islamic-related architecture, but it must be remembered that direct Muslim rule in Sicily lasted barely a century and a half, as opposed to nearly eight centuries in Spain. This makes what has survived all the more remarkable. Sicily's surviving 'Islamic' architecture was built mainly under Norman patronage: the Norman Palace, the Churches of San Cataldo and San Giovanni degli Eremiti, and the magnificent Cappella Palatina, the latter probably the most remarkable work of syncretic 'Islamo-Christian' architecture in existence (Pls 74-76). No mosques have survived apart from a few fragments incorporated into Palermo Cathedral, and outside Palermo there are only the occasional fortifications and bridges.

FREDERICK II: KING OF SICILY AND JERUSALEM, HOLY ROMAN EMPEROR, SULTAN OF LUCERA

The twelfth century saw a gradual latinisation of Sicily—discriminatory against the native Orthodox Greeks as much as against the Muslim Arabs, culminating in an anti-Arab pogrom in 1160. But a revival of Muslim-Christian culture occurred under the Normans' Hohenstaufen successors. Indeed, the high point was the reign of the Hohenstaufen Emperor Frederick II from 1215 to 1250. Frederick was grandson of both Frederick Barbarossa and Roger II, and was at once king of Sicily, Holy Roman Emperor and King of Jerusalem. He spoke Arabic fluently and continued to employ Muslims not only in his administration but, most of all, in his army. This came about in an extraordinary manner.

In the 1220s a Muslim emirate revived in western Sicily under Amir Ibn 'Abbad, which even minted its own coins. This posed a direct challenge to Frederick's authority, prompting him in 1222 to attack Ibn 'Abbad's capital at Iato which surrendered, and Ibn 'Abbad was executed. Muslim rebellion continued, however, so that Frederick decided upon complete expulsion from the island. Hence, in 1224 Frederick settled 40,000 Sicilian Muslims at his residence in Lucera in southern Italy. Lucera then became a self-governing Muslim enclave in Christian Italy: it was autonomous, it had its own mosque, it was governed under shari'a law. Frederick even insisted upon asserting their rights against Christian opposition—a church was actually demolished to allow them to build their mosque on the site—earning Frederick the nickname 'Sultan of Lucera'.

These Sicilian and southern Italian Arabs—the 'Saracen infantry'—participated in all of Frederick's subsequent wars, including the Sixth Crusade led by him in 1226. His campaigns in northern Italy in the 1230s in an increasingly bitter struggle against the papacy and their Angevin allies were fought with the aid of his Saracen units—up to ten thousand, for example, in the siege of Ravenna in 1237. Frederick's successor Manfred maintained his father's Muslim connections, both diplomatically in continuing relations with Muslim rulers and militarily by maintaining the Saracen soldiers. The Saracen infantry remained loyal to the Hohenstaufen cause to the last in the series of wars of the later thirteenth century culminating in the Sicilian Vespers of 1282, fighting loyally alongside Manfred and Conradin against Charles of Anjou and the papacy.

After the collapse of Hohenstaufen resistance in Italy with the execution of Conradin, the last of Frederick's line, in 1268, Charles of Anjou still treated the Hohenstaufen's Muslim allies leniently and recognised their rights. The Muslims of Lucera continued to fight in subsequent Angevin wars in many parts of the Mediterranean, even on occasion against fellow Muslims in Tunis. This came to an end in 1300 when Charles ordered that all mosques in Lucera be destroyed and Muslims either to convert or face death.

This quite extraordinary history of Muslims and Christians living and fighting alongside each other within Europe thus ended. It was an episode that ultimately ended in failure—both the collapse of Lucera and the execution of the young prince Conradin were tragic events—but it was toleration that characterised it above all: it demonstrated that the two faiths could coexist. The story has inspired operas—Verdi's *Sicilian Vespers* and Szymanowski's *Krol Roger* for example—it witnessed great events and produced great figures. Out if it, Emperor Frederick II of Hohenstaufen, at once both German and Roman, Mediterranean prince and oriental potentate—not to mention King of Sicily, King of Jerusalem, Holy Roman Emperor, Sultan of Lucera, Antichrist, Beast of the Apocalypse, Wonder of the World—emerges as one of the most extraordinary figures of the Middle Ages. In his patronage of the arts, toleration of Islam and challenge to the oppression of the medieval Church, Frederick has been seen as anticipating the Renaissance princes. But it would be a mistake to overstate either Frederick's achievement or the era in which he lived, and David Abulafia's magisterial biography of the emperor concludes that he was after all a man of his era. Steven Runciman sees this era as one of the turning points in the history of the Mediterranean world.[3]

The Arab presence in both Andalusia and Sicily took root and lasted for many centuries. In this context it is important to recall that both experienced extensive colonisation by Phoenicians in the first millennium BC. This earlier Phoenician colonisation, therefore, forms an essential background to later Arab presence, and it is tempting to regard the two as essentially one process. In this context, the area of Arab penetration where we turn to next had never witnessed earlier Phoenician colonisation, and hence was far shorter-lived with less long-term consequences—which makes it all the more astonishing.

ACROSS THE ALPS: THE SARACENS OF SWITZERLAND (MAP 7)

In about 889 some twenty Muslim sailors—presumably corsairs—from al-Andalus landed in Provence near St Tropez and raided up and down the coast and further inland. The raids were consolidated by reinforcements from Spain and Africa, and the stronghold of Fraxinet was taken and used as a base for further campaigns. Fraxinet is probably the modern town of Garde-Frainet near Fréjus, where there are remains of strong fortifications.[*] By 906 they had seized control of much of Provence and Dauphiné, occupying the Alpine passes as far north as Lake Geneva and advancing eastwards to the borders of Liguria. From the mountain strongholds which they seized and fortified they raided much of Piedmont and Montferrat. The immediate vicinity of Garde-Frainet became devastated by the raids, and the passes through the Alps

---

[*] The name supposedly is an Arabic one, possibly derived from *Farakhshan*.

were barred by Muslim strongholds, interrupting the normal traffic between France and Italy. In 940 both Fréjus and Toulon were captured by the Muslims and their populations expelled.* After about 940 most of Switzerland was divided between the Magyars (one of whose raids extended through southern Germany, Burgundy, across the Alps and into northern Italy) and the Muslims, with the southern Swiss cantonments of Valais and Grisons coming under the Muslims. We do not know the names of any of these Muslim leaders, although one of the abbey records mention a Muslim chief called 'Sagitus' in 935 (perhaps Sajid or Sa'id—or even Sarjis, 'Sergius?')

Hugh, the Count of Provence and brother-in-law of the Byzantine Emperor (Constantine Porphyrogenitus), counter-attacked in 941, aided by naval reinforcements sent from Constantinople. In 942 it was possible to lay siege to Fraxinet, but Count Hugh then switched sides and allied himself with the Muslims against his own rival, the Holy Roman Emperor Berengar. Under an agreement with Hugh, the Muslims were allowed to remain in southern Switzerland centred on the Great St Bernard Alps (between Valais in Switzerland and Aosta in Italy). The Muslims of Great St Bernard accordingly settled in the area and inter-married with the local population. Nice and Grenoble are also recorded as being taken and settled by Muslims at this time.

Despite attacks on the Muslims by the Magyars (encouraged by the Christian powers) from their bases in Alsace in 952, the Muslims continued to advance, reaching St Gall in northern Switzerland in the 950s. Contemporaries were impressed by their skill at mountain warfare, and the remains of the towers and other fortifications they built around St Gall still survive. In desperation the new Holy Roman Emperor, Otto II, was forced to enter into negotiations with the Caliph 'Abd al-Rahman III of Cordova, who was regarded as ultimately responsible for the renegade colony of Fraxinet. Accordingly, a delegation was sent to Cordoba, but apart from recording the magnificence of the Caliphal court, it is not known whether 'Abd al-Rahman exerted pressure (or even whether he was in a position to do so) to rein in Fraxinet's raiding activities.

Be that as it may, it marks the beginning of the decline of the Arabs of central Europe. They were driven out of Great St Bernard in about 960, but were still in possession of Provence and Dauphiné in 962. In 965 they

---

* The first, but not the last, time that Toulon became Muslim: in 1543-4 Toulon was made an Ottoman naval base under Barbarossa by agreement with the French, becoming effectively—albeit temporarily—an extension of the Ottoman Empire.

7. *The Arabs in south-eastern France, Switzerland and northern Italy.*

were forced to evacuate Grenoble. In 972 the Muslims holding the Alpine passes captured the holy man St Mayeul (or Majolus) of Cluny whilst on pilgrimage and held him for ransom. St Mayeul was held in enormous veneration by the Christians of France (indeed, he was even offered the

137

papal throne, which he refused). Whilst he was treated with respect by the Saracens, it galvanized the Christians into response. The Muslims of the town of Gap were taken and massacred, and gradually all of Dauphiné was reconquered by Christian forces let by Guillaume, Count of Provence. The great Muslim stronghold of Fraxinet was besieged and eventually taken in about 965 and its defenders routed. The Muslim villages and farmers of Provence, however, were allowed to remain as serfs attached to the churches, and some pockets of Muslim settlers were still recorded in the Alps as late as 1000. After this, the religion seems to have died out and the Arabs (or Berbers) merged into the local population. Thus ended this 'strange Islamic State encapsulated within a wholly Christian land'.[4]

Part of Muslim Savoy was called Maurienne, supposedly after the Moors, but since this name was known as early as the sixth century its occurrence is coincidental. The Côte d'Azur of southern France is also locally known as the Côte de Maures. A locality near Modane is known as Vallon Sarrazin, 'Saracen', and Sarrazin remains a prominent family name in Switzerland and France. Some graves in Basel are traditionally identified with the Saracens and several fortresses were recorded to have been constructed in Piedmont by the Muslims. Contemporary accounts mention in particular the fortress of Frascenedellum, identified today either with Frassinito on the Po or Fenestrelle. The town of Riez in Basses-Alpes still celebrates its liberation from Muslim hands every year during Whitsun. Remains of Muslim towers and other fortifications around St Gall still stand. Some towers along the coasts of France and Italy are thought to be Muslim according to local tradition (in fact Arabic sources refer to *ribats* being constructed in Languedoc by 'Uqbah as early as 734).[5] Inscriptions survive in St Pierre Montjoux in Great St Bernard in 'pseudo-Arabic', and there have been numerous finds of Arab coins throughout the region.[*]

Fraxinet in Provence, therefore, had been a Muslim centre for some eighty years, a Muslim centre furthermore known to have amassed great wealth. Whilst this is hardly comparable to Cordoba or Palermo or even Bari, it nonetheless formed the centre of substantial Muslim penetration into and colonisation of south-eastern France, northern Italy and Switzerland. Such penetration was more than mere casual raids. Contemporary records refer to villagers and farmers who were Muslim, so they came to stay and settle, and the fortifications they built to protect these colonies still stand. The raids,

---

[*] Although the coin finds alone do not necessarily confirm an Arab occupation—cf the Abbasid coin hoards discovered in Scandinavia, discussed in Chapter 9.

therefore, were followed up by colonisation; the Muslims' aimed at more than the mere amassing of wealth or slaves, but permanent occupation.

The story is an extraordinary one, and not only because it is so little known. In fact it was a sideshow: a sideshow not only to the greater story of the Arabs' expansion worldwide but even to their expansion into Europe, taking second place to Andalusia or Sicily, and their eighty or so years there had no real lasting influence on Switzerland, Provence or anywhere else they occupied—and there are even many uncertainties in the reconstruction given above. But that is not the point. The story illustrates just how much the Arabs in the Middle Ages were not the outside, peripheral and transient culture they are often thought of in relation to Europe. In the constant interplay and political jockeying between the different powers of Europe—Holy Roman Empire, Byzantine Empire, French dukes, Magyar mercenaries—the Arabs were viewed as merely another power, albeit a minor one, to court against one another. The story demonstrates just how much they had become a people *of* Europe.*

---

* References to Saracens from Fraxnith and elsewhere are by the monk Ekkehard IV from St Gall, who in about 1050 wrote a history of his monastery between the years 883 and 973 based mainly upon oral testimony. Paradoxically, the fact that there are no Arab sources, only Latin, is probably the main guarantor of the veracity of these events: Arab sources might well have exaggerated them, whilst it would be in the interests of the Latin sources to play down the penetration of Arabs into the heart of Europe. The above account is drawn mainly from Reinaud 1836, translated into English by Sherwani (1964). Reinaud's account is drawn mainly from Luitprand, supplemented by medieval chronicles and various abbey records, supported by strong local tradition in those parts; there does not seem to be any Arabic sources (and if there were, Reinaud would have known of them), so we do not have any Arabic names, either of places or persons. Hugh Kennedy (1996: 97) confirms that there are only Latin sources for these events. The mid-eleventh century *Life of Eucharius of Orleans* refers to 'the Ishmaelites [Arabs], who have left their homeland in order to march into the Province of Aquitaine.' Quoted in Carbini 2001: 33. See also Hitti 1964: 605; Cardini 2001: 22-31; Arkoun 2006. I am also greatly indebted to Monika Raudnitz for very valuable comments.

Chapter 9

THE WORLD'S DEBATE
Tragedy of the Crusades and the Legacy of Intolerance

Whether we regard the Crusades as the most tremendous and most romantic of Christian adventures or as the last of the barbarian invasions, they form a central fact in medieval history. Before their inception the centre of our civilisation was placed in Byzantium and in the lands of the Arab caliphate. Before they faded out the hegemony in civilisation had passed to western Europe.

Steven Runciman

It is a grand story. It involves great feats of heroism, as well as acts of unspeakable savagery; it is a story of the sort of faith and ideals that appear so very foreign to us now, as well as of raw cynicism that is all too familiar. But it is as one of the greatest true epics that we remember the Crusades. The story covers many centuries and involves many peoples; it takes us halfway across the globe from everyday scenes in our own land to some of the most exotic and remote in the world; it incorporates obscure events now forgotten about as well as those that still dominate headlines today. Not since the Trojan Wars has there been a grander epic tale, and the names of its heroes—Richard the Lionhearted and Saladin, Frederick Barbarossa and St Francis of Assisi, Baibars, Baldwin and Bohemond—ring through history along with Achilles, Odysseus and Priam.

But unlike the Trojan Wars, the Crusades are almost a part of us today as they were in the Middle Ages. We are constantly being reminded of them in everyday life, from the toy soldiers we play with as children to the aggressive speeches of war-mongering politicians, from opera's *Tancredi* to cinema's Indiana Jones. All fantasies perhaps? But the Crusades, surely, are still being fought out today: on the killing fields of Afghanistan, in the basements of Bradford and in the skies above our heads. No fantasy that. Indeed, it was not for nothing that over two hundred years ago Sir Edward

Gibbon entitled his own story of the Crusades 'The World's Debate'. Some fifty years ago Sir Steven Runciman, whose words form the opening remarks, saw them as the birth of modern history.

As a Near Eastern archaeologist painstakingly piecing together the trivia and bits and pieces of the far more distant past, one cannot help but be overwhelmed when, on glancing up as it were, one is confronted by the silent colossi of the gigantic Crusader castles that still to this day dwarf almost all other antique remains in the Near East (Pls 77, 78). Overwhelmed, overawed—and baffled. The great civilisations of Greece and Rome, of the Arab Caliphate and the Ottoman Sultanate, seem comprehensible in comparison to the European Middle Ages. All those ideals, that faith, such extraordinary episodes as the Children's Crusade or the theological disputes, the motivation that made thousands get up and go to places they only had the vaguest of notions of. What motivated them?

On one hand the Crusades concerned nothing more than the tiny strip of land euphemistically known as the 'Holy Land,' almost unnoticeable on the western extremity of the vast Asian land mass. On the other hand they concerned events from Central Asia to the far western limits of Europe. Similarly, the peoples involved: on one level simply the Franks and the Saracens, the two main protagonists. But the 'Franks' were not the French in the modern sense, and the 'Saracens' even less the Arabs as we understand them. (Indeed, the most famous Saracen, Saladin, was not an Arab at all, but a Kurd.) The 'Saracens', then, were Kurds, Turks and Egyptians, in addition to Arabs, whilst the 'Franks' were English, Germans, Italians and—above all—Normans, as well as French.[*] To these can be added Hungarians, Germans, Genoese, Pisans, Byzantines, Armenians, Iranians, Assassins, Chorasmians, Mongols, all of whom became intimately bound up with the story. In the end, the Crusades also concerned the Moors, the Spanish, the Jews, the Maltese, the Portuguese, the Cathars, the Hussites, the Swedish, the Lithuanians, the Livonians, and many others as well, in addition to the original protagonists. The World's Debate indeed!

---

[*] It is interesting that an anonymous eleventh century Italo-Norman text, the *Gesta Francorum*, asserts the myth that both Turks and Normans had a common ancestry, both being descended from the Trojans. Hence, both were natural enemies of the despised Greeks. If the Turks would only convert to Christianity, it was argued, no nation would be their equal. See Cardini 2001: 83 and 142.

THE FIRST CRUSADE (MAP 8)

Jerusalem was one of the first cities captured by the Arabs in the early years of Islam, but this posed no problems either for its resident Christians or for pilgrims: as fellow 'peoples of the book', Christians were protected and the Christian holy places respected. The move of the Caliphate to Baghdad in the eighth century turned Islam's back on the West as we have seen, resulting in the emergence of independent dynasties in Egypt, who maintained control over the Christian holy places, culminating in the rise of the Fatimids of Egypt at the end of the tenth century. By the eleventh century the Muslim authorities posed no threat to the holy places: the Fatimids were mainly lenient rulers (indeed, they ruled over a substantial Coptic Christian population in their own land) and a steady stream of pilgrims from all over Western Europe as far away as Iceland came down through the lands controlled by the Byzantine Empire in south-eastern Europe and Anatolia. In other words, Arab Muslims had been governing the Christian holy places and Christian populations for four centuries without there being the slightest thought of or need for a Crusade. What changed?

Matters changed following the arrival of the Turks after the Battle of Manzikert in 1071, when most of Anatolia and the Near East fell to the Seljuk Empire.* In 1071 Jerusalem was captured, followed by Damascus in 1075 and Antioch in 1085. Hitherto, the holy places were in the hands of the Umayyads and Fatimids who, though Muslim, inherited centuries of shared traditions and dealings of mutual benefit with the Mediterranean and Europe: the last of the house of the Umayyads, after all, escaped the collapse of their dynasty to found a neo-Umayyad court in the West, whilst the Fatimids themselves hailed from Tunisia which, under successive Roman and Visigothic rule, culturally still shared many characteristics with Europe. With the coming of the Turks, all that was to change. The Turks were not necessarily more hostile to Christianity than the Arabs had been. But originating far off in innermost Asia, they had no common ground with Europe and Christianity. More importantly, the pilgrimage route across Anatolia was cut, posing an immediate threat to the very existence of the Byzantine Empire, hitherto Christendom's eastern-most flank. The Emperor Alexius in Constantinople, therefore, appealed to the Western Christian powers for aid. The appeal went far beyond what he could have conceived—and was ultimately to rebound on Constantinople itself.

---

* This is examined more fully in Volume 3, *Sultans of Rome: The Turkish World Expansion.*

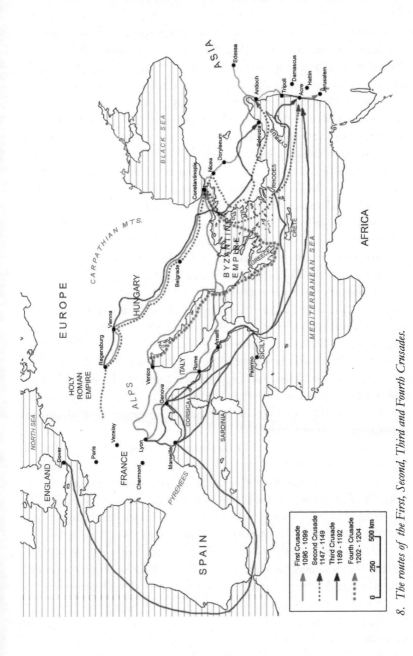

8. The routes of the First, Second, Third and Fourth Crusades.

The papacy was familiar with the concept of Holy War through the Christians of Spain, who in turn may have received the idea from the Muslims themselves with their concept of *jihad*. Strictly speaking the idea is anathema to Christianity, and the papal authorities underwent considerable theological contortions to justify it, mainly in terms 'sacred violence' (likened, for example, to the need to amputate a diseased limb to save the whole body). The idea of Holy War was first mooted by Pope Gregory VII in 1070s, but in 1088 Gregory was succeeded by one of the greatest of medieval popes, Urban II. Urban first emphasised the dangers to eastern Christianity at the Council of Piacenza in 1095, and then at the Council of Clermont in November 1095, announced that a special public session was to be held for a great announcement. Three hundred clerics were present and huge multitudes gathered, too many for the cathedral, so the session took place in a field outside the city to the east. Urban was blessed with formidable powers of oratory, and in describing threats to Christendom and the appeal to arms, electrified his audience. The Crusade* was launched, to gather at Constantinople on 15 August the following year.

The enthusiasm was even greater than Urban expected. The assembly dispersed through Europe, preaching the Crusade as far away as Scotland, Denmark and Spain. Soon, many great noble houses of medieval Europe began to answer the call. Raymond, Count of Toulouse, was the first noble to join, followed soon by Robert II of Flanders, Stephen, Count of Blois, Godfrey of Bouillon, the Duke of Lorraine, along with his brothers Eustace and Baldwin, then Bohemond the son of Robert Guiscard, the Norman ruler of southern Italy. Hugh of Vermandois, younger son of Henry I of France was soon to follow.

Before setting out for the Crusades, the unleashing of the Crusading zeal inevitably rebounded onto the 'infidels' nearer to home: the Jews. Exacerbated by the need to finance the Crusades by borrowing from the Jews, not to mention the Crusading emphasis on Jerusalem, the scene of the crucifixion, the Crusades were coloured by bloodshed even before they begun. In May 1096 there was an attack on the Jews of Spier, most of whom were able to shelter under the protection of the bishop and only twelve were killed. But a precedent was set, and five hundred were killed at Worms, despite the bishop's protection, and more pogroms were carried out elsewhere in Europe.

---

* The term 'Crusade' is technically an anachronism, as is their conventional numeration (First, Second, Third Crusades, etc), being a relatively late term applied retrospectively in the fourteenth century. 'Military expeditions' or 'pilgrimages' were the contemporary terms used.

Meanwhile, preparations were being made in Constantinople, albeit with considerable apprehension: the Emperor Alexius had wanted Western mercenaries, but entire armies were on the march, and Alexius was understandably worried, particularly on receiving news of the first army entering imperial territory at Belgrade at the end of May 1096—three months early. This was the 'People's Crusade', led not by a knight but by Peter the Hermit.

Peter the Hermit was an itinerant monk of obscure origins, but probably Flemish. He is described as short, stocky, ugly, filthy and ragged, and always rode on a donkey which became his hallmark. Such wandering holy men were common in the Middle Ages, but Peter had the power to move men that contemporaries described as semi-divine. Peter was not at Clermont, but he took up Urban's cause and travelled throughout France and southern Germany preaching the Crusade amongst the ordinary people. He finally set off from Cologne on 12 April 1097 with a Crusade numbering twenty thousand, but it was an undisciplined rabble, not an army: a motley collection of enthusiasts comprising mainly peasants that included womenfolk, children, some brigands and a few junior noblemen.

Fighting had already broken out in passing through Hungary, and by the time they reached Sofia a quarter were already lost through starvation, fighting, captivity and desertions. Peter held an audience with Alexius in Constantinople who was not impressed by this rabble, hurriedly sending them on before they caused trouble with Constantinople's own home-grown and notoriously fickle rabble. They crossed the Bosphorus in early August 1096. There was immediately pillaging around Nicomedia and in-fighting between German, Italian and French contingents. In September the French members of the People's Crusade raided as far as Nicaea, the Seljuk capital, penetrating the outskirts where they tortured and butchered its Christian inhabitants. The Turks managed to drive them off, but the German contingent, not to be outdone, raided beyond Nicaea, capturing a fortress. The fortress was besieged by the Turks and the Germans surrendered. All were slaughtered, creating panic in Peter's main camp near Nicaea, which was then ambushed by Turks and most were killed. The People's Crusade had achieved nothing.

Meanwhile, the Crusade proper was beginning to arrive in Constantinople. The first to arrive in December 1096 was Godfrey of Bouillon, the 'perfect Christian knight', who represented the epitome of Crusading ideals, along with his brothers Eustace and Baldwin, and other armies started to arrive at the end of March 1097. After giving their oath of allegiance to Alexius—many of them grudgingly so—they crossed the Bosphorus. The following month Bohemond and his nephew Tancred with their Norman army from southern Italy arrived at Constantinople. Both took the oath of allegiance with Alexius before crossing the Bosphorus to join Godfrey's army, but the same day another army under Raymond of Toulouse (Raymond of St Gilles) arrived, who swore a modified oath to Alexius. The last army to arrive was led by Robert of Normandy, eldest son of William the Conqueror, and his brother-in-law Stephen of Blois. Altogether, the armies probably totalled some 60-100,000 soldiers.

Heavy fighting was first encountered at Nicaea, which the Crusading army captured and turned over to Byzantium. The Crusaders gained their first major victory against the Seljuks in Battle of Dorylaeum at the end of June in 1097, and the road through Anatolia lay open. At Heraclea the army split, with Tancred and Baldwin entering Cilicia whilst the remainder continued on to Antioch. Tancred captured Tarsus and left Cilicia with garrisons at Tarsus, Adana and Mamistra. This campaign culminated with Baldwin's founding of the County of Edessa, the first Crusader state guarding the Crusaders' eastern flank, captured from the Turks with Armenian help.

The remaining army under Godfrey, Raymond and Bohemond, soon rejoined by Tancred, besieged Antioch in October 1097, a city held by the Seljuks but with a mainly Christian population. The Crusaders were overawed by size and opulence of Antioch, a city second only to Constantinople at that time. Antioch's formidable fortifications, however, meant a long siege: by the winter, famine, cold and desertions were beginning to take their toll and the army was slowly diminishing. Finally, after a seven month blockade, the Crusaders under Bohemond feigned retreat. Then in June 1098, using local contacts inside the walls, they entered the city and there ensued a general massacre and looting. The last barrier to Jerusalem was removed.

Bohemond remained and founded the Principality of Antioch. The rest of the army under Raymond of Toulouse set out January 1099 for Jerusalem—Raymond himself walked barefoot, as befitted a pilgrim. It was still not easy going, and they had to fight their way southwards along the Orontes valley and then to the coast. Ramleh was occupied on 3 June and then Bethlehem shortly afterwards by Tancred. On 7 June 1099 the army camped before Jerusalem (Pl. 79). A first assault failed, and by now the army was beginning to suffer from the intense heat. Then on the night of 13-14 July a general assault was ordered. A breach was made and Godfrey was the first to enter. There ensued a general massacre, killing all they met, women and children as well as men, Christians as well as Muslims. Raymond of Aguiles writes:

> Wonderful sights were to be seen. Some of our men (and this was more merciful) cut off the heads of their enemies; others shot them with arrows, so that they fell from the towers; others tortured them longer by casting them into flames. Piles of heads, hands and feet were to be seen in the streets of the city. It was necessary to pick one's way over the bodies of men and horses. But these were small matters compared to what happened at the Temple of Solomon, a place where religious services were normally chanted. What happened there? If I tell the truth it will exceed your powers of belief. So let it suffice to say this much, at least, that in the Temple and porch of Solomon, men rode in blood up to their knees and bridle reins. Indeed it was a just and splendid judgement of God that this place should be filled with the blood of the unbelievers since it had suffered for so long from their blasphemies.[1]

After satiating their blood-lust, the Crusader leaders met to decide who was to rule Jerusalem. There were intrigues for the throne with considerable rivalry among the princes. Godfrey of Bouillon, the 'perfect Christian knight', was elected but died soon after of an illness. There followed further intrigues. Bohemond of Antioch had been captured by the Turks and imprisoned in central Anatolia. Of the other senior commanders, Robert of Normandy, Robert of Flanders, Hugh of Vermandois and Stephen of Blois had all returned to Europe. In the end Baldwin, Count of Edessa and founder of the first Crusader state was called for, entering Jerusalem in November 1199. Thus, Baldwin, 'the penniless younger son of the Duke of Boulogne' in the words of Runciman, was crowned King of Jerusalem in the Church of the Nativity in Bethlehem on Christmas Day 1100. 'His coronation was a glorious one and a hopeful ending to the First Crusade.'[2]

THE SECOND AND THIRD CRUSADES

The capture of Jerusalem and the coronation of Baldwin I was not, of course, an end in itself: Jerusalem, far from being an end, was merely the beginning. It might have seemed an end to many of the Crusaders—it was after all the ultimate goal that inspired the Crusade in the first place—and after its capture many of the Crusaders performed their pilgrimages to the holy places and returned to Europe. It was this loss of manpower caused by the retiring Crusaders that eventually led to the Second and Third Crusades.

For the end was far from being in sight. The kingdom had to be secured and consolidated as well as merely created, and the ensuing years, therefore, was a period of almost continuous warfare and expansion. Galilee was made a principality—as much to placate Tancred (who was made its Count) as to secure the rich agricultural land of northern Palestine so essential to supplying Jerusalem and the infant kingdom. But strategic planning was called for as well. The establishment of the principality of Antioch, with its hinterland secured by the County of Edessa, safeguarded the overland route from Constantinople. But Anatolia was inherently unstable, and the supply lines to Europe—for pilgrims (the original cause of the Crusades) as much as for soldiers and goods—could never be guaranteed. Secure, permanent access to Europe could only be guaranteed by sea, so to ensure this all the sea ports of the Levantine coast had to be captured. Latakia, Tortosa, Gebail, Tripoli, Beirut, Tyre, Sidon, Acre, Caesarea, Ascalon, Gaza—all the fabled Phoenician ports of antiquity.

But it was not only the western flank that had to be guarded. The key to the security of Jerusalem itself was not so much the west, but its hinterland to the east, and in order to safeguard this the Crusaders had to expand eastwards as well—a problem the Romans before them encountered, when they had to annex the Nabatean kingdom in Transjordan to ensure the safety of their conquest of Palestine. Hence, the Crusaders extended their rule across the Jordan, following the ancient King's Highway of the Bible, and with their headquarters at Kerak in Moab, extended down through Edom to the head of the Red Sea at Aqaba, establishing a stronghold on the off-shore island of Graye (modern Farun).

That the Crusaders were able to expand in such a way—as well as take Jerusalem in the first place—was as much due to the disunity of the Saracens as to their own military prowess. The Near East at the time was controlled by a series of rival petty emirs—Aleppo, Damascus, and the declining power of the Fatimids in Egypt being the main ones—as well as numerous minor rulers in between. Most of these emirs or princes were Turks, descendants of the Turkish chiefs who originally came with the Seljuk invasions of the eleventh century, but who then set themselves up as independent rulers, often controlling little more than a town or even a castle. As often as not these petty princes seemed more concerned with fighting each other than with the Crusader outsiders—indeed, there were many cases of these princes allying themselves *with* the Crusaders against a rival prince. To us, dominated still by the 'them and us' impression of the Crusades, this might seem utterly cynical, or at least odd. But one must bear in mind that these Turkish princes were virtually as much newcomers as the Franks; both were exerting their rule over native Arab populations, who were in any case Christian as well as Muslim.

But with or without such minor re-adjustments of loyalties, the deep divisions in the Near East made the establishment of the Kingdom of Jerusalem and its dependencies a much easier task than it might have been, so that for most of the mid-twelfth century the Crusading states reached their limits and a working balance of power was established. What upset this was the rise of a new leader, Zangi of Aleppo. Zangi, and even more his son, Nur al-Din, were the first leaders strong enough to seriously challenge the Crusaders. This resulted in the loss of Antioch's essential flank, the County of Edessa in 1144. But more important than the strategic loss was the moral loss: to the Saracens, Edessa had demonstrated that the Franks were not invincible and that a Frankish state could be recaptured for the faith; to the Franks, it demonstrated that there was a continual threat to their possessions, and that they were not as secure as it seemed.

This inspired the Second Crusade. The kings of Europe gathered: Roger II, the Norman king of Sicily, Louis VII of France and Conrad of Germany, answered the call by Pope Eugenius and the fiery speeches of St Bernard. Louis and Conrad set out for the East in 1147, the latter leading a formidable army, assembling at Constantinople in September.

The Crusade was an unmitigated disaster. Roger II was regarded with suspicion by both kings, who declined his offer to provide sea transport, so taking the long overland route through Constantinople instead. Even before reaching Constantinople there was open discord between the French and German armies. Crossing Anatolia the German army was annihilated by the Seljuks at Dorylaeum and Laodicaea, while the French suffered such heavy losses that only a fraction of its forces managed to make it through to the Holy Land in 1148. Worse blunders were to come. Conflict arose between the newly arrived Crusaders, with their narrow views of the Crusades merely in terms of killing Muslims, and the resident Crusaders in the Holy Land, who saw that the only way for the Crusaders to survive was to come to some amicable working arrangement with the Muslims. Accordingly, an open breach occurred, with the newly arrived Crusaders fired by their narrower religious zeal holding sway, and an assault was planned on Damascus in 1148 which hitherto had enjoyed friendly relations with the Crusaders. The armies reached right to the walls of Damascus and ravaged the suburbs and surrounding countryside, but in the end were forced to retreat, with heavy losses, having achieved nothing (Pl. 50).

It was the turn of the tide. For apart from the humiliation and heavy losses of manpower, more than anything else it demonstrated to the Muslims the non viability of living alongside the Christian powers, however unstably. It became a 'them and us' situation: for the Muslims, the only goal could be their ultimate eviction from the Holy Land.

Accordingly, the Muslims went on the offensive, first under Nur al-Din of Aleppo and then under the greatest leader that the Crusades produced: Saladin (Salah al-Din). Saladin was able to overthrow the last of the declining Fatimid rulers of Egypt in 1171, initiating the rule of his own dynasty, the Ayyubids. Having taken Egypt, he was then able to extend and consolidate his rule to all of Syria, thus bringing about the unification of the entire Near East under one strong centralised rule for the first time since the Umayyads. The result of this for the Franks was inevitable: the writing was on the wall.

Matters came to a head in 1186, when the notorious Frankish lord of Kerak, Reynald of Chatillon, carried out another of his unprovoked attacks on a caravan of unarmed Muslim pilgrims, refusing to make restitution despite a truce between the two sides. For Saladin, there could only be one outcome, and war became inevitable.

The rest can be told fairly quickly. Saladin accordingly mustered a huge army, and the Franks and Muslims met in a great battle at the Horns of Hattin in Galilee on 4 July 1187 (Pl. 80). The Crusading army was annihilated. Almost all of the great Crusader lords were either killed or taken prisoner. The King of Jerusalem himself, Guy de Lusignan, was the chief captive. Other captive lords included Reynald de Chatillon. The flower of the Crusading spirit was wiped out in a blow.

Contrasting sharply with the Crusaders, Saladin's treatment of the prisoners was lenient and courteous, with most, including King Guy, being allowed to purchase their freedom—with the one important exception of Reynald of Chatillon, whom Saladin personally beheaded. Most of the remaining Frankish possessions in the Holy Land fell to Saladin in a matter of mere weeks following Hattin: Acre, Jaffa, Beirut, Sidon, Geble, Latakia, Sahyun, with Jerusalem itself falling after only a fortnight's siege. Indeed, the entire Christian foothold in the Levant was only saved at the eleventh hour by Conrad of Montferrat's heroic defence of Tyre.

The loss of the holy city to Saladin inspired the legendary Third Crusade in the 1190s, attracting the participation of Europe's greatest kings: Frederick Barbarossa of Germany, Philip Augustus of France and Richard the Lionhearted of England. Although great feats of arms were carried out by both sides, the Third Crusade was hardly more successful than the Second. The German army under Frederick Barbarossa had to fight its way heavily across Anatolia, with many losses on the way, only for Frederick to die tragically by drowning almost within reach of the Holy Land at Seleucia on the Cilician coast in 1190. The French and English armies under Philip and Richard reached the Holy Land by sea, and whilst much was made of the personal relationship between Richard and Saladin—gifts were exchanged and each obviously held the other in high regard—the two never met, and the Crusade largely resulted in stalemate. The only lasting achievements of the Third Crusade—and these were important ones—were the conquest of Cyprus by Richard the Lionhearted whilst en route to the Holy Land, and the recapture of Acre after he arrived, the siege of which had already begun by Guy de Lusignan. The former provided the Crusaders not only with an important off-shore springboard for the Holy land (indeed, the Crusading Kingdom of Cyprus under the Lusignan family lasted down to the fifteenth century, long after the last of the Crusading possessions on the mainland had gone for good) and the tragedy of Barbarossa and previous disastrous attempts at maintaining the land route across Anatolia had demonstrated the importance of ensuring a regular, secure sea route to the Holy Land. The other achievement—the reconquest of Acre—enabled the Kingdom of Jerusalem to live on in the Holy Land with its capital at Acre—though it was still officially known as the 'Kingdom of Jerusalem'—for another one hundred years. Although the siege was begun by King Guy de Lusignan after his release by Saladin, on its capture the royal title was handed to Conrad of Montferrat, as reward for his heroic eleventh hour saving of the Crusader possessions, rather than to Guy, still discredited from the disaster of Hattin. Guy was consoled with the Kingdom of Cyprus.

Facing stalemate in the Holy Land and challenges to his rule back home in England, Richard had little option but to negotiate a peace with Saladin in 1192, leaving the interior of Palestine (including Jerusalem) and Syria with the Muslims and the coastal strip to the Franks, with the rights of pilgrims being recognised by both sides. Richard left for home (albeit with further adventures—not a part of this story) and Saladin died of fever shortly afterwards. The Third Crusade was at an end.

LATER AND LESSER CRUSADES

It is not intended here to recount all of the Crusades that followed the famous Third, but only to highlight some of them—not necessarily in chronological order—that shed some particular light on the Crusading movement.*

Although there were later Crusades—indeed, there were four more full Crusades, and many lesser ones—with great feats of arms and new conquests—parts of Egypt, even Jerusalem itself was won back briefly in 1229 by the Emperor Frederick II—and legendary new leaders—Louis IX of France being the most famous—the spirit had gone out of the Crusading movement after the Third. Its military back had been broken at Hattin, and the brutal cynicism of the Fourth Crusade had demonstrated the spiritual bankruptcy of the movement as well—even the moral driving force of the Crusades in the first place seem to have evaporated. Indeed, the Fourth Crusade is perhaps the most shameful episode in the whole history of the Crusades, for it was directed not at the Holy Land nor even at the Muslims, but at the very power that had called in the Crusades in the first place: Constantinople, Christendom's first and greatest city. Mutual discord and suspicion between eastern and western Christendom had a long history buried deep in theological disputes, with political suspicion of Frankish motives dating well before the Crusades. The Crusades exacerbated all of this: with the passing of great western armies across Byzantine territories in the following centuries, accusations of duplicity were flung on both sides, reaching flash-point on numerous occasions. This came to a head in 1204 when the armies of the Fourth Crusade, transported in Venetian ships, breached the impregnable walls of Constantinople—the only time since their construction by Theodosius in the fifth century that they had ever been breached—and subjected that great city, the greatest in the world, to the most brutal pillaging it had ever experienced. Indeed, it was a sacking far worse than that which occurred when the Muslims themselves, under Mehmet the Conqueror on 1453, finally penetrated its walls.

---

* There was even an extraordinary proposal for a Crusade from one of the Mongol rulers. This is discussed in Volume 4, *The Gates of Europe*.

To give them their due, there was guilt felt in the capitals of Europe—the pope later even condemned the Crusade—and the Fifth Crusade was to some extent an attempt at restitution, to restore some of the moral right to the movement. Hence, it attracted perhaps the holiest and greatest idealist of all the great Crusading leaders, the morally irreproachable Louis IX of France, later canonised. But it failed to save the Crusading movement. Apart from its lack of success—Louis himself was captured in Egypt, and only released after payment of an immense ransom—Europe was turning instead to building more idealised Jerusalems in their own green and pleasant lands, rather than the increasingly unattainable goal of the real Jerusalem in the harsh, sun blasted lands of the East.

Constantinople remained for a while as yet another Frankish kingdom in the East, and whilst the Byzantines under the Emperor Michael VIII Palaeologus were able to win back his historic city in 1261, Constantinople remained but a shadow of its former self. No longer a great Christian empire, it became little more than a city-state—although still officially called the Empire of Rome—of only local importance, until the Ottoman Turks under Mehmet the Conqueror delivered the *coup de grâce* nearly two centuries later. The real tragedy of the Fourth Crusade and sack of Constantinople was that it did more than anything else to hasten the eventual capture by the Turks and the advance of Islam into Europe.

The idea of Jerusalem and ideals of the Crusades still managed to capture some spark of imagination, despite the calamities and disillusion, throughout the thirteenth and fourteenth centuries—and from surprising quarters. The greatest of all European holy men of the Middle Ages, St Francis of Assisi, journeyed east in 1219 during the Fifth Crusade on an idealistic mission. Mystics such as St Francis have always been far more familiar in the east than the west, so the Saracens treated this simple, dirty and incredibly gentle man of God with great sympathy and patience, but whilst pressing him with costly gifts (which he naturally refused), sent him back to the Franks.

A far more quixotic—and tragic—mission of pure idealism was the so-called 'Children's Crusade' in 1212. It was preached by a twelve-year old French shepherd boy, Stephen, who appeared at King Philip of France's court claiming he had a letter for the king given to him by Christ in person. King Philip did the natural thing, and merely told him to go back home, but Stephen was not to be put off and saw himself as a Christ-anointed leader who would win back Jerusalem where his elders had failed. Stephen must at least have been gifted with extraordinary powers of eloquence, for the children of France responded to his call in their thousands, claiming that the seas would part for their passage as the Red Sea had for Moses. Even the credulous Middle Ages were overawed, and contemporaries speak of 30,000 boys and girls gathering at Vendôme, not one of them over twelve years of age. This is clearly an exaggeration, but there must certainly have been several thousand. The Children's Crusade under their inspired boy leader marched to Marseilles, where there was rather touching childish dismay that the waters of the Mediterranean did not part for them as promised. Many then returned home, disillusioned. They were the lucky ones. The remainder were offered free passage to the Holy Land on seven vessels by two unscrupulous Marsaillaise merchants, Hugh the Iron and William the Pig. Eighteen years were to pass before news of the fate of the Children's Crusade would reach Europe. The ships—after losing two in a storm—were taken by previous arrangements to Algeria, where the children were all sold in the slave markets, never to be heard of again.

The remaining days of the Crusades can be told fairly quickly. Just as the Second Crusade produced a great leader of the Saracens in the person of Saladin, so did the Fifth Crusade in Baibars, originally a Turkish slave who established himself as sultan in Egypt, founding the Mamluk dynasty (which literally means 'slave') in 1261. But Baibars was a very different stamp to Saladin, and whilst 'a statesman of the highest calibre' in the words of Runciman, 'was unimpeded by any scruple of honour, gratitude or mercy.' He accordingly pursued the Franks with the ruthlessness and relentlessness of a vendetta, and with his successor, Sultan Qalawun, finally brought an end to the last Crusader possessions on mainland Asia. It was Baibars who took the impregnable Hospitaller fortress of Krak des Chevaliers in 1271, and between 1261 and 1277 he picked off most of the Frankish strongholds one by one. It was Qalawun's son Khalil al-Ashraf who finally took Acre in 1291, with the last of the Franks finally being expelled from Tortosa later that same year. The Franks held on for a little while longer on the Island of Ruad, just off Tortosa, until 1302, and apart from a brief re-occupation of Ruad from Cyprus in 1518, were never seen in the Holy land again. The Crusades had come to an end. Just as it was the Turks who sparked off the Crusades in the first place, it seemed fitting that it was the Turks who would see its end. Henceforward, the Near East became a Turkish world: the Arabs, it seemed, had forfeited Islam to these newcomers from far-off Central Asia.

THE LEGACY OF INTOLERANCE

The spectacular Seljuk advance almost to within the gates of Constantinople implied an undeniable—and perhaps irresistible—threat to Christendom. Europe, only beginning to emerge from chaos and millenarian pessimism of its Dark Ages, was spurred into response.

The Crusades are one of the most romanticised episodes of European history. Their ideals, it is true, were of the noblest by the terms of their day: to recapture Jerusalem and liberate the Christian holy places from the Muslim. The First Crusade in 1097 consisted of many thousands of fighting men—mostly French and Normans—and achieved precisely that: most of the Levant was quickly captured, with principalities established in Edessa, Antioch and Tripoli. On Christmas Day in the year 1100, Baldwin—the dispossessed knight and holy adventurer—was proclaimed King if Jerusalem. A title hearkening back to the heroic era of David and Solomon. The Crusades, it appeared, had fulfilled the loftiest of ideals.

To the Saracens, however, heirs as they were to the ancient civilisations of the Near East, the knights of the cross appeared as little more than barbarian pillagers. Their acts of brutality in the lands they conquered shocked even them, inured as they had been to centuries of invasions: the sadistic and treacherous exploits of Reynald de Chatillon make sickening reading by the standards of any day, let alone the ideals of which the Crusaders were supposedly torchbearers. But it is not the barbarity of the Crusaders alone for which their ideals must be questioned. It was, after all, the Middle Ages when few had little to recommend themselves over the next, and no single side had any monopoly of barbaric acts. The Crusades were a tragedy more because of the untold damage they inflicted upon the very religion it was supposed to be upholding: Christianity. The Levant at the time of the Crusades still had large populations of Christians—indeed, it has been argued that Christians still formed a majority (as they did in Lebanon until quite recently)—but the Crusaders were undiscriminating in whom they slaughtered so that much of the Christian population was prompted to convert to Islam simply out of self defence. After losing much of their possessions in the Holy Land, the armies of the Fourth Crusade in 1204 turned upon the greatest stronghold of Christendom itself, Constantinople. This was Christendom returning home to its eastern roots only to end up devouring itself.

It was not all necessarily one-sided. Crusader kingdoms did after all hang on in parts of the Levant for several centuries, and in Cyprus for several more, and this could not have been achieved without at least some co-operation from the local population. Hence, there were more than just a few instances of Saracen princes allying themselves with Crusader knights against fellow Saracens. The great Crusader fortresses, too, were administered much as their European counterparts: as feudal fiefdoms. Such an administrative network would not have been possible without collaboration—or at least compliance—from the populations they administered. Indeed, the Muslim writer Ibn Jubayr, when travelling in the Crusader states in 1184 makes a point of remarking how much better Frankish rule over Muslim subjects were than the neighbouring Muslim rulers themselves.[3] Rule, throughout history, is always a two-way process involving the co-operation of both rulers and ruled, and the Crusader states were no exception; the rule by the holy knights of their fiefdoms was, by the standards of the day, generally reasonable enough. For the Levantine peasant in any case there would be little difference as to whom one paid taxes: Arab, Turk or Frank.

The medieval romances glorified the Crusades as man's greatest adventure in the name of God. Such a view of the Crusades is now dead. Sir Steven Runciman ends his monumental *History of the Crusades* with the words:

> 'The triumphs of the Crusades were the triumphs of faith. But faith without wisdom is a dangerous thing. In the long sequence of interaction and fusion between Orient and Occident out of which our civilization has grown, the Crusades were a tragic and destructive episode. The historian as he gazes back across the centuries of their gallant story must find his admiration overcast by sorrow at the witness that it bears to the limitation of human nature. There was so much courage and so little honour, so much devotion and so little understanding. High ideals were besmirched by cruelty and greed, enterprise and endurance by a blind and narrow-minded self-righteousness; and the Holy War itself was nothing more than a long act of intolerance in the name of God, which is a sin against the Holy Ghost.'[4]

Powerful words and very true ones. But perhaps this is judging the Middle Ages too harshly from a modern liberal standpoint, and more recently it has become the fashion to add the Crusades to our already overburdened Western guilt complex as yet another act of European aggression against the Middle East—there is even a movement for 'us' to 'apologise' for the Crusades (to whom?). Others write off the Crusades as 'no more than a superficial epic external to Europe.'[5] More cynical writers a little over-obsessed with the economic causes of history have written off the Crusades as merely another invasion of the Near East by barbarians in search of loot, with the Crusades running out of steam as soon as the occupation of the Holy Land was no longer economically viable.

But such a judgement is also attributing twentieth-century criteria to the Middle Ages, and in any case does not stand up to historical scrutiny. To begin with, the chief 'economic adventurers' of the European Middle Ages were not the Normans, French, English or Germans, but the Italian merchant states: Genoa, Pisa and Venice. These were at first completely against the Crusades, enjoying profitable relations already with the Muslim powers. In any case, funding a Crusade was a huge cost which Medieval Europe could little afford. But more important, the ideals that inspired the Crusades cannot be written off so cynically, for ideals did play a major role— perhaps *the* major role. True, many of the first Crusaders such as Tancred or Bohemond were little more than adventurers in search of conquest, whilst Reynald of Chatillon was a barbarian of the most unsavoury kind. Even if one can question the motives of some of the great heroes of the Crusades, such as Godfrey of Bouillon or Richard the Lionhearted—and they have been questioned—such astonishing phenomena as the Peoples' Crusade or the Children's Crusade can only be explained in terms of *ideals*: sheer, raw ideals on a scale that seems utterly inconceivable in this day. Can anybody today who has children (as I do) understand not only the faith of the thousands of children who answered Stephen's call, but, more important, the faith of the parents who allowed them to go?

The heritage and aftermath of the Crusades go far beyond such a simple statement. To the Arabs they were seen—and with justification— merely as barbarians. More important, the Crusaders sowed a discord between Christian and Muslim that plagues the world to this day. The first Muslims treated Christianity with open admiration and even emulation. This soon became modified under the first Arab empires to toleration and respect. But the Crusades changed all that forever, and subsequent history between these two such closely similar religions, that share the same God and even many of the prophets and traditions, is one of distrust, dislike and hostility.

But what of its legacy in the West? To quote Runciman again, 'Before their inception the centre of our civilization was placed in Byzantium and in the lands of the Arab Caliphate. Before they faded out the hegemony in civilization had passed to western Europe. Out of this transformation Modern History was born.' And it went beyond that. For more than anything else, the Crusades meant that Western Europeans, hitherto an inward, insular, backwaters people, looked and went outwards beyond their borders. Having once tasted overseas expansion, Europe and the world would never be the same. Just as ancient Roman expansion into the Mediterranean came about as a direct consequence of their contact with the Phoenicians, Western Europe's contact with their descendants proved a heady one. It comes as no coincidence, therefore, that during the Crusades the first Europeans journeyed overland through Asia to China, and soon after their end the first Europeans were rounding Africa to India and crossing the Atlantic to discover America. The age of European expansion had come.

Chapter 10

THE ARABIAN LAKE
Arab Seafaring and the pre-European World System

Whereas European merchants trading in the Middle East seem to have had very little influence on the culture of the unreceptive Muslim societies in whose ports they were essentially quarantined, the Muslim traders established colonies throughout the Asian world, carrying not only their goods of trade but their culture and religion. Through them, Islam was transmitted to India, Ceylon, Malaysia and Indonesia. There, it coexisted with the Hindu and Buddhist cultures that were being diffused from India and China along the same routes. This intermingling and coexistence gave a continuity and coherence to the Indian Ocean arena that, ever since the rise of Islam, the Mediterranean had lacked.

Janet Abu Lughod[1]

Our history books are conventionally littered with chapter headings such as 'The Age of Expansion' or 'The Age of Exploration', almost invariably referring to the Western European expansion after the fifteenth century: the world is perceived as being discovered by 'us'. Indeed, the former is the title of a major Thames and Hudson publishing venture in 1968 edited by Hugh Trevor-Roper, and subtitled *Europe and the World 1559-1660*, hence conceived entirely in those terms. Chapters on the 'Empires of Islam' and 'The Oriental World' (a vague lump-all term!) are left to the very end—almost footnotes, as it were, to an idea that is seen as essentially European. Another similarly titled work from the same era on the same subject is J H Parry's *The Age of Reconnaissance: Discovery, Exploration and Settlement 1450-1650*. Although Europe is neither included nor implied in the title, the work covers solely Western European exploration.

In fact both Parry's and Trevor-Roper's works are excellent and can still be read with profit today—and are not, furthermore, necessarily incorrect in their approach. Without perspective history is meaningless; there is nothing innately wrong with such a perspective, and it is a natural assumption to make that our present world system originated with the expansion of the European seaboard powers. But it is only a part of the story—and not necessarily the main part. (Russian expansion to cover more of Asia than all of the Western European powers combined did, for example, rarely gets a mention.) Even an earlier work, such as Percy Sykes' *History of Exploration*, published in 1934, includes chapters on Chinese and Arab exploration. A more contemporary work, such as Felipe Fernández-Armesto's *Pathfinders: A Global History of Exploration* published in 2006, takes a far more even-handed approach beginning with the expansion of our species out of Africa, while in his earlier (2000) *Civilizations*, Vasco da Gama does not put in an appearance until three-quarters of the way through the book. Beginning everything with Adam (in fact Eve) or the Big Bang is perhaps making history a little too holistic, but certainly nowadays no balanced study of navigation or exploration can omit the outstanding achievements of, say, the Australian Aborigines or the Polynesians.

THE CAMEL OR THE DHOW

Or of the Arabs. Arabia is, it must be remembered, a peninsula jutting into the Indian Ocean: a seaboard country as much as (or more than) a desert one. Hence, when it came the turn of the Arabs for world expansion under the early years of Islam, it was natural that they would look to the Indian Ocean and become seafarers as well as camel herders—'ships of the desert' is a metaphor that can work both ways. Long before the European seaboard countries made the Atlantic their own, the Indian Ocean was an Arab lake. Even the Qur'an contains references to Indian Ocean trading—'ships of plank and twine' (Pl. 88). This is one of the reasons why Islam, at first no more 'eastern' or 'western' than Christianity was, remains today mainly an Eastern religion. Arabia's position as a peninsula gave it several more natural advantages in the making of a world system: both sides of it are bounded by major waterways that formed essential channels of communication between the Indian Ocean and Mediterranean worlds throughout history. The Red Sea reaches like a finger towards the Mediterranean almost touching it, the shortest line of communication resulting in canals being excavated to connect the two in ancient and modern times. The Persian Gulf* on the other

---

* Traditionally, it has always been known as the 'Persian Gulf', in Arabic *Khalij al-Fars*, after the Iranian province of Persia or Fars that comprises most of its north-eastern shore. The ancient

side of the peninsula is hardly a lesser channel of communication, despite being much further from the Mediterranean, for the waterway is extended by the two great rivers that empty into it: the Tigris and Euphrates. These rivers—particularly the Euphrates—extend the Indian Ocean virtually to within reach of the Mediterranean: the great bend of the Euphrates east of Aleppo is less than 200 kilometres from the Mediterranean coast near Antioch over easy, well-watered country. Thus, the Mediterranean and Indian subcontinent were brought surprisingly close together by the Gulf in antiquity by a route that almost completely avoided the insecurity of the great land routes, mountains and deserts that characterise so many of the overland routes across Asia.

Indeed, it was the Persian Gulf—and mainly the Arabian side—that formed probably the first major international maritime communications system in history in the third millennium BC when it became a channel between two of the world's earliest civilisations, the Sumerian of Mesopotamia and the Harappan of the Indus Valley. Even earlier, Ubaid pottery and its copies of the fifth millennium, probably originating around the city of Ur in southern Iraq, has been found along the Arabian side of the Gulf coast as far as the eastern Emirates, with a particularly high concentration on Bahrain and the mainland immediately adjacent. The height of Sumerian civilisation after 3500 BC sees an increase in outward movement from the Sumerian cities, with strings of colonies established in Syria and the southern mountains of Anatolia, as well as a reaffirmation of the older connections down the Gulf coast. At the other end of this Gulf corridor lay the Indus Valley. The Indus civilisation (sometimes called Harappan) shares with the other great riverine civilisations in Mesopotamia and Egypt the distinction of being amongst the world's first (although the Indus civilisation is slightly younger than the other two). But the Indus civilisation was the most widespread, with Indus sites being discovered as far away as the Oxus River in Central Asia to the north, Oman to the west, and Gujerat to the south. This makes it by far the most widespread—as well as most sea-borne—in early antiquity, a gigantic area by any standards. It is

---

Arab geographers invariably referred to it thus. However, the term 'Arabian Gulf', first coined by a Baghdad journalist in the 1930s, has become more fashionable due to pressure from Arab nationalism. More recently, it has become more diplomatic to refer to it simply as 'the Gulf'—to the confusion of Americans, who had already monopolised that term for their own Gulf (of Mexico)! The ancient Mesopotamians called it the 'Sea of the Rising Sun', for obvious reasons, or the 'Lower Sea' (as opposed to the 'Upper Sea', or Mediterranean). By the time of the Greek and Roman writers, the term 'Persian Sea' had come into general use, anticipating the medieval and modern 'Persian Gulf'.

an indigenous culture, although it may have received some stimulus from Mesopotamia, with which it remained in commercial contact throughout its history. The Indus civilisation very roughly spanned the years 3200 to 1800 BC.

Ancient Mesopotamian texts refer to trade to the east with the lands of *Dilmun, Magan* and *Melukha*. The identification of 'Dilmun' or 'Tilmun' with Bahrain and the adjacent areas of the Arabian mainland and possibly Failaka Island off Kuwait is now undisputed. 'Magan' or 'Makan' is probably Oman, and there is now increasing consensus that 'Melukha' is to be identified with the Indus civilisation. Magan is often cited as the source of copper, imported by both Mesopotamia and the Indus, so is probably associated with the abundant traces of ancient copper mining and smelting that have been found in Oman and some of the eastern Emirates. 'Dilmun', centred on Bahrain, has given its name to the ancient civilisation of the Gulf, although the cultures of the Emirates further east are generally called 'Umm an-Nar', after the site in Abu Dhabi where it was first excavated. The period is roughly 2500 to 1800 BC, corresponding almost exactly with the height of the Indus civilisation with which it had so much in common. Both Dilmun and Umm an-Nar boast monumental buildings. The Umm an-Nar culture is characterised by massive, stone-built tombs, such as the one at Hili in al-'Ain. Dilmun has large elaborate temples, such as those excavated at Barbar and Qal'at al-Bahrain on Bahrain. Dilmun is further characterised by astonishing numbers of tumulus burials, with some 150,000 of them being recorded on Bahrain alone, the largest necropolis of the ancient world.

The trading network of the Dilmun civilisation spanned the Arabian sea, their partial control of which is seen from their own distinctive style of stamp seals, copied from the Indus style, which they issued. Indeed, it was with the Indus civilisation that Dilmun probably had the greater links. The grid plan of Ra's al-Qal'a on Bahrain about 2000 BC is possibly related to Harappan grid plans. It contained Harappan style sherds, Harappan standard weights, and Harappan style Persian Gulf seals. Indus seals have also been found in the tumuli and typical Indus pottery has been found elsewhere on the island. Elsewhere on the Gulf and the Arabian peninsula, Indus seals have been found in many places along the coastal littoral. The Umm an-Nar culture in Oman has Harappan beads, pottery similar to those found in Baluchistan, and similarities with Harappan weapons. The period 2400-2100 sees the beginnings of these Indus connections, with carnelian beads and pottery designs. By 2000 BC there is a continued spread of Harappan wares and a dense occurrence of Harappan-related artefacts throughout Oman and the Emirates to around 1800 BC. The main sites where this is seen are Ras al-Junayz, which may have been an actual Harappan colony, Hili and al-Maysar. Local seals are in the Harappan style depicting Indian animals, such as the zebu bull. At Maysar one seal was found with the Indus script on it. Oman was a major copper supplier to both Mesopotamia and the Indus in the third millennium, and characteristic copper ingots have been found from Tell Chuera in Syria to Lothal in India.

The Arabian littoral of the Gulf, therefore, despite its apparent lack of natural advantages (no rivers, little fresh water, no timber, little resources apart from copper, minimal agriculture apart from the occasional date palm) boasted international cities, wealth, monuments and eclectic art styles as early as the third millennium BC, with communities from the Indian Subcontinent at one end and the Middle East at the other, and commercial connections that spread beyond. This belies the traditional image of Arabia as simply desert- and camel-centred, turning its back on the sea, with its people essentially inward-looking until Islam. Thus, the people of the Arabian littoral exactly reflected their counterparts on the Mediterranean littoral of Arabia, the Phoenicians. Both were exceptional in their early control of the sea-lanes and their ability to turn this to commercial advantage.[*]

Of course, the Arabs are even less the same people as our ancient Dilmunis and Maganis than they are Phoenician (although equally, there is no evidence that they are not). But it nonetheless comes as no surprise to observe the modern-day Arabian littoral of the Gulf reasserting a tradition in the same place thousands of years old: trade, international communications, communities from the Indian Subcontinent and the Middle East, eclectic styles. It has become fashionable to disparage the superficial boom-cities of the Emirates and others along the present Gulf coast, with their seven-star sail-shaped hotels, indoor ski-slopes, artificial islands, gold-tinted skyscrapers and expatriate communities outnumbering indigenous inhabitants (Pls 96, 97). But this is to do them an injustice. As well as being the latter-day descendants of Dilmun and Magan, places such as Dubai or Abu Dhabi are the contemporary equivalents of the sadly vanished international communities of the Mediterranean, such as Smyrna, Alexandria or Beirut. The oasis city of al-'Ain/Buraimi, administrated jointly by two states (Abu

---

[*] Indeed, there is some suggestion in the ancient sources that the Phoenicians actually colonised parts of the Gulf coast: ancient Tylos on Bahrain, for example, was thought to be derived from Tyre. There is, however, no hard evidence for this.

Dhabi and Oman), is a lesson in power sharing that ought to be learnt by other states in the region. Such states have allowed peoples from as far off as the Philippines, South Africa and Britain—not to mention more disadvantaged peoples nearer to home such as Palestinians or Baluchis—not only to partake in the wealth, but to walk away with their gains. In an era and a region where 'money no object' has become a byword, spending on artificial island resorts or golf courses in the desert may appear crass, but are infinitely better options than the spending on weapons and warfare that the region has more typically suffered from. These Gulf states are, above all, lessons in tolerance. Few can boast as much.

THE ARABIAN SEA BEFORE ISLAM (MAP 9)

In the first century AD, a trader in Somalia called Iamblos (who was probably a Syrian) sailed to Ceylon and spent several years there before continuing on to Pataliputra, modern Patna in north-eastern India and returning overland. Pliny recounts how another merchant venturer sailed to Ceylon at about the same time, returning with gifts from its ruler. To these can be added a handful of references to named traders mentioned on documents—mainly ostraca and graffiti—found at some of the Red Sea ports referring to Egyptians, Greeks, Romans, Arabs and Indians resident in the ports.

The most remarkable of the Classical sources for this trade is the mid-first century AD *Periplus of the Erythraean Sea*. It is an anonymous maritime manual and navigational aid written in Greek for merchants sailing from the Red Sea to trade with east Africa, south Arabia and India. Most of the information it contains appears to be from personal experience. The importance of the *Periplus* as a document has been rated as highly in the history of exploration as the accounts of Marco Polo or Columbus. It describes the sea route to India from the Red Sea ports of Myos Hormos and Berenice, thence the ports of Mouza, Ocelis and Qana in south Arabia, thence either to Barbaricon and Barygaza in north-western India or to Muziris in southern India. The journey time averaged about six months. The routes into the Persian Gulf and down the east coast of Africa are also indicated, and information about the ports for much of the western and northern Indian Ocean as a whole is given. Some of the main land routes are also outlined, particularly into the interior of India from its west coast ports and into Central Asia from the mouth of the Indus. There is much

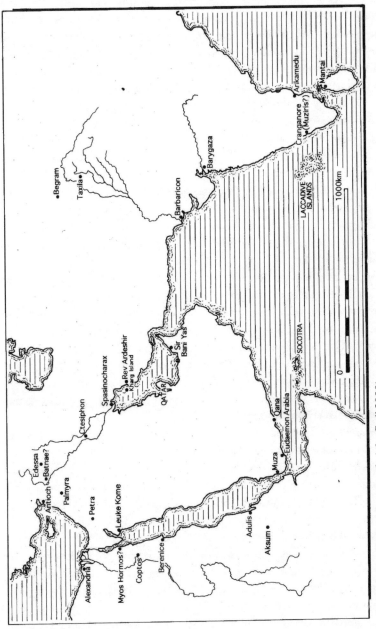

9. Pre-Islamic Indian Ocean trade (after Ball 2000).

165

information that would naturally be of concern to a navigator: supplies, safe anchorages and prevailing winds (in particular the monsoons). The *Periplus* is also a mine of information of prime importance for the economic historian: the products of particular lands, trade opportunities in particular ports, the movements of particular products, the peculiarities of the natives, etc. Altogether, it ranks with Strabo's *Geography* as one of the most important sources of the ancient historical geography of Asia that has come down to us.

There is consequently a huge amount of archaeological evidence in India—mainly in the south—to complement this literary evidence. The most dramatic was revealed by the excavations at Arikamedu, a small coastal settlement on the Coromandel coast just to the south of Pondicherry, where excavations by Mortimer Wheeler in the 1940s revealed large quantities of imported pottery, table ware and glass-ware from the Mediterranean, leading to its interpretation as a Roman trading colony. Wheeler sums up the excitement that was felt at this astonishing discovery when he writes that 'the imagination of the modern enquirer kindles as he lifts from the alluvium of the Bay of Bengal sherds bearing the names of craftsmen whose kilns lay on the outskirts of Arezzo. From the woods of Hertfordshire to the palm-groves of the Coromandel, these red-glazed cups and dishes symbolise the routine adventures of tradesmen whose story may be set only a little below that of King Alexander himself.'[2] But a more cautionary note is provided by David Whitehouse, himself an excavator of the ancient trading ports of the Indian Ocean: 'The question, of course, is: do 150 fragments of Mediterranean amphorae, 50 fragments of Arretine ware, a handful of Roman glass, two pieces of Roman lamps, one engraved gem, and what may be a Roman stylus, deposited over a period of more than 200 years, really add up to a "colony of Westerners"? The answer, I suspect, is no. … Until we find distinctive "colonial" architecture or a Greek or Latin inscription, I think we would do well to regard the possibility of a Roman community at Arikamedu as a hypothesis that cannot at present be tested.'[3]

The interpretation of Arikamedu as a Roman trading colony in India is thus now hugely modified or even denied—indeed, many Indian archaeologists rightly regard the modern interpretations as 'retrospective post-neo-colonialism'. But it is evidence of trade, if not of Romans. The existence of maritime trade between the ancient Near East and India hardly requires the *Periplus* and Arikamedu to demonstrate: such a trade was in place thousands of years before the *Periplus* was written or Arikamedu built, as we have seen. But it was revolutionised with the exploitation of the monsoons in about AD 40-50 by the peoples of Arabia and the increasing demand for luxury goods—particularly spices—by Rome. The two most important ports in India for the Roman trade were Barygaza and Muziris. Barygaza is the modern city of Broach in Gujerat; Muziris was in the south but has never been identified. A secondary sea route reached the mouth of the Indus at Barbaricon in north-western India. Both of these kingdoms stretched into Central Asia. Arabians most likely controlled this trade rather than Romans or even Alexandrians.

After the fifth century the Nestorian church became prominent in the trade. The Nestorians were a Christian grouping centred in Syria who were persecuted by the orthodox court in Constantinople, being forced to flee progressively further eastwards. The Nestorians established a number of communities in the Indian Ocean, where St Thomas was said to be the Apostle, with bishoprics throughout southern Iran, southern Mesopotamia, northern Arabia and western and southern India. Metropolitans were established in Charax, Rev Ardeshir (modern Bushehr) and Qatar, and descendants of these Nestorians form the Christian population of Kerala in India today. One of our main sources for the Indian Ocean trade, the *Christian Topography* of Cosmas Indicopleustes, was Nestorian. Being mainly Syrian in origin, the Nestorians were simply bridging the tradition that had begun by the Palmyrenes and Phoenicians and was to achieve culmination with the Muslim Arabs.

It is highly unlikely that ancient Mediterranean vessels—essentially galleys or the big grain-transporting tubs the Romans used—could have sailed the Indian Ocean. They would not have stood up to the heavy wear and their rig was too primitive for sophisticated manoeuvring. The traditional vessel of the Indian Ocean, the Arab stitched vessel or *sambuq*, was far more seaworthy, as tests have shown, and probably the only type of vessel that would have made the crossing in ancient times (Pls 87-94). This in itself suggests a greater role in the trade for the Arabs (and the Indians, where the stitched dhows probably originated). The Arabs were, after all, as actively involved in the Mediterranean sea trade as they were in the Indian Ocean, a role they inherited from the Phoenicians. This brings us to the great age of Arab maritime expansion.

THE AGE OF SINDBAD (MAP 10)

A fourteenth century Jewish book originating in Barcelona known as the Sarajevo *Haggadah* was one of the first books to depict the world in the round. It presumably provides a link between Arab seafaring knowledge surviving in Andalusia with the first Iberian voyages that established the world as round. For the Arabs of Spain were heirs to a huge maritime tradition far to the east of Spain. As early as the middle of the eighth century—the first century of Islam—accounts survive of the Malabar Coast and China written by the Omani merchant Abu 'Abayda 'Abdullah. By this time the focus of Indian trade had shifted to the Persian Gulf rather than the Red Sea or other parts of Arabia because of the rise of Baghdad as the capital of the new 'Abbasid Caliphate, particularly under its greatest ruler Harun al-Rashid (786-809). Basra had taken over from the earlier port of Spasinu-Charax at the head of the Gulf, becoming one of the greatest ports on the Indian Ocean as it channelled the wealth of Asia to an increasingly luxurious Baghdad. We have already seen (Chapter 6, above) how this revolutionised Western Europe. Only marginally behind Basra was the older Sasanian port of Siraf, the traditional home city of Sindbad the Sailor. Sirafi merchants controlled much of this trade and grew notoriously rich (Pls 81-83).

Accounts survive of merchants sailing from Basra and Siraf to Muscat, the Malabar Coast, the Maldives, Sri Lanka, Malacca, the South China Sea and finally Hanchow in China. The voyage was some six thousand miles, taking 120 days according to an account in 851 by the merchant Sulaiman of Siraf. By the seventh century the first Arab merchant colony was established at Cannanore on the Malabar Coast, followed by merchant colonies in Chinese ports in the eighth century. The accounts of such voyages by Sulaiman of Siraf and Abu Zaid of Siraf in about 900 form the basis of the legends of Sindbad the Sailor.

In 878 Chinese rebels massacred the Arab communities in Chinese ports. The following years consequently saw a rise of colonies in Cochin, Calicut and Cannanore in India, with Chinese products sent to India by junk rather than by Arab dhow. By the tenth century Persian Gulf and Omani seafarers ventured south to East Africa in search of teak, ivory and slaves. A string of colonies were established at Mogadishu, Lamu, Mombasa, Pemba, Zanzibar, Dar as-Salaam and Madagascar. Mandu, on the North Kenyan coast near Lamu, has remains of a ninth-tenth century colony which have been excavated, probably a colony of Siraf. Further extensive early Islamic remains have been excavated off the coast of Tanzania at Kilwa.

The decline of Baghdad after the tenth century led to a decline of the trade through the Gulf. The centre of the Gulf trade moved from Siraf to the island of Kish further down the coast. But the event that most led to the decline of Persian Gulf trade was the Mongol invasions of the thirteenth centuries. This did not extinguish trade as such—far from it, as Mongol courts from Tabriz to Peking rapidly outdid either Rome or Baghdad in their demands for luxury items. However, the Mongol invasions did mean that for the first time in history, virtually all of Asia from the Mediterranean to the Pacific was united under one power: the overland trade routes became safe and flourished, at the cost of the sea routes.

In 1498 there occurred at Malindi on the East African coast an historic meeting between two men, both sailors, that would change the world. It was a meeting of two worlds between an Omani navigator, Ahmad ibn Majid, and a Portuguese explorer, Vasco da Gama. Da Gama was trying to reach India, but had little idea of how to get there, of the science of navigation, of what it entailed. Ibn Majid was heir to the Arab science of navigation and a knowledge thousands of years old of the Indian Ocean and its monsoons. He was able to pass this on to the Portuguese. And when, on finally 'discovering' India when he reached Calicut on 20 May 1498, da Gama to his acute embarrassment was greeted almost immediately in Spanish by an Arab from Tunisia. 'May the Devil take you! What brought you here!'[4]

Such anecdotes might well be apocryphal—the historic meeting between Vasco Da Gama and Ahmad ibn Majid in fact is certainly considered to be so[5]—but they form appropriate metaphors nonetheless. A much blunter—and certainly less romantic—account of the meeting is given in a contemporary chronicle from the Hadhramaut, which writes: 'In this year the vessels of the Frank appeared at sea en route for India, Hormuz and those parts. They took about seven vessels, killing those on board and making some prisoners. This was their first action, may God curse them.'[6] The Europeans had arrived in the Indian Ocean.

FIRST IN, LAST OUT

The rise of the European powers overseas was never either one-way or unchallenged and the Indian Ocean trade continued to remain largely in local hands and not European. In particular, two Arab powers maintained a strong trading and colonial presence throughout the period of European domination of the Indian Ocean: Yemen and—especially—Oman. The Yemeni contribution came mainly from the area of Hadhramaut, appropriately facing the Indian Ocean. The isolation of Hadhramaut from the rest of Arabia probably encouraged the Hadhramis to form links with Asia and Africa since early times. Hadhrami merchants are first recorded travelling to the west coast of India in 1220, later forming important merchant colonies throughout India and even forming the officer corps of the Nizam of Hyderabad's army. After the sixteenth century businessmen from Tarim formed a trading network around Java and Sumatra, extending their activities in the nineteenth century to Singapore where they were partly responsible for its foundation. The capital of the Kathiri Sultanate in the Hadhramaut was Tarim in the sixteenth century before it moved to Saiyun. Accordingly, Tarim today boasts some of the most extraordinarily eclectic buildings anywhere in the Indian Ocean (Pls 84, 85). Most show close links with South-east Asian architecture, derived from the very strong trading links that the Hadhramaut had there, but there are elements of Indian, traditional Arabian and high Victorian architecture as well.

The greatest of the Arab seafaring powers was undoubtedly Oman, whose maritime traditions go back many thousands of years. The ports of Sohar and Muscat rose to power in the early Islamic period, the former in particular becoming a major maritime entrepot in the following centuries that rivalled Siraf. An Omani overseas presence is recorded on the Makran coast (modern Pakistan) even before the Arab conquests there of Muhammad ibn Qasim in 711, and Omanis were establishing colonies in East Africa as early as the 690s. Although not specifically recorded, there is no doubt that the Arab maritime expansion throughout the Indian Ocean as far as China described above would have included a substantial Omani presence. There was a decline after the tenth century along with the decline of the 'Abbasid Caliphate and of trade generally, but contact between Oman and the East African coast was maintained throughout the tenth and eleventh centuries.

With the collapse of Sohar on the north Omani coast the centre of Omani trade moved southwards to Dhofar, probably because of its closer proximity to the Red Sea and the east coast of Africa, always the main focus of Omani trade. Dhofar was also the centre of the frankincense trade, much declined since antiquity but there was some revival of demand in this commodity from China. This remained the main centre until the fourteenth century when the focus shifted northwards once more to Qalhat, Sur and eventually Muscat. This was probably a response to the rise of the Mongol Empire and consequent shift in trade—and demands for luxury goods—to Mongol Iran. However, the East African trade was not neglected at this time, and the Omani colonies of Mogadishu, Lamu, Malindi, Mombasa Kilwa and Pemba increased during the fourteenth and fifteenth centuries.

After the sixteenth century, the Europeans began to dominate the region, particularly when Portuguese superior fire-power led to some subjugation of Omani colonies—Muscat itself was occupied. This was largely led by the great Portuguese conqueror Alfonso de Albuquerque, Viceroy of the Indies. He landed on the Malabar coast in 1503 and conquered Goa, which he made the seat of Portuguese power in Asia. To protect their position he established a string of forts around the Indian Ocean, including a number along both sides of the Persian Gulf. The greatest of these was the Island of Hormuz which controlled the entrance to the Gulf, which Albuquerque seized in 1515 and made a Portuguese possession.

Oman fought back in the mid-seventeenth century under Imam Nasr ibn Murshid, driving the Portuguese out of Oman and reoccupying Muscat in 1649, with the whole East African coast from Mogadishu to Cape Delgado once more under Omani control by 1698. The Omani colonial empire reached its height under the reign of Sultan Sayyid ibn Sultan from 1807 to 1856. He organised a strong navy with frigates built in East India Company docklands in Bombay. So important had the East African possession become to Omani commercial interests that in 1832 he transferred the capital to Zanzibar. The year 1869, however, saw the opening of the Suez Canal leading to the decline of Oman and of its colonies. By the late nineteenth century its colonies in East Africa had been reduced to Zanzibar, Pemba and Kilwa, as well as a few enclaves on the Makran coast. Zanzibar and Pemba became British Protectorates in 1890. Following the independence of Zanzibar in 1963 the Omanis were evicted and Zanzibar was linked with Tanganyika to form Tanzania in 1964. The Omani colonial empire in the Indian Ocean, however, still clung on, with its last overseas colony, Gwadar in Pakistan, finally being handed over to Pakistan in 1974 after an Omani presence on the Makran coast of almost thirteen hundred years and a presence in East Africa of much the same length of time. Not one of the European colonial empires could boast half of much.

This Arabian presence left its mark all around the western Indian Ocean in a unified culture that is immediately recognisable. From whichever direction one approaches—from the inland areas of Kenya, Arabia, Iran or the Deccan in India—on reaching the shores one leaves the respective cultures of the various countries behind and enters a world that is as familiar in Mombasa as it is in Cannanore—or Bushehr or Mukalla or Muscat. The Arabic language and the Islamic religion are, of course, enormous unifying factors—and the linguistic influence has been particularly strong on the Swahili coast. It is a world above all of the dhow, but also of everyday patterns of life, designs, architecture, utensils, food, smells and all the intangibles that serve to define and unite a civilisation rather than divide it (Pls 86-95). Most of all, it is a culture that reaches deep down, far deeper than the superficial overlay of the relatively recent European arrivals. It is an important lesson in a present world system that appears to be the result of the European expansion: there existed another cultural expansion that began earlier than the European, paralleled it throughout, and appears just as permanent.

AN ARABIAN LAKE

When viewed from outer space we are not 'Earth' but a water planet.* Our geographical divisions perhaps ought, therefore, be defined by our seas rather than our land masses. This is already becoming more common usage. The Mediterranean has long been viewed as a distinct cultural unit in its own terms and, following Fernand Braudel's magisterial *The Mediterranean and the Mediterranean World*, the Black Sea now follows suit. In the modern world we have a North Atlantic Treaty Organisation (becoming more and more stretched beyond its initial watery definition admittedly) and we now talk about the 'Pacific Rim' countries. Increasingly, the Indian Ocean is now also viewed as central to the cultures on their peripheries rather than the other way round.[7] At no time was this more so than the medieval to modern period.

Historian Felipe Fernández-Armesto uses the travels of Ibn Battuta to illustrate just how much the Indian Ocean had become an Arab lake by the fourteenth century.[8] We will look at the great Maghrebi traveller more in the next chapter, but Fernández-Armesto's illustration is worth pursuing for a moment. Ibn Battuta was able to find ample employment using his training as a *qadi*—a judge using Islamic jurisprudence—throughout his travels in the Indian Ocean, teaching and giving judgement in Arabic (if not using it in everyday activities in the bazaars). He travelled on ships commanded by

---

* Indeed, even as a species we comprise 70 percent water.

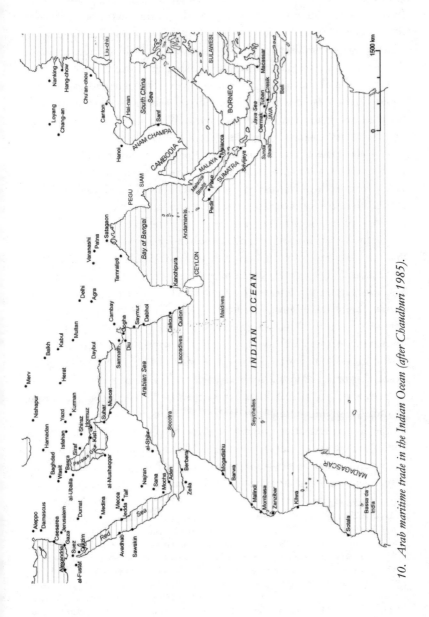

10. Arab maritime trade in the Indian Ocean (after Chaudhuri 1985).

Arabs and was welcomed, in Arabic, by Arab expatriate communities as far away as the east coast of China. He was able to share his experiences with fellow Arabs in the remotest corners of the world—even, on occasion, a fellow Maghrebi—and Arabic had become the *lingua franca* of commerce and international communication with Arab colonies stretching all the way down the east coast of Africa, the west coast of India and further to South-east Asia and the skirts of the Pacific. So thoroughly had the Indian Ocean become a part of the Arab-dominated international system that one almost feels disappointed at Ibn Battuta's achievement. When the Western Europeans first penetrated this area and this system—at first the Portuguese, followed soon by the Spanish, Dutch, English and French—they not so much opened up the Indian Ocean, but simply entered a ready-made system. Without the earlier Arab world system before them, the European world penetration and eventual domination would have been substantially different.

Of course, it would be just as much a mistake to assume that the Arabs made the Indian Ocean their exclusive monopoly as to assume that the Western Europeans were the only outsiders to penetrate and take advantage of it. Following on from major maritime expansion during the Sasanian period, the Iranians continued to be major participants of the Indian Ocean trade during the Islamic period, and even today one hears Persian spoken in Dubai Creek almost as much as Arabic. Siraf on the Iranian side of the Gulf dominated much of the trade of the early Islamic period with colonies as far as Manda off the coast of Kenya (although the 'Iranian' as opposed to the 'Arab' character of Siraf is a matter of dispute). The seaboard peoples of India also participated: there are ample records of Indian shipping putting in at Arabian sea ports, and the western reaches of the Indian Ocean are littered with Indian place-names, from Farj al-Hind ('the Gates of India') at the head of the Persian Gulf to the Island of Socotra (from Sanscrit *Sukhatara-dvipa*, 'the most pleasant land') off Yemen.* In 1025 a naval campaign by Rajendrachola from southern India

---

* *Sukhātara-dvīpa* or (alternative version) *Sukhāvatīvyūha* ('Land of Bliss') figures very highly in Buddhist sacred literature. The *Sukhāvatīvyūha* is in fact the name of an ancient Buddhist sacred text referring to the utopian land of *nirvana* in the western heaven. By the time of the 5th century AD the *Sukhāvatīvyūha* was one of the most popular texts of Buddhism, rivalling the *Lotus Sutra*. The text carries very little in the way of historical or geographical information, but does describe the land as full of trees of the 'seven jewels' adorned with lotus lakes of the 'seven jewels.' It is also described as being very easy to reach, albeit presumably in the mystical sense. Xinru Liu (*Anicent India and Ancient China. Trade and Religious Exchanges AS 1-600*, Delhi 1988, p. 99) writes: 'The theories of utopian lands often drew their inspiration from long-distance trade and travel. Anecdotes of foreign countries and exotic alien goods provided the best food for the imagination.

was mounted against the Srivijaya Empire of Sumatra. The period also sees the rise of the Swahili people of the East African coast who began to take an active part throughout the ocean.

Countries from beyond the Indian Ocean long anticipated the arrival of the Europeans. Chief of these was Ottoman Turkey, whose naval power extended across the Indian Ocean with possessions on the west coast of India before the Portuguese arrived. The Indian Ocean was the stage for the Turkish-Portuguese war in the sixteenth century, and for a while the eastern spice trade in the late sixteenth century was recaptured by Turkey from Portugal. As late as the early seventeenth century an Ottoman trading station was established at Atjeh in the East Indies.* More curiously—if only because it was more unusual—was the Chinese penetration of the Indian Ocean in the early fifteenth century during the time of the outward looking Yongle Emperor of the Ming Dynasty. These expeditions, commanded by the admiral Zheng He, were carried out in the 'treasure ships,' fleets consisting of up to several hundred large ocean-going vessels and crews numbering in their thousands. The largest of the treasure ships were four hundred foot long nine-masted giants (compared to Columbus' eighty-five foot, three-masted *Santa Maria*), with hulls divided into water-proof compartments—easily the largest and most sophisticated ships in the world at the time. Altogether, Zheng He commanded seven expeditions, bringing back precious woods, tortoise-shell, pearls, ivory, rhinoceros horn and—on occasion—even giraffes to astonished viewers back in Beijing.† Over several voyages they sailed throughout South-east Asia, all the way around India, right up the Persian Gulf and all the way down the east African coast—almost exactly replicating the earlier Arab voyages in reverse. In this connection, it is important to remember that Zheng He himself was a Muslim. For, impressive though the Chinese and Turkish—and Portuguese—achievements were so far from their own shores, none would have been possible if the Indian

---

The *Sukhāvatīvyūha*, developed in the commercial atmosphere of north India during the first few centuries AD, became one of the most influential statements of Buddhist doctrine in China.'

* Ottoman activities in the India Ocean are explored more in Volume 3, *Sultans of Rome.*

† The huge size of the treasure ships in contrast to the tiny *Santa Maria* forms a dramatic front cover illustration of Hobson 2004. The best account remains Louise Lavathes (1994), *When China Ruled the Seas. The Treasure Fleet of the Dragon Throne, 1405-1433* (Oxford). Even more popular has been Gavin Menzies *1421: The Year China Discovered the World* (2003) and now his *1434: The Year a Chinese Fleet Sailed to Italy and Ignited the Renaissance* (2008). 'Ming Chinese maritime, artistic, technological and scientific achievements were without doubt impressive and are well acknowledged, but unfortunately in overstating the case and making quite preposterous claims, Menzies merely ends up doing Chinese civilisation a disservice. Such books can be relegated to fantasy rather than history.

Ocean had not been made into a Muslim lake—and a familiar, integrated world system—by the Arabs long before.

In this connection it is also important to remember the Arabs' most impressive and long-lasting achievement in the Indian Ocean: the islamisation of South-eastern Asia. For it is often forgotten that today the demographic centre of Islam is not Arabia or the Middle East, where we most associate Islam, but South and South-east Asia: Malaysia and Indonesia are the largest Muslim countries in the world, with Bangladesh, India and Pakistan following close behind (compare Indonesia with a Muslim population of 111 million, for example, with the most populous Arab country, Egypt, with a Muslim population of 58 million). Arab arms never extended to South-east Asia: its islamisation was achieved solely through trade and proselytisation, a direct result of making the Indian Ocean an Arab lake.

So thoroughly did the Arabs penetrate the Indian Ocean that the total absence of their presence in the largest country of all bordering the ocean seems almost inexplicable: Australia. There is more evidence for the presence of the Chinese on the western seaboard of Australia (and even then fairly tenuous) than for Arab. In 1944 a hoard of five Arab copper dirhems dating between the tenth and early fourteenth century was found just off the coast of Australia's Northern Territory. Interestingly, the coins were from medieval Arab trading port of Kilwa off the coast of Tanzania which, at first sight, seems to fit neatly into the pattern of Arab Indian Ocean exploration. Kilwan coins, however, were never circulated much outside eastern Africa, and four Dutch coins dating 1680 to 1784 were also found in the same place (although not necessarily part of the same hoard). The site has never been excavated, so the problem remains unresolved and the question of a medieval Arab discovery of Australia remains open.[9] The historian Geoffrey Blainey makes the interesting observation that it was only by a quirk of history that it was people from north-western Europe who first colonised south-eastern Australia: historically, it would have been more logical for people from south-eastern Asia to have colonised the north. Hence, Australia became a dry-farming economy based on cereals with its demographic centre in the south-east with a largely European population. But if patterns of history and geography are anything to go by, the demographic centre would more logically have been in the moister, tropical rainforest regions of northern Australia, with a paddy-field based economy peopled by colonisers from south-eastern Asia.[10] Such a rice-eating Asian 'Australiastan' would almost certainly have been a part of the Arab lake—and Muslim.

66 Stalactite ceiling decoration in the Alhambra at Granada.

67 Interior decoration in the Alhambra at Granada.

68 The Generalife Palace at Granada.

69 The church at Almonaster la Real in Andalusia converted from a 10th century mosque: the minaret and projecting mihrab are apparent.

70 *Minaret of the former*
Almohad mosque in Niebla.

71 *Interior of the former Almohad mosque at Jérez de la Frontera in Andalusia.*

72 *The Moorish castle of Almodovar del Rio in Andalusia.*

73 *The modern railway terminal in Seville, reviving the Moorish style.*

74 *The interior ceiling of the Cappella Palatina in the Norman palace at Palermo.*

75 *The church of San Cataldo in Palermo reflecting the Fatimid styles of Egypt.*

76 The interior of San Cataldo at Palermo, with the wholly Near Eastern style of squinches.

77 The Crusader castle of Sahyun in Syria.

78 The Hospitaller castle of Krak des Chevaliers in Syria, probably the greatest of the Crusader castles.

79 Jerusalem from the Mount of Olives overlooking the Haram al-Sharif with the Mosque of al-Aqsa and the Dome of the Rock, built within Herod's Temple temenos.

80 The Horns of Hattin in Galilee, scene of Saladin's great victory over the army of the Second Crusade, probably the most decisive battle of the Crusades.

81 The bay of Taheri on the Persian Gulf, site of the early Islamic port of Siraf.

82 Remains of the great mosque at Siraf.

83 An excavated residential area at Siraf.

84 The eclectic Indian Ocean style of one of the mansions at Tarim in Yemen.

85 The main mosque in Tarim.

86 The port of Mukalla facing the Indian Ocean in Yemen.

87 A traditional dhow off the port of Kangan on the Persian Gulf.

*88 A derelict sewn dhow on the beach at Shihr in Yemen. (This looks to be the same vessel
photographed by Alan Villiers in 1939: see Hourani and Carswell 1995: Pl. 8).*

89 Traditional Red Sea vessels at Hodeida in Yemen.

90 *A traditional harbour scene at Kangan in Iran.*

91 *The traditional dhow building port of Kong in Iran.*

92 Dhow construction on the sea front at Kong.

93 Ocean-going wooden dhows under construction at Kong.

94 The previous photographs of Kong were taken in the 1970s. This and the following, taken in the early years of the third millennium, demonstrate the strength of tradition of traditional dhows in the Gulf.

95 Dhow construction down the coast from Kong.

96 Dubai Creek.

97 Traditional and modern in Abu Dhabi.

Chapter 11

A UNIVERSAL WORLD
Arab World Travel and World Views

I heard this wizard down the University say that the Klatchians invented nothing. That was their great contribution to maffs, he said. I said 'What?' an' he said, they come up with zero.

Dun't sound that clever to me, ... Anyone could invent nothing. I ain't invented anything.

My point exactly ... *Nothing* didn't need inventing. It was just there. They probably just found it.

It's having all that desert.

Terry Pratchett[1]

As Terry Pratchett's 'Disc World' protagonist rightly points out, inventing nothing is a huge achievement. By inventing nothing the Arabs—the model for Terry Pratchett's fictional 'Klatchians'—in one stroke made a giant leap forward for all mankind, with the concept of zero underpinning all subsequent scientific achievements that rest upon mathematics. Without nothing, landing on the Moon would have been inconceivable.

It also underlines how Arab civilisation was characterised by curiosity and worldliness since its beginning. Journeys in the mind were matched by physical journeys throughout the world, motivating the Arabs to reach Spain and China as much as it motivated them to arrive at the answers to abstruse and abstract mathematics.

The historian J M Roberts writes, 'Few non-Europeans other than Turks even entered Europe ... and we still do not really know why.'[2] To be fair, Roberts is simply raising such issues rather than citing Western superiority, and his overview on the worldwide spread of European values on the whole is a balanced one. But the issue he raises—the view that Europe has always remained somehow exclusive, un-penetrated by and separated from the East—has given rise to the idea of 'fortress Europe', manifest, for example, in controversies surrounding Turkey's entry to the European Union or in immigration generally.

As for 'the reason why', great lengths have been travelled to explain how the European mind has some in-built curiosity and worldliness that others do not. The outgoing curiosity of Europeans has commonly been contrasted with the traditional incuriosity and inwardness of Asians, cited in discussions of European expansion into the East, whether in antiquity or in modern times. This fallacy still enjoys surprising currency.[3] Outwardness supposedly motivated Marco Polo, Vasco da Gama and other European traveller-explorers as far back as the Middle Ages. This was at a time when the places they travelled to, such as China or India, were civilisations immeasurably superior to contemporary Europe on all levels but one: intellectual life supposedly remained essentially inward-looking in contrast to assumed European curiosity and outwardness.

In the latest foray into the 'West versus East' controversy initiated by Edward Said, the historian John M Headley in his challenge to 'the historical studies of moral posturing against the West' contrasts the inwardness of Islam with the universalist traditions of Christianity, arguing that universalism is exclusively a product of Western Europe.[4] But Islam has a greater history of universalism, tolerance and inclusiveness than the Christian church, characterised as it has been for much of its history by intolerance and exclusiveness. Headley further claims that any ideas of universalism, compassion and human rights are merely isolated instances in other cultures, lacking the sustained continuity of the West—but such isolated cases do nonetheless create some ground for receptivity of Western values!

The previous chapters are, I hope, sufficient to refute such views. It remains, therefore, to summarise just some of those travellers from distant Araby or Barbary who either rivalled Marco Polo or went in the opposite direction, and to note just some of the ideas of universality which we owe to the Arabs and to Islam.

The Sultanate of Peru:
Arab travellers in Europe and beyond

To many in the West, travelling is a luxury that is enjoyed more and more as mass tourism has increased to overtake just about every other industry in the world. But travel is more than a mere luxury to the Muslim: it is a commandment. It is embodied in one of the five pillars of Islam, where every Muslim is enjoined if possible to perform the pilgrimage to Mecca at least once in a lifetime. The *hajj*, therefore, has instilled the idea of travel since the beginning of Islam.

The huge range of eighteenth and nineteenth century 'orientalist' travel literature presented Europe as an outgoing and curious society, with the Arabs as essentially inward and static. The backlash against this— begun by Edward Said and now a literary industry almost as prolific as the orientalist literature which prompted it—has been a much-needed corrective but in some ways also misses the point. For there has also been an Arab 'occidentalist' literature looking the other way: at the West as an object of curiosity, of one culture looking down upon another. This did not just belong to the 'high' period of Arab Islamic civilisation—the great age of the Caliphs prior to the Mongol invasions—but has been a part of Arab literature down to the modern period when Arab culture has supposedly been in decline. A complete history of Arab travel and exploration is not possible here (and Arab maritime exploration is given in the previous chapter). But a summary of some of its achievements, including some of those who journeyed into the West, is not out of place—and puts 'us' in our place.

Arab travel writing certainly has a venerable pedigree with 'Abbasid Baghdad being a natural centre. Ibn Hauqal from Baghdad travelled the length and breadth of the Muslim world in the tenth century and wrote a general description of the world. Al-Mas'udi, also born in Baghdad 987, was blessed with extraordinary intellectual curiosity, spending most of his life during the first half of eleventh century travelling from Morocco and Egypt to India and China. As well as absorbing much of what he saw, al-Mas'udi absorbed Greek and pre-Islamic Persian literature, and his account of the world entitled *The Meadows of Gold* is one of the most important sources for the period. Baghdad was not the only centre where such 'world descriptions' were compiled. Al-Idrisi, born in Ceuta in Morocco at the end of the eleventh century, travelled in Europe and eventually settled in Palermo at the court of Roger II for whom he wrote *The Delight of those who seek to wander through the regions of the world* (much of it a compilation). Another was Ibn Jubayr, born in Valencia in 1145, who also travelled the Mediterranean and the Muslim world. His observations are rather more in-depth than al-Idrisi's compilations giving, amongst other descriptions, a picture of Palermo under William II.

Europe outside Spain and Byzantium was a comparative backwater during the early Islamic period, so there was little need and less interest in travel there. Nonetheless, Arab travellers did reach the further corners of Europe: the Arab ambassador al-Ghazal, for example, was sent by 'Abd al-Rahman II of Cordoba on a mission to the Viking court in Denmark in 845. The perspectives of Europe by such writers are salutary: their accounts often resemble nineteenth century European accounts of embassies to Africa.[5] In the travels of Ibrahim ibn Yaqub from Cordoba to central Europe in c. 965, 'What is not in doubt is that this diplomat from Muslim Spain looked on the exotic peoples of the European interior with the curiosity of a modern anthropologist surveying the tribes of Papua.'[6] In 921 the 'Abbasid Caliph al-Muqtadir sent a special envoy to the Khan of the Bulgars on the Middle Volga near modern day Kazan. Ibn Fadlan, who accompanied the mission, wrote a detailed account of the often gruelling journey. He also wrote of the manners and customs of the 'barbaric tribes' they encountered, notably the Vikings, the Russians and the Bulgars. Another traveller, al-Mazini of Granada (1080-1179), visited Russia in 1136 and reported on the trade in fossil mammoth ivory.

Undoubtedly the greatest of all Arab travellers—indeed, one of the greatest of all time—was the Moroccan Ibn Battuta who travelled the world between 1325 and 1354. Born in Tangier in 1304 of a judicial family, he died in Marrakesh 1377. He set out on his first journey at the age of twenty-one on a *hajj*, but by the time he got no further than Egypt there is a first hint of his passion 'to travel the earth.' On completing his pilgrimage he then travelled through the inner Islamic lands—Iraq, Persia and Azerbaijan—making it a rule 'never to cross the same road a second time' before returning to Mecca. This proved to be a good base for his third journey to Yemen and around Arabia to Oman and the Persian Gulf. Ibn Battuta's fourth journey was more ambitions. In 1332 he travelled through Egypt, Syria and Anatolia to Crimea and the lands of the Golden Horde in southern Russia. After a brief diversion to Constantinople, he returned to southern Russia, then continued through Khiva, Bokhara, Samarkand, Balkh, Khorasan and Afghanistan, describing the devastation left behind by the Mongol invasions, to India, arriving on the banks of the Indus in 1333. He travelled through—and described—India, entering the service of Sultan Muhammad ibn Tughluq at Delhi as *qadi* or judge, before being appointed the sultan's special envoy to the Mongol Emperor of China in 1342. He does not seem to have taken his appointment too seriously, for his route—and his insatiable curiosity—took him through Central India, the Malabar coast, Calicut and the Maldives, where he remained for eighteen months as *qadi*, before continuing to Ceylon, Bengal, Assam and Sumatra, eventually arriving in Peking. After further travels in China, in 1347 he returned via Sumatra to Malabar and thence to the Persian Gulf, Baghdad, Syria and Egypt to Mecca in 1348 and then through Egypt, Tunisia and Algiers—with a brief diversion to Sardinia—to eventually arrive in Fez, twenty-three years after leaving his homeland. Not content to rest in Morocco, he travelled again to Andalusia before setting out on another major journey in West Africa, crossing the Sahara twice to the Muslim Empire of Niger.

Ever since the days of al-Idrisi, Morocco seems to have nurtured a tradition of travel and outwardness generally (it was Morocco, after all, who proposed the opening up of the West Indies to Moroccan colonisation to Queen Elizabeth in 1603, and Morocco was the first country in the world to recognise the newly independent United States of America in 1786). The seventeenth and eighteenth centuries sees this tradition continuing. Between 1611 and 1613, Ahmad ibn Qasim al-Hajari travelled through France and the Netherlands. Originally a Morisco from Spain, he grew up knowing Arabic even though mere knowledge of the language was punishable by the Spanish authorities at the time by burning at the stake. In 1595 he was forced to flee Granada to Morocco, where he entered the service of the court of Marrakesh. In the early seventeenth century all remaining Moriscos in Spain were forcibly expelled by a decree of Phillip III and their possessions confiscated. As someone well versed in European ways, as well as being a fluent Spanish (and apparently French) speaker, Ahmad bin Qasim was selected to lead a Moroccan delegation to Europe to plead the cause of the dispossessed Moriscos and seek restitution (ultimately unsuccessful).

As a visiting ambassador Ahmad ibn Qasim was naturally well treated and lavishly entertained by leading families and government circles in both the Netherlands and Spain. Much of the account of his travels comprise dialogues where, at various dinners and soirées for the benefit of the visiting Arabs, Ahmad would delight at arguing the superiority of Islam—but arguing solely from the *Christian* point of view, making a point of quoting the Gospels rather than the Qur'an to his hosts to demonstrate the rightness of Islam. Any passage from the Gospels that was quoted to him he was immediately able to cap with another to prove his point, demonstrating a knowledge of the Gospels that was generally far superior to that of his Christian hosts.[7]

Another Arab traveller in Spain towards the end of the seventeenth century was the Moroccan ambassador Muhammad ibn 'Abd al-Wahab al-Ghassani. He expresses repugnance of the sport of bull-fighting, 'for the torture of animals is not permitted either by the law of God or by the law of nature,'[8] as well as shock at the still barbaric and unjust nature of the Inquisition. He is openly cynical at how the rich 'eat all day long ... whatever meat they wish' during the fast of Lent. But by no means everything met with the ambassador's disapproval: Muhammad openly admired the system of hospitals and the exemplary work of the friars who cared for the sick, only wishing in 'their convictions and gentle manners and humility' that they would be Muslims.[9] He also comments on the curious sport of ice-skating in Madrid (noting that visiting English and Flemish were the most skilful), as well as the new system of putting 'news in the mould, from which he prints thousands of papers which he sells very cheaply. ... Whoever desires to learn the news buys a paper from him, which they call a *gaseta*. The reader finds many items of news, but there is always exaggeration and inaccuracy stemming from the desire to satisfy people's curiosity.'[10] Little changes it seems.

Muhammad demonstrates a sound grasp of current European politics and recent history. His observations extended to such events as far apart as the Ottoman second siege of Vienna in 1683 at one end of Europe, to England's 'Glorious Revolution' and the accession of William of Orange in 1688 at the other. He was also fully conversant with such nuances as the religious differences and the very complex system of dynastic alliances and genealogies between the ruling houses of Europe.

Later in the seventeenth century, a Chaldean Christian priest from Baghdad, Ilyas Hanna al-Mawsuli, travelled through Europe visiting Italy, France, Spain and Portugal before crossing the Atlantic and travelling through Central and South America. Although a Christian and not a Muslim, in travelling so extensively through the lands of the Spanish Empire, Ilyas ostensibly would have experienced two drawbacks: his religion and his citizenship. The Chaldean, or Assyrian, church of Iraq (better known as 'Church of the East'), separated from the main Orthodox church after the Council of Ephesus of 431 because of its views on the nature of Christ. Hence the Catholic (and Orthodox) churches regarded these 'Nestorians' as heretical. However, in the sixteenth century one branch of the Chaldean church entered into communion with Rome. Hence, although they maintained their Syriac liturgy, they were no longer viewed as heretics by the Catholics.

Ilyas' other drawback was that, being a native of Iraq, he would have been a citizen of the Ottoman Empire, bitter enemies of the Spanish, hence viewed with suspicion as a possible spy despite his Christianity. It seems unclear just how Ilyas avoided this problem—he claims merely to have found favour in his celebration of mass in Madrid (perhaps the novelty of the Syriac liturgy impressed his hosts?)—his travels were nonetheless undertaken with official Spanish consent.

Ilyas sailed first to Venezuela and then down through Colombia, Panama and Ecuador to Lima in Peru, where he celebrated mass (in Syriac). From Lima he travelled around both Peru and Bolivia, before turning northwards once more eventually to the 'Sultanate of Yenki Dunia', Turkish for 'New World' as he called the Spanish Viceroyalty of Mexico. In fact throughout his American travels Ilyas refers to both the Spanish sovereign and the former Inca Atahualpa as 'sultans'. He also refers to the village heads of native villages as 'shaikhs', to Spanish governors as 'pashas', and all references to the pope and to Christ are as 'sayyid pope' and 'sayyid Christ' respectively. And—naturally—he would have prayed to Allah. Ilyas comments upon the appalling way in which the Spanish treat the native Indians as well as on numerous other aspects of the Spanish New World, such as its administration, the church, and the methods of extracting silver. On reaching Mexico Ilyas contemplates taking a ship across the Pacific to the Spanish Philippines, but in the end this charming Iraqi priest returns across the Atlantic to Spain with increased wealth, a pet parrot and a lifetime of stories.

A UNIVERSAL VIEW

The *hajj* imposes internationalism upon Islam: every year members of the religious community from every corner of the world must gather. No other religion has ever imposed internationalism to this extent. This is perhaps the ultimate embodiment of the ancient Arabian religious emphasis on congregation that we reviewed in Chapter 6 on communal gathering that is manifested in the vast courtyards of ancient Semitic pagan temples from Palmyra to Marib, a practice that was adopted as core rituals into both Christianity and Islam. The only other time of obligatory internationalism was during the time of the ancient Persian Empire, when delegates from all corners of the empire (which comprised much of the then known world) would gather at Persepolis every year, but these were never the vast mass gatherings of the *hajj*.

Hence, since its beginning Muslim Arab civilisation has had an intellectual world view with universal concepts of history and human behaviour. In the ninth century, for example, Ibn Khurradadhbih and al-Ya'qubi compiled precise descriptions of the known world, thus beginning a long tradition of Arab geography. The historian al-Tabari (838-923) wrote a massive, multi-volume history of the world, beginning with the creation and ending in 915, and the historical works of al-Idrisi and al-Mas'udi that we have reviewed above belong within this tradition. Another *World Geography* was compiled by the Andalusian Ibn Sa'id (1214-74). Between 1224 and 1228 in Mosul and Aleppo, Yaqut (originally a Greek from Asia Minor), compiled his massive *Geographical Dictionary*, an encyclopaedic compilation in alphabetical order of all known geographical information. The period from the tenth century also saw encyclopaedists, such as Ibn al-Nadim. The idea of universal enquiry became a feature of Islamic scholarship, and Ibn Battuta's travels are as much a part of this as the encyclopaedists' compilations are. Perhaps the first of the great polymaths was al-Biruni in the eleventh century, followed by Nasir al-Din Tusi in the early thirteenth century. In the early fourteenth century the idea of universal history culminates in the work of Rashid al-Din, the first true universalist. These scholars were Iranians and Central Asians rather than Arabs, but they wrote in the Arabic language (as well as in others) and they drew upon a rich tradition of broad scholarship that flourished under Islam—and long before the idea of universalism began with the great polymaths of the European Renaissance.

The greatest intellectual giant of the Arab Middle Ages was Ibn Khaldun (1332-1400). His very background illustrates the universal—or at least international—world that the Arabs had created by that time. Born in Tunis to a Spanish-Arab family (the founder of the family originally migrated from Yemen to Spain), he entered the service of sultan of Granada in 1362 as a special envoy to the Castilian court. After only two years, however, Ibn Khaldun retired to Morocco to begin work on his monumental *Muqaddimah*, or the *Introduction to History*. In 1382 he went to Cairo where he lectured at al-Azhar, and in 1401 Ibn Khaldun met and conversed with the great conqueror Tamerlane in Damascus.

The first volume of his massive *Introduction to History* is a Prolegomena on the theory of history. It also acts as a 'Mirror of Princes', a guide to good (Islamic) government, a literary genre which has its origins in the *Andarznameh* of pre-Islamic Iran. The Prolegomena is a theory of human development, the first history to consider environmental and geographical factors, as well as ethnic and philosophic. It also considers more intangible factors in human history, such as the influence of diet on cultures, rather than racial and genealogical: 'Man is the child of customs, not the child of his ancestors.'[11]

Ibn Khaldun developed the principle of consensus or 'group feeling' *('asabiyah)*, the most frequently used term in the entire work, as the basis of the nation and civilisation, as a principal underpinning all history and human activity in general. This is summed up in his definition of 'Civilization. This means that human beings have to dwell in common and settle together in cities and hamlets for the comforts of companionship and for the satisfaction of human needs, as a result of the natural disposition of human beings towards co-operation in order to be able to make a living, as we shall explain. Civilization may be either desert (Bedouin) civilization as found in outlying regions and mountains, in hamlets (near) pastures in waste regions, and on the fringes of sandy deserts; or it may be sedentary civilization as found in cities, villages, towns, and small communities that serve the purpose of protection and fortification by means of walls. In all these different conditions, there are things that effect civilizations essentially in as far as it is social organization.'[12] Ibn Khaldun's principle of *'asabiyah* still has resonance today. It has recently been revived, for example by Peter Turchin in *War and Peace and War: The Life Cycle of Imperial Nations*, and his idea of civilisation is reflected and amplified by universal historians from Fernand Braudel's magisterial studies of civilisation to Felipe Fernández-Armesto more recent works on the same subject.

Ibn Khaldun emphasises the urban and economic basis of society and gives a broad and comprehensive view of world history as a unit rather than component parts, or mere lists of rulers and states. Most of all he views the study of history as an essential tool for understanding present societies: 'The past resembles the future more than one drop of water another.'[13] If Herodotus was the founder of history, Ibn Khaldun was the founder of historical science. Ibn Khaldun's universalist message is echoed in subsequent Arab and Islamic intellectual tradition, and his views remain valid today.

Despite the occasional foray by Ibn Fadlan and a small handful of other early Arab travellers in Europe, in all this universal curiosity and exploration

Europe is conspicuous by its absence until the modern period. The Arab histories, travellers and geographers pass over Europe almost in silence—the great traveller Ibn Battuta chose to travel to West Africa rather than into darkest Europe after the return of his epic journey to China. It is tempting to see this omission as Islamic civilisation being blinkered to anything beyond the world of Islam: to them, Europe was outside and therefore irrelevant. But Arab writing is copious concerning India, the Indian Ocean, China and South-east Asia, and the mining of the pre-Islamic learning of ancient Greece was so extensive that Islam can claim to be as much heirs to Hellenism as Europe is. Europe is passed over not so much in arrogance but because it had so little to offer: no works of scholarship, no great cities, no great power that challenged them, few goods worthy of trade. The Arab intellectual achievement may have been universal, but it was not unselective nor indiscriminate. After all, the obscurest of ancient Greek pharmacopoeias were translated into Arabic, but there are no Arabic translations of Homer or Herodotus. An obscure Greek pharmacopoeia was of use to Arab learning: western Europe simply was not. Herodotus, for example, was often derided—even in ancient times—not so much for his inaccuracies but for his curiosity for non-Greek cultures, whilst William of Tyre's history of the Muslim states has not survived merely because nobody wished it worth preserving; his history of the Crusades, on the other hand, is still in print today.[14]

Much has been made of the Muslim view of the world in terms of the *Dar al-Islam* versus the *Dar al-Harb*, the 'realm of serenity' versus the 'realm of chaos'. The idea that this one-sided view of a superior Islamic civilisation is theoretically in perpetual conflict with the non-Muslim world out of which Islam can only triumph world-wide, somehow marks Islamic civilisation as different. This facet of Islam, with its subsequent concept of the *jihad*, obsesses modern Western misconceptions almost as much as the obsession over head-scarves for women.

Such a one-sided view of the world in terms of 'us and them' is a characteristic of many civilisations: Greeks versus barbarians, for example, Chinese versus non-Chinese. The historian Bernard Lewis notes that it was only in Europe that sovereigns were kings of specified narrow units—kings of 'France', of 'England', of 'Denmark', etc.—but in the Middle East sovereigns were unspecified. Sultans of 'Turkey' or 'Egypt', or Shahs of 'Persia' were solely European constructs; sultans and shahs themselves saw themselves as unrestricted and universal; the titles were not limited to specific lands (unless they were something very broad, such as 'sovereign of Islam').[15]

Internationalism, multi-culturalism, pluralism, universalism, the idea of different communities and religious groups living together: such ideas characterised the great ages of Islam. This has characterised Arab societies since. In the recent past the great multi-cultural communities of the Mediterranean, such as Smyrna or Beirut or Alexandria, existed within Islam, while today such communities flourish in the Emirates. The decree of Emperor Theodosius in 385 prohibiting all religious worship in the empire apart from Christianity has no counterpart in Islam.

OUT OF ARABIA

The expansion out of Arabia changed Europe in almost every way. The Phoenicians brought a new system of writing, new religious ideas, new ways of laying out cities and new crops (such as the olive) as well as new agricultural techniques.* When the Arabs in their turn came, the new ideas, techniques and items (both utilitarian and luxury) grew into a flood. With them came nautical instruments, astronomy, mathematics, navigation, cartography, new textiles, oranges, cane sugar, rice, many spices, glazed pottery, much glass technology, paper, the compass (albeit passed on by the Arabs from the Chinese) and our numeric system—not to mention the idea of nothing. Many Arab engineering devices, some appearing for the first time in Europe in the sketch books of Leonardo da Vinci, were known in the Islamic world many centuries previously.[16]

The Arabs even brought Europe's own Classical legacy back to Europe. Much of the learning of the Greek and Roman word had been lost to Europe but preserved in translation—Aramaic as well as Arabic—in the centres of learning in the east, at first the Aramaic centres of Nisibis and Edessa and then in the translation schools of 'Abbasid Baghdad. They contributed more than lost Greek classics to the European intellectual revival. For example, the idea of the college derives from the Islamic *madrasa*. The

---

* The archaeologists Monica Barnes and David Fleming, make a closely argued and persuasive case of how just one ancient Near Eastern agricultural development, underground irrigation canals, reached the far west and beyond to the New World. Underground irrigation canals were probably developed in ancient Persia where they are known as the *qanat* or *kariz*. The idea spread eastwards to China and was carried westwards to North Africa by the Arabs (or perhaps earlier by the Phoenicians) where they are known as the *foggara*. From there the Arabs took the idea across the Mediterranean, where they occur in Andalusia. The technique was then further carried by the conquistadors to America, where they remain in use in the desert areas of northern Peru. See Barnes & Fleming 1991.

university (that is, the awarding of degrees) is solely a medieval European development, not necessarily rooted in the *madrasa* as is often thought. But the ideas of scholasticism and humanism, which underpinned both the Renaissance and the Enlightenment and which was long considered exclusively Western European developments, are rooted in the Muslim Arab intellectual tradition.[17]

Perhaps the idea that the Arabs contributed most was the idea of universalism, of universal enquiry. A tradition that may reach back to the earliest (and now lost) Phoenician works of Sanchuniathon and Marinus of Tyre. Of course, in stressing the above very brief list of Phoenician and Arab contributions to the West, I do not mean to shout that 'everything came from the East.' On the contrary, the European achievement and expansion is huge, and hardly requires reiterating. But neither did 'everything come from the West' and if there is one lesson to be learnt from the idea of universalism—and one which this work must stress above all—it is that the Eurocentric view of the present world solely in terms of European expansion cannot be valid.

This may be stating the obvious—and is doubtless obvious to readers who have reached this far. But the Eurocentric view still prevails. On the very day that this book went to the press[*] I was given the latest issue of the *BBC History Magazine* (Vol. 10, no 7, July 2009). The issue was devoted to the fortieth anniversary of the Moon landings. As a part of this, the editors asked twelve prominent historians 'to nominate alternative moments in the past that they consider to be giant leaps for mankind.' With the sole exception of Felipe Fernández-Armesto who (characteristically) chose the moment when the first hominids learnt to eat meat in Africa, *all* chose European achievements. Three chose (predictably) Greek: politics, democracy and Ptolemy. One chose French (Villedieu's *Doctrinale*) and one Italian (Galileo). And six chose British giant leaps forward for all mankind: Magna Carta, Harvey's discovery of the circulation of the bloodstream, the Royal Society, Hooke's microscopy, the invention of the steam engine, and the wisdom in granting India its independence. Non-European 'leaps' from, the invention of paper, the alphabet and algebra to Hammurabi's law code, Marinus' geography or Ulugh Beg's star charts do not even rate a whisper.

I rest my case.

---

[*] 1 July 2009

NOTES

INTRODUCTION

1   Stephen Runciman opens his *The Emperor Romanus Lecapenus and his Times* (1929) with these lines.
2   Roberts 1985: 176.
3   In the classic 1969 and 1973 BBC Television series, *Civilisation* and *The Ascent of Man*. See Clark 1969: 1-2; Bronowski 1973: 3-4.
4   Braudel 1981-4, 1: 64; 1973: 757.
5   Herodian III, i, 4.
6   Schafer: 102.
7   Ibn Khaldun, for example, writing in the 14th century uses the 'East' meaning Middle East and the 'West' as meaning the Maghrib.
8   Hobsbaum 1997: 218.
9   Braudel 1981: 412 and 509.
10 Roberts 1996: 582.
11 Hobsbaum 1997: 217.
12 Schafer 1965: 102.
13 Trevor-Roper1968: Foreword.
14 The quotation from the rear jacket publicity of Headley 2008. Headley's aim, stated in the introduction, is to pose a challenge to the 'moral posturing' popular in American academia since the 1960s, but throughout does not cite a single source of those he is challenging.
15 Diamond 1997: 16.
16 Even on occasion almost falling back on 'conspiracy theory:' a conspiracy by the Western academic establishment against the Orient, e.g., Said 1993: 21-322.
17 The title of Sachs 2002.
18 Said 1993: 407.

2 THE NEAR EAST'S FAR WEST

1   From pp. 30-32 of the 1986 Penguin Classics edition.
2   Moscati 1968: 129.
3   *Aeneid* I, 421-7.
4   Lancel 1995: 24.
5   Lancel 1995: 403-4.
6   Ludwig 1942: 64.
7   Fantar 1987: 113.
8   Jidejian 1968: 16.
9   Headley 2008: 16.

3 GLITTERING KINGDOMS

1   Hitti 1957: 406.
2   MacDonald 1993: 388.
3   Although the Idumaeans of Judaea and Herod himself have been labelled 'Arab' by Shahid 1984a: 145-60.
4   Ball 2000: 37-47. See, however, Young 2003.
5   Strabo 16. 2. 21.
6   Ball 2000: Chapter 7.
7   Hitti 1957: 406.
8   Bowersock 1983: 147.

4 ROME'S ARAB HALF CENTURY

1   Herodian VI, viii, 8.
2   Millar 1993 is sceptical, but Levick 2007 assumes the connection.
3   Gibbon I: 112.
4   Levick 2007: 42.
5   Dio LXXIX. 23. 3.
6   Al-Fassi 2007, writing mainly about the Nabateans. Women also traditionally held a high position at Edessa: their distinctive head-dress, as depicted on mosaics and sculpture, in fact survived in the region until the 19th century. See Segal 1970: 38-40.
7   Levick 2007: 56.
8   Ward Perkins 1981: 389-91; Ball 2000: 419-31.
9   Herodian, quoted in Levick 2007: 88.
10 Herodian IV, vi, 1-5. See also Dio LXXVIII. 4-6; *Augustan History* Caracalla: 252-4.
11 Dio LXXVIII. 22. 1.
12 Gibbon I: 149.
13 *Augustan History* Heliogabalus: 312. John Malalas: p. 158.
14 Herodian V, vi, 1.
15 Gibbon I: 143-8.
16 Kleiner 1992: 362-3.
17 *Augustan History* Alexander. Dodgeon & Lieu 1994: 21.
18 Herodian VI, viii, 8.
19 Gibbon I: 149-66; Aurelius Victor 24.
20 See Dodgeon & Lieu 1994: 75-6.

5 IMPACT OF THE ABSTRACT

1   Herodian V, iii, 5.
2   Roberts 1985: 42-3 & 314. See also 81-116: 'The Birth of the West,' where Christianity is seen as fundamental to the definition of Europe.'
3   Cardini 2001: 128-134.
4   Le Goff 2005: 4.
5   'Christianity is an essential reality of Western life: it even marks atheists, whether they know it or not.' Braudel 1993: 23.
6   A.W. Redgate, *The Armenians* (Oxford 1998): rear jacket & xii.
7   E.g., Orlando Figes, *Natasha's Dance: A Cultural History of Russia* (London): 378, to take just one example, but numerous more could be cited.

8   Ball 2000: 37-47. See now, however, Young 2003.
9   Herodian V, iii, 5.

6 MUHAMMAD, CHARLEMAGNE AND ROME

1   Hodges & Whitehouse 1983: 19.
2   Lewis 2008.
3   McKetterick 2008: 103-6.
4   Ahmed Rashid (2000) *Taliban* (London): 111-2.
5   Braudel 1973: 759, when writing of the sixteenth century Mediterranean.
6   Pirenne 1939; Ashton 1976: 85-6 & 148; Whitehouse & Hodges 1983; Barford 2001: 245.
7   Davies 1996: 266.

7 CALIPHS IN EUROPE

1   Gibbon, ch. 52.
2   Almond 2009: 16.
3   Lewis 2008: 132.
4   Quoted in Lewis 2008: 130.
5   Gibbon, *loc. cit.*.
6   Lewis 1982: 20.
7   Lewis 2008.
8   Herrin 1987: 233-5.
9   Burnett in Agius 1994.
10   Cardini 2001: 76.
11   Almond 2009: 28.
12   Ibn Khaldun: 341 and 372-5.
13   Braudel 1973: 804.

8 ACROSS THE ALPS

1   Quoted in Carbini 2001: 33.
2   Almond 2009: 53.
3   Abulafia 1988; Runciman 1958.
4   J Calmette, *L'effondrement d'un empire et la naissance d'une Europe*, 117. Quoted in *Encyclopaedia of Islam*, 'Fraxinetum', Leiden 1999.
5   Hitti 1964: 605.

9 THE WORLD'S DEBATE

1   Raymond of Aguiles.
2   Runciman 1951-4, Vol 1: 326.
3   Lewis 1982: 98.
4   Runciman 1051-4, Vol 4: 480.
5   Le Goff 2005: 112.

10 THE ARABIAN LAKE

1   Janet Abu Lughod 1989: 242, in the context of the thirteenth century.
2   Wheeler 1954: 178-9.
3   Whitehouse 1990: 490.
4   Quoted in Brotton 2002: 168
5   Fernández-Armesto 2006: 180-1.
6   Quoted in Chaudhuri 1985: 65.
7   For the Mediterranean, see for example Ludwig 1942 and Braudel 1972. The first to view the Black Sea as a distinct unit was Ascherson's superb work (1995), and now there is King 2004. For the Indian Ocean see for example Chaudhuri 1985, who acknowledges Braudel's precedent. Both Fernández-Armesto's ground-breaking works (2000 and 2006) also recognise this.
8   *Civilizations* 2000, 'The Muslim Lake': 456-9.
9   Estenson 1998: 42-4.
10 Blainey 1983.

11 A UNIVERSAL WORLD

1   Terry Pratchett, *Jingo* (London 1997: 41), in a dialogue between Serjeant Colon and Nobby about the 'Klatchians,' thinly disguised Arabs. Mr Pratchett's publishers, the Orion Publishing Group, have kindly given permission to reproduce this quotation.
2   Roberts 1985: 232.
3   See, for example, Warmington 1974: 1 (written in 1928), Roberts 1985 or, most recently, Headley 2008.
4   Headley 2008: Chapter 2. The quotation is from the publicity on the inside jacket cover.
5   Lewis 1982: 93-4.
6   Davies 1996: 324-5.
7   Matar 2003.
8   Quoted in Lewis 1982: 274.
9   Matar 2003: 159.
10 Matar 2003: 160.
11 Ibn Khaldun: 300.
12 Ibn Khaldun: 41-2.
13 Ibn Khaldun: 12.
14 A point noted by Lewis 1982: 300.
15 Lewis 1982: 202.
16 Hill in Agius 1994.
17 For the transmission of Greek learning, O'Leary 1949 is long considered a classic. See now also Gutas 1998. For scholasticism and humanism, see Makdisi 1990.

BIBLIOGRAPHY

Abulafia, David, *Frederick II. A Medieval Emperor.* London 1988

Abu-Lughod, Janet L, *Before European Hegemony. The World System A.D. 1250-1350.* New York & Oxford 1989

Agius, Dionisius A & Hitchcock, Richard (eds). *The Arab Influence in Medieval Europe.* Folia Scholastica Mediterranea. Middle East Culture Series Vol. 18. Reading 1994

Ahmad b. Mājid al-Najdī, *Kitāb al-Fawā'id fī usūl al-bahr wa'l-qawā'id of Ahmad b. Mājid al-Najdī.* Translated as *Arab Navigation in the Indian Ocean Before the Coming of the Portuguese* by G R Tibbetts. London 1981

Ahmad, Maqbul S, *Arabic Classical Accounts of India & China.* Shimla 1989

al-Fassi, H A, *Women in Pre-Islamic Arabia: Nabataea.* Oxford 2007

Almond, Ian *Two Faiths, One Banner. When Muslims marched with Christians across Europe's battlegrounds.* London 2009

Al-Rawas, Isam, *Oman in Early Islamic History.* Reading 2000

al-Tabari, *The History of al-Tabari.* 27 vols Albany 1987-96

Anonymous, *The Ship of Sulaimān.* Translated by John O'Kane. London 1972

Arkoun, Mohammed, *Histoire de l'Islam et des musulmans en France du Moyen-Age à nos jours,* Albin Michel 2006

Ascherson, Neal, *Black Sea. The Birth of Civilisation and Barbarism.* London 1995

Ashtor, E, *A Social and Economic History of the Near East in the Middle Ages.* London 1976

Aubet, M E, *The Phoenicians and the West.* Cambridge 1993

Ball, Warwick, *Rome in the East. The Transformation of an Empire.* London 2000

Barnes, Monica & Fleming, David, 'Filtration-gallery irrigation in the Spanish New World.' *Latin American Antiquity* 2, 1 (1991): 48-68

Bartlett, Robert, *The Making of Europe. Conquest, Colonization and Cultural Change 950-1350.* London 1993

Blainey, Geoffrey, *The Tyranny of Distance. How Distance Shaped Australia's History.* Sydney 1983

Bowersock, G W, *Roman Arabia.* Cambridge Massachusetts 1983

Boxer, C R, *The Dutch Seaborne Empire 1600-1800.* London 1965

Boxhall, P, Arabian Seafarers in the Indian Ocean. *Asian Affairs* 20, 3 (1989): 287-295.

Braudel, Fernand, *A History of Civilizations.* London 1993

Braudel, Fernand, *Civilization and Capitalism.* 3 vols, London 1981-4

Braudel, Fernand, *The Mediterranean and the Mediterranean World in the Age of Phillip II.* 2 vols. London 1972-3

Braudel, Fernand, *The Mediterranean in the Ancient World.* London 2001

Breton, Jean-François, *Arabia Felix from the Time of the Queen of Sheba. Eighth Century B.C. to First Century A.D.* Notre Dame Indiana, 1999

Bronowski, J, *The Ascent of Man.* London 1973

Bronowski, J & Mazlish, Bruce, *The Western Intellectual Tradition. From Leonardo to Hegel.* London 1960

Brotton, Jerry, *The Renaissance Bazaar. From the Silk Road to Michelangelo.* Oxford 2002

Butcher, Kevin, *Roman Syria and the Near East.* London 2003

Cardini, Franco, *Europe and Islam.* Oxford 2001

Carr, E H, *What is History?* London 1961

Cary, M & Warmington, E H, *The Ancient Explorers.* London 1963

Casson, Lionel, *Ships and Seafaring in ancient times.* London 1994

Chaudhuri, K N, *Trade and Civilisation in the Indian Ocean. An Economic History from the Rise of Islam to 750.* Cambridge

Clark, Kenneth, *Civilization.* London 1969

Culican, W, *The First Merchant Venturers.* London 1966

Davies, Norman, *Europe East & West.* London 2006

Davies, Norman, *Europe. A History.* London 1996

Dawson, Christopher, *The Making of Europe. An Introduction to the History of European Unity.* London 1934

Diamond, Jared, *Guns, Germs and Steel.* London 1997

Dodgeon, Michael H & Lieu, Samuel N C, *The Roman Eastern Frontier and the Persian Wars AD 226-363. A Documentary History.* London 1994

Doe, Brian, *Monuments of South Arabia.* Naples & Cambridge 1983

Dunn, Ross E, *The Adventures of Ibn Battuta. A Muslim Traveler of the 14th Century.* Berkeley 1986

Dunstan, G R, *The Human Embryo. Aristotle and the Arabic and European Traditions.* Exeter 1990

Elton, G R, *The Practice of History.* Sydney 1967

Estensen, Miriam, *Discovery. The Quest for the Great South Land.* New York 1998

Fantar, M H, 'Kerkouane: A Punic City at Cape Bon'. In Khader & Soren 1987

Ferguson, Niall ed., *Virtual History. Alternatives and Counterfactuals.* London 1997

Fernández-Armesto, Felipe *Civilizations.* London 2000

Fernández-Armesto, Felipe, *Pathfinders. A Global History of Exploration.* Oxford 2006

Frye, Richard N, *Ibn Fadlan's Journey to Russia. A Tenth-Century Traveller from Baghdad to the Volga River.* Princeton 2005

Geary, Patrick J, *The Myth of Nations. The Medieval Origins of Europe.* Princeton 2002

Gibbon, Edward, *The History of the Decline and Fall of the Roman Empire.* 7 vols. Ed. J B Bury. London 1900

Goody, Jack *Islam in Europe.* Cambridge 2004

Goody, Jack, *The East in the West.* Cambridge 1996

Goody, Jack, *The Theft of History.* Cambridge 2006

Groom, Nigel, *Frankincense and Myrrh. A Study of the Arabian Incense Trade.* London & Beirut 1981

Gutas, Dimitri, *Greek Thought, Arabic Culture. The Graeco-Arabic Translation Movement in Baghdad and Early 'Abbāsid Society 2nd-4th/8th-10th centuries.* London 1998

Hall, Richard, *Empires of the Monsoon. A History of the Indian Ocean and its Traders.* London 1996

Halliday, Fred, *Islam and the Myth of Confrontation. Religion and Politics in the Middle East.* London 2003

Harden, Donald, *The Phoenicians.* London 1962

Headley, John M., *The Europeanization of the World. On the Origins of Human Rights and Democracy.* Princeton 2008

Herrin, Judith, *The Formation of Christendom.* London 1987

Hillenbrand, Carole, *The Crusades. Islamic Perspectives.* Edinburgh 1999

Hitti, Philip K, *History of Syria.* London 1957

Hitti, Philip K, *History of the Arabs. From the Earliest Times to the Present.* London 1964

Hobsbaum, Eric, *On History.* London 1997

Hobsbawm, Eric & Ranger, Terrence, eds, *the Invention of Tradition.* Cambridge 1983

Hobsbawm, Eric, *On History.* London 1997

Hobson, John M, *The Eastern Origins of Western Civilisation.* Cambridge 2004

Hodges, Richard & Whitehouse, David, *Mohammed, Charlemagne and the Origins of Europe.* London 1989

Holt, P M (ed), *The Cambridge History of Islam.* 2 vols, Cambridge 1970

Hourani, Albert, *A History of the Arab Peoples.* Cambridge Massachusetts 1991

Hourani, George F, *Arab Seafaring in the Indian Ocean in Ancient and Early Medieval Times.* Revised and expanded

by John Carswell. Princeton 1995

Howard-Johnston, James, *East Rome, Sasanian Persia and the End of Antiquity.* Aldershot 2006

Hoyland, Robert G, *Arabia and the Arabs. From the Bronze Age to the Coming of Islam.* London 2001

Huntingdon, Samuel P, *The Clash of Civilizations and the Remaking of the World Order.* New York 1996

Ibn Battuta, *The Travels of Ibn Battuta. A.D. 1325-1354.* Transl. H A R Gibb. 3 vols Cambridge 1958-73

Ibn Khaldun, *The Muqaddimah. An Introduction to History.* Tr. Rosenthal. London 1967

Jidejian, Nina, *Byblos through the Ages.* Beirut 1968

Jones, Alan (ed), *University Lectures in Islamic Studies. Volume 2.* London 1988

Kennedy, Hugh, *The Prophet and the Age of the Caliphate.Islamic Near East from the Sixth to the Eleventh Century.* London 1986

Kennedy, Hugh, *Muslim Spain and Portugal. A Political History of Spain and Portugal.* London 1996

Khader, A & Soren, D (eds) *Carthage: A Mosaic of Ancient Tunisia.* New York 1987

King, Charles, *The Black Sea. A History.* Oxford 2004

Kleiner, Diana E E, *Roman Sculpture.* Yale 1992

Lancel, Serge, *Carthage. A History.* Oxford 1995

Lavathes Louise, *When China Ruled the Seas. The Treasure Fleet of the Dragon Throne, 1405-1433* Oxford 1994

Le Goff, Jacques, *The Birth of Europe.* Oxford 2005

Levick, Barbara, *Julia Domna. Syrian Empress.* London 2007

Lewis, Bernard, *Cultures in Conflict.*

Christians, Muslims, and Jews in the Age of Discovery. New York 1995

Lewis, Bernard, *The Muslim Discovery of Europe.* London 1982

Lewis, David Leavering, *God's Crucible. Islam and the Making of Europe, 570-1215.* New York 2008

Lowenthal, David, *The Past is a Foreign Country.* Cambridge 1985

Ludwig, Emil, *The Mediterranean saga of a Sea.* New York 1942

MacDonald, M C A, 'Nomads and the Hawran in the late Hellenistic and Roman periods. A reassessment of the epigraphic evidence. *Syria* 70 (1993): 303-413

Mack, Rosamond E., *Bazaar to Piazza. Islamic Trade and Italian Art, 1300-1600.* Berkeley 2002

Makdisi, George *The Rise of Humanism in Classical Islam and the Christian West. With special reference to scholasticism.* Edinburgh 1990

Markoe, Glenn E., *The Phoenicians.* Berkeley 2000

Matar, Nabil (ed. & tr.), *In the Lands of the Christians. Arabic Travel Writing in the Seventeenth Century.* New York 2003

Matar, Nabil, *Turks, Moors & Englishmen in the Age of Discovery.* New York 1999

McKetterick, Rosamond, *Charlemagne. The Formation of a European Identity.* Cambridge 2008

Millar, Fergus, *The Roman Near East, 31 BC-AD 337.* Cambridge Massachusetts, 1993

Ministry of Information and Culture, Sultanate of Oman 1979, *Oman. A Seafaring Nation.* Muscat

Moscati, Sabatino (ed.), *The Phoenicians.* London 2001

Moscati, Sabatino, *The World of the Phoenicians.* London 1968

Nasr, Seyyed Hossein, *Science and Civilization in Islam.* Lahore 1968

Nasr, Seyyid Hossein, *Traditional Islam in the Modern World.* London 1987

Nielsen, J S, 'Islam and Europe', in: *University Lectures in Islamic Studies* Vol 2, ed. Alan Jones London (1998): 19-29.

O'Leary, De lacy, *How Greek Science Passed to the Arabs.* London 1949

O'Shea, Stephen, *Sea of Faith. Islam and Christianity in the Medieval Mediterranean World.* London 2006

Owens, E J, *The City in the Greek and Roman World.* London 1991

Palmer, Andrew, Brock, Sebastian & Hoyland, Robert 1993, *The Seventh Century in the West-Syrian Chronicles.* Liverpool

Parry, J H, *The Age of Reconnaissance. Discovery, Exploration and Settlement.* London 1963

Pirenne, Henri *Mohammed and Charlemagne.* New York 1927

Potts, D T, *The Arabian Gulf in Antiquity.* 2 vols, Oxford 1990

Rashid, Ahmed, *Taliban.* London 2000

Reinaud, Jacques, *Invasion des Sarrazins en France, et de France en Savoie, en Piemont et en Suisse.* Paris 1836

Rietbergen, Peter, *Europe. A Cultural History.* Oxford 1998

Roberts, J M, *A History of Europe.* London 1996

Roberts, J M, *The Triumph of the West.* London 1985

Rodinson, Maxime, *Europe and the Mystique of Islam.* London 1988

Rosenthal, Franz, *The Classical Heritage in Islam.* London 1992

Ross, Steven K, *Roman Edessa. Politics and Culture on the Eastern Fringes of the Roman Empire, 114-242 CE.* London 2001

Runciman, Steven, *A History of the Crusades.* 3 vols. Cambridge 1951-54

Runciman, Steven, *The Sicilian Vespers.*

A History of the Mediterranean World in the Later Thirteenth Century. Cambridge 1958

Sachs, Jonathan, *The Dignity of Difference.* London 2002

Said, Edward W, *Culture and Imperialism.* London 1993

Said, Edward W, *Orientalism. Western Conceptions of the Orient.* London 1978

Schafer, Edward H, *The Golden Peaches of Samarkand.* Berkeley 1965

Seaman, Khalil I, (ed) *Islam and the Medieval West. Aspects of Intercultural Relations.* Albany 1980

Segal, J B, *Edessa 'The Blessed City'.* Oxford 1970

Shahid, Irfan, *Rome and the Arabs.* Washington 1984

Sherwani, Haroon Khan, *Muslim Colonies in France, Northern Italy and Switzerland. Being the English translation of Reinaud's "Invasions des Sarrazins en France, et de France en Savoie, en Piemont et en Suisse".* Lahore 1964

Simpson, St John (ed.), *Queen of Sheba. Treasures from Ancient Yemen.* London 2002

Starr, Chester G, *The Influence of Sea Power on Ancient History.* New York & Oxford 1989

Stoneman, Richard, *Palmyra and its Empire. Zenobia's Revolt against Rome.* Ann Arbor 1992

Sykes, Percy, *A History of Exploration from the earliest times to the present day.* London 1934

Tibbetts, G R, *Arab Navigation in the Indian Ocean Before the Coming of the Portuguese.* Being a translation of *Kitāb al-Fawā'id fī usūl al-bahr wa'l-qawā'id of Ahmad b. Mājid al-Najdī.* London 1981

Trevor-Roper, Hugh (ed.), *The Age of Expansion. Europe and the World 1559-1660.* London 1968

Trimingham, J Spencer, *Christianity among the Arabs in Pre-Islamic Times.* London & Beirut 1979

Tubb, Jonathan, *Canaanites.* London 1998

Turcan R, *The Cults of the Roman Empire.* Oxford 1996

Turchin, Peter, *War & Peace & War. The Life Cycles of Imperial Nations.* New York 2006

Ward Perkins, J B, *Roman Imperial Architecture.* London 1981

Warmington, E H, *The Commerce Between the Roman Empire and India.* London 1974

Wheeler, R E M, *Rome Beyond the Imperial Frontiers.* London 1954

Whitehouse, D, 'The *Periplus Maris Erythraei*' *Journal of Roman Archaeology* 3 (1990): 489-493

Wickham, Chris, *Framing the Early Middle Ages. Europe and the Mediterranean, 400-800.* Oxford 2005

Young. G K, 'Emesa and Baalbek: Where is the Temple of Elahgabal?' *Levant* 35 (2003): 159-162

Zahran, Yasmine, *Philip the Arab. A Study in Prejudice.* London 2001

Zahran, Yasmine, *Zenobia between Reality and Legend.* Oxford 2003

INDEX